Sacred Modernity

Postcolonialism across the Disciplines 12

Postcolonialism across the Disciplines

Series Editors
Graham Huggan, University of Leeds
Andrew Thompson, University of Exeter

Postcolonialism across the Disciplines showcases alternative directions for postcolonial studies. It is in part an attempt to counteract the dominance in colonial and postcolonial studies of one particular discipline – English literary/ cultural studies – and to make the case for a combination of disciplinary knowledges as the basis for contemporary postcolonial critique. Edited by leading scholars, the series aims to be a seminal contribution to the field, spanning the traditional range of disciplines represented in postcolonial studies but also those less acknowledged. It will also embrace new critical paradigms and examine the relationship between the transnational/cultural, the global and the postcolonial.

Sacred Modernity

Nature, Environment,
and the Postcolonial Geographies
of Sri Lankan Nationhood

Tariq Jazeel

Liverpool University Press

First published 2013 by
Liverpool University Press
4 Cambridge Street
Liverpool L69 7ZU

British Library Cataloguing-in-Publication data
A British Library CIP record is available

ISBN 978-1-84631-886-3 cased

Typeset in Amerigo by Carnegie Book Productrion, Lancaster
Printed and bound by CPI Group (UK) Ltd, Croydon CR0 4YY

For Maite

Contents

Map and Figures

Acknowledgements

This book has been a long time in the making, and it would not have been possible without the generous help of many people and institutions along the way.

I must thank the Departments of Geography at the Open University and the University of Sheffield who have provided funding to enable the research in Sri Lanka on which parts of this book are based. The UK's Arts and Humanities Research Council (AHRC) provided me with a Research Leave Fellowship that enabled the completion of this manuscript, for which I am extremely grateful.

In Sri Lanka over the years many people have gone out of their way to help me during the course of my research. To them I am indebted. In particular I would like to thank Michael Mack, Nirmala de Mel, Auntie Aurasie, Channa Daswatte, Chandi Jayawickrama, Phillip Weeraratne, Varuna de Silva, Robert Verrijt, Amanda Weerasinghe, Dila Weerasinghe, Ro, Dinesh, Harindra Dasanayake, Nira Wickremasinghe, Sasanka Perera, and Anoli Perera. Staff and reading room assistants at the Department of Wildlife Conservation, the Wild Life and Nature Protection Society, and the Associated Newspapers of Ceylon Ltd assisted me beyond the call of their duty, particularly Eshani Nanayakara, Hasini Sarathchandra, Vishantha Mendis, Mishani Goonatilake, and Mr Chandrasena. Thank you also to the International Centre for Ethnic Studies (ICES) and the Colombo Institute for the Advanced Study of Social Sciences, who both provided institutional support and affiliations for me in Colombo. Many thanks also to the hugely inspirational *theertha* art's collective in Colombo.

Colleagues and graduate students past and present at the University of Sheffield have provided a supportive and intellectually stimulating environment in which many of the ideas in this manuscript fomented. Many have offered invaluable advice on the project, comments on sections of the manuscript at various stages of its development, as well as fantastic practical assistance. Thank you especially to Peter Jackson, whose support and advice have been an anchor for me. Thank you also Charles Pattie, Grant Bigg, Eric Olund, Jessica Dubow, Richard Phillips, Megan Blake, Pat Noxolo, Paula Meth, Glyn Williams, Katharine Adeney, Margo Huxley, Graham Allsopp, and Paul Coles.

Beyond the University of Sheffield I also must thank Steve Pile, Nigel Clark, Parvati Raghuram, Jenny Robinson, Alison Blunt, Catherine Nash, David Scott, Patrick Deer, James Duncan, Steve Legg, Alex Vasudevan, Nayanika Mookherjee, Ambika Satkunathan, Rajesh Venugopal, Charan Rainford, Malathi de Alwis, Tham Shanaathanan, Cathrine Brun, Kanchana Ruwanpura, Beth Greenhough, and Jean Franco for advice, comments, and conversations that have one way or another proved instrumental to the development of this manuscript. I have also been lucky enough to benefit from the intellectual generosity of a number of friends and colleagues who have commented on sections or fragments of the manuscript at draft stage: Colin McFarlane, Mustafa Dikeç, Richard Phillips, Brian Larkin, Sasanka Perera, Anoli Perera, and especially Leah Gibbs, thank you all so, so much. In addition, thank you to my editor at Liverpool University Press, Alison Welsby, who has been fantastic.

Thank you to my family – Dad, Myn, and especially Riz and Mum – for always being interested in the stuff I do, and for indulging me in conversations about those things. And Riz, thank you also for the images you helped me get hold of.

Though he did not live to see this book published, my former PhD supervisor Denis Cosgrove has been, and continues to be, a constant source of inspiration. His guidance, creativity, constant support, and critical acuity remain with me and underpin this manuscript. Thank you Denis, always. Never forgotten.

Finally, I owe my biggest thanks to Maite Conde, whose critical insight, friendship, love, and support have been like oxygen. She has read every word of this manuscript, and forced me always to think more lucidly about what it is I am trying to say. She has lived with this book as much as I have, and has always given me encouragement as well as the best advice I could hope for. I hope that by dedicating it to her she will feel it has in some small way been worth it. Thank you Maite.

Introduction

The National Atlas of Sri Lanka has seventy-three versions of the island –
each template revealing only one aspect, one obsession: rainfall, winds,
surface water of lakes, rarer bodies of water locked deep within the earth.
    The old portraits show the produce and former kingdoms of the country;
contemporary portraits show levels of wealth, poverty and literacy.
Michael Ondaatje, Anil's Ghost (2000), p. 39

Nature is something of an obsession in Sri Lanka. Visitors to the island and
residents alike never stop marvelling at the abundance of flora, fauna, and
the succession of staggeringly beautiful landscapes with which the country
seems to have been blessed. But if Sri Lankan nature captivates, it has rarely
ever been strictly 'natural'. Commonplace understandings of the country's
nature are deeply entwined with narratives of history, culture, and religion. As
Michael Ondaatje remarks in his novel *Anil's Ghost*, even the *National Atlas of Sri
Lanka* seamlessly intertwines aspects of Sri Lanka's non-human composition
– rainfall, winds, water – with historical portraits of ancient kingdoms. In
fact, the very first lines in the *National Atlas* begin: 'The ancient chronicle
Mahavamsa records that Sri Lanka was divided into regional units and that
village boundaries were established over the whole country. Moreover,
evidence from rock inscriptions show that every Buddhist monastery had its
boundaries strictly fixed and defined' (1988: 11). Buddhist history, it seems, is
inscribed in the environmental fabric of this state-consecrated geography of
the island; Buddhism sits in the place of environmental origins. It is no wonder
then that Ondaatje's novel *Anil's Ghost* implicates palpable human experiences
of Sri Lankan landscape and nature within the country's troubled political
present; experiences that as the novel suggests are so often redolent with the
weight of the country's Sinhala history and Buddhist religion.

1

Sacred Modernity takes Ondaatje's intervention seriously. The book explores the relationship between nature and Sinhala-Buddhist nationhood in Sri Lanka, particularly in the context of the normalization of ethnicized social relations and identities. It focuses on the ways that dominant discourses, materialities, and not least the poetic registers of Sri Lanka's natural environment form part of an ongoing spatial production of ethnicized identity and difference. But a central part of this task is the methodologically problematic sense in which the very concepts 'nature' and 'religion' are only partially able to make visible the political contours of environmental formations in the Sri Lankan context. In this sense, this book struggles both with and against the grain of the words 'nature' and 'religion', and specifically their conceptual capacities to bring into representation ordinary and everyday spatial formations that cohere around environmental experience, and that, as I argue throughout the chapters that follow, are more usefully understood aesthetically.

Despite these methodological problematics, ultimately *Sacred Modernity* aims quite straightforwardly to reveal the implication of Sri Lanka's environment and natural history within productions of ethnicized identity and difference that have fuelled the violently contested politics of postcolonial Sri Lankan nationhood. The book makes visible the mechanics of a pervasive spatialized politics in a context where, despite the end of a bitter twenty-six-year civil war in May 2009, a state-endorsed Sinhala-Buddhist hegemony continues apace to minoritize non-Sinhala, non-Buddhist otherness within the national polity; Tamil and Muslim groups in particular, as well as voices openly critical of Sinhala nationalism. In fact, in the immediate aftermath of the civil war the triumphalist flag-waving that crept across central and southern cities and villages alike clearly betrayed the deep-seated elisions between the Sinhala-Buddhist nation and the Sri Lankan nation state, and hence the cultural and political hegemony that characterizes postcolonial Sri Lanka (see Jazeel and Ruwanpura 2009; Weiss 2011). It is to some of the naturalizations and everyday environmental formations that make these kinds of political elisions and articulations seem so much common sense to so many that this book pays particular attention.

In this sense the book aims to tease out, to make visible that is, strains of ethno-nationalism that do not announce themselves as nationalism or nationalist political projects per se, but instead pass for the ordinary, the taken-as-given, the natural, in fact. It is my argument that these taken-as-givens are all the more powerful and thus worth considering in relation to Sri Lankan politics for the ways they help shape what many believe to be a geographical imagination in and of the country that in fact both precedes and transcends politics. This kind of work seems all the more urgent now that the war is over and the pieces of a once fractured state are settling into a worryingly orchestrated structure where the machinations of ethnicized homogeneity, power, and hierarchy are squeezing spaces for non-Sinhala difference, for the criticism of an increasingly dynastic and nepotistic government, and for civic dissent. For it is precisely this kind of political power that draws its energies and legitimacy from foundationalist and essentialist claims that Sri Lanka is a natural home for Therevada Buddhism, and that it is historically Sinhala all the way back. It is the enabling conditions for these kinds of politico-historical claims that this book excavates.

Empirically the book explores the ethnicized spatial politics of Sri Lankan nature through two prominent sites in and through which environmental relations are both curated and experienced; sites that precisely because of the access to nature they so readily afford are overlooked in actual discussions of state power and the political. First, the country's most famous national park, Ruhuna, in which Sri Lankan nature articulates itself primarily through the registers of landscape, conservation, and fauna and flora. Second, a genre of contemporary architecture known as tropical modernism that since pioneering efforts in the 1950s consciously seeks to frame the Sri Lankan environment and its tropicality as key symbolic and experiential domains. Both are actively assembled in ways that produce space and nature on particular terms. Both, in this sense, help constitute a politics of everyday and modern life.

As I argue, through both park and architecture we can trace a common environmental aesthetic that I call *sacred modernity*; one whose political connotations in the Sri Lankan context merit the labour of this book. In Chapter 1 I set out a methodology of sorts for making this *sacred modernity* visible through both park and architecture. The book departs from a long line of intellectual work across the social sciences and humanities that collectively regards nature itself to be in some senses socially constructed. That is to say, whereas nature is undeniably a material artefact and participatory space, poststructuralism has shown us nature's inherent conceptual instability, pointing out how its manifold meanings and valences are always textually and historically derived. In addition, one thing that is consistent about nature is that given its foundational import in Enlightenment thought, claims of origin, essence, and 'the real' are all too frequently made in its name. And as I have just emphasized it is precisely the Sri Lankan state's proclivity to mobilize nativist narratives of the nation state's Sinhala-Buddhist origin that necessitates we take Sri Lankan nature and environment seriously as domains connected to the political.

Chapter 1 also emphasizes that, like nature, religion is another of those post-Enlightenment concepts that is in some sense constructed; that is to say, along with nature, religion is also part of modernity's dialectic. This is of some importance in the Sri Lankan context because whilst Buddhism is constituted as a formally organized religion it is also present in Sri Lankan society as a metaphysics, an aesthetic, a structure of feeling that the word 'religion' cannot quite capture. Hence, illogical as it may sound, *sacred modernity* is not by any means a religious aesthetic, but it *is* one in which Buddhism and its ethnicizing politics are implicated. As Chapter 1 stresses, the ability to read from both park and architecture the politicizing aesthetics of what I refer to as *sacred modernity* hinges upon a radically contextual attunement to the contingency and instability of two post-enlightenment concept-metaphors, nature and religion, whose very presence in Sri Lanka is yoked to colonialism and the forms of geographical modernism so linked to the island-state's colonial spatial histories.

Following Chapter 1, the book is organized in two main parts that focus on Ruhuna National Park and tropical modern architecture respectively. Though Ruhuna and tropical modern architecture are necessarily very different kinds of spaces through which Sri Lankan nature and environment are made present, in both I argue one can trace the common characteristics of a sacred modern environmental aesthetics that spatially does the work of hegemony in contemporary Sri Lanka. As the two parts of the book show, both park and architecture are examples of a kind of spatial rationality through which considerable work has gone into making Sri Lankan nature and the environment palpably present in particular kinds of ways. But, as the book argues, it is not just their spatial rationalities that make each of these sites modern as such. It is also their mutual proximity to the political project of nationhood. Before proceeding, it is worth introducing both Ruhuna National Park and tropical modern architecture respectively.

Ruhuna (Yala) National Park

Since its conversion from colonial game reserve in 1898 to National Park in 1938, Ruhuna, or Yala as it is commonly known, remains the most popular of Sri Lanka's well-developed network of national reserves. Located in the arid southeast of the island some 309 miles from Colombo (see Map 1), the park receives over 200,000 visitors annually, and in the early 2000s income generated from nature tourism at Yala accounted for more than half the revenue of Sri Lanka's Department of Wildlife Conservation (Pethiyagoda, in de Silva and de Silva 2004: vii). The park's popularity is in part due to its wealth of native flora, fauna, mega-fauna (including leopards and elephants), and its veritable abundance of avifauna. However, just as it is popular for wildlife tourism and scientific research, Yala is also a landscape rich in the national and historical imagination because of a plethora of archaeological remains dotted throughout. As such, the poetics of park experience is a popular currency exchanged through a variety of means and media within Sri Lankan society: newspaper accounts, poems, in photographic, documentary and scholarly mediums, and not least in everyday conversation. Part I of the book comprises three chapters that offer a sustained engagement with expressions of Sri Lankan nature made present through Ruhuna's pervasive and contested landscape histories and aesthetics, as well as through the apparently benign domains of flora and fauna and their connections to the nation.

As I outline in Chapter 2, Ruhuna's enclosure as a space of nature is indissociable from a late nineteenth-century colonial desire to civilize British Ceylon's unruly and economically unproductive wilderness zones and peripheral landscapes. However, the park's postcolonial trajectories are more

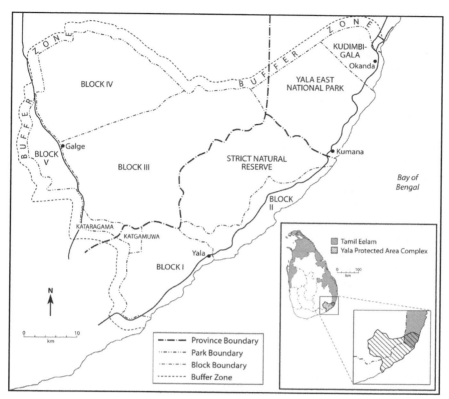

Map 1 Ruhuna (Yala) National Park, drawn by Paul Coles, University of Sheffield Cartographic Services, after H. W. Jayawardene (ed.), *Yala National Park* (Colombo: Fauna International Trust, 1993), p. 8.

complicated precisely because flora and fauna are not the only attractions in the park. As a result of extensive late colonial and then anti-colonial archaeological praxis between the early and mid-twentieth century, the park's substantial archaeological ruins are now both woven into its fabric and central to its popular meanings. In Chapter 3, I argue that the liberal distribution of these ruins throughout the park has participated in an imaginative decolonization of space, lodging the park in the popular and national imagination as a landscape congruent with the former Sinhalese kingdom 'Ruhuna'. The Ruhuna kingdom itself – often referred to as the twin cradle of Sinhala civilization (twinned with the Kandyan kingdom) – was the second-century BCE jungle refuge of the Sinhalese hero king, Dutthugemenu, who in mythic Sri Lankan historiography recorded by the *Mahavamsa* eventually defeated the South Indian Tamil 'invader' Elara in battle. In other words, and as Chapter 3 shows, the park's landscape history itself is a spatialization of what in Sri Lanka is a familiar, nationalist historical refrain of Sinhala rootedness, Tamil invasion, and Sinhala re-conquest. These historiographical landscape striations and spatializations are themselves registered and (re)inscribed through the affective economies the park commonly affords its users; what, drawing on Jacques Rancière's (2004) work, I refer to as a 'distribution of the sensible'. Sinhala spatial history is known, and made present, precisely through the non-dualistic Buddhist environmental aesthetics that Ruhuna National Park commonly affords its nature tourists.

Through Sri Lanka's civil war in particular, the park was also a strategic space, straddling as it does both sides of the border that demarcated the Liberation Tigers of Tamil Eelam's (LTTE) imaginative geography of Eelam itself, the independent Tamil homeland the LTTE fought for twenty-six years to realize (see Map 1). Chapter 4 shows how the park itself accordingly became a site of many contested claims, encounters, and not least surveillance by both State and the LTTE. And these contestations have themselves been fought around the terrain of biodiversity, environmental knowledge, and aesthetics; for example, around the semantic meanings of 'jungle' and 'tiger', the cyclical loss and securitization of the park's affective affordances, and the right of the state – as well as wildlife NGOs – to render transparent to its gaze bodies that move through park space.

Tropical Modern Architecture

For its part, Sri Lanka's 'tropical modern' architecture, sometimes referred to as just 'tropical' or 'vernacular' architecture, is a lot less obviously historio-graphically marked. As a style of building, it emerged principally through the efforts and work of a few key Sri Lankan architects who trained and qualified in London from the late 1940s onwards before returning to their homeland to practise professionally. Upon their return they begun to experiment with how best to adapt the modernist styles they had learnt in Europe to Sri Lanka's tropical environmental conditions. These were architects also involved in self-conscious and deliberate attempts to fashion Ceylon's own form of architectural modernism just as the colony was getting to grips with independence. They were trying to fashion an avowedly 'post-colonial' architecture of sorts ('anti-colonial' would be misleading given these architect's proximities to colonial privilege). Architects like Minnette de Silva, Geoffrey Bawa, and to a lesser extent Valentine Gunesekera were using architectural tools acquired through training and networking in Europe and North America to fashion what they thought to be a quintessentially Sri Lankan modernism that drew on the newly independent post-colony's own cultural, historical, and intellectual resources; a 'native' modernism of sorts that, whilst interna-tionalist, could provide a corrective to colonialism's violent interruptions in the post-colony's national identification and determination. They have ended up forging a style of building that takes as a central challenge built space's incorporation of, and attunement to, Sri Lanka's natural environment; a style that has now been popularized and proliferated as the cutting edge of modern

Sri Lankan architectural style. Bringing the analysis of Sri Lankan nature more squarely into the domain of what is often evoked as the quintessential Sri Lankan environment, Part II's three chapters collectively explore the political implications of the tropicality that modernists both architecturally negotiate and work hard to make present through their designs.

Like Sri Lanka's mid-twentieth-century artistic modernist movement 'the '43 Group', tropical modernists have variously looked to an understanding of Sinhala 'tradition' and 'folk culture' to inspire their articulations of a uniquely Sri Lankan architectural modernity. Tropical modernism's continuities with Ruhuna National Park's sanctioned and effectively nationalist landscape history speak volumes about the idioms of Sri Lankan nature more generally, and these connections are explored in Chapter 5. Central within tropical modernism is a belief that the architecture itself is a mere extension of the Sri Lankan landscape and environment. At stake here then is a key question regarding how the Sri Lankan environment is tacitly understood by these architects as well as by users of the spaces they build? And, as Chapter 5 stresses, this architecture produces spaces through which a Buddhist aesthetics in particular is made palpably present, both ornamentally and historically.

There are a number of building techniques that architects have adopted and adapted to fashion such built spaces, most of which Chapter 6 explores in some depth. These techniques aim at somehow bringing the outside environment into built space. Or, to put this differently, tropical modernists aim at deploying architectural techniques that create the experiential illusion of a merging of self and world, the fundamental dismantling of a division between outside and inside, or nature and culture, that tropical materialities practically necessitate; what I refer to in Chapter 6 as the attempt to produce fluid space. In essence, this architectural modernity works hard at fashioning a non-dualistic environmental aesthetics that itself participates in the instantiation of a 'distribution of the sensible' (Rancière 2004) consistent with those aesthetic dimensions of nature tourism in Ruhuna National Park. As Chapter 6 also stresses through the testimonies of users of this architecture, Buddhist philosophy and thought is often heavily implicated in this kind of aesthetics, and, by extension, I argue, those aesthetics sit within the domain of Buddhism's ethnic striation as Sinhala in the Sri Lankan context.

Importantly, however, there is often little political intent in the production or use of tropical modernism: neither are non-Sinhala and non-Buddhist users by any means prohibited from bringing their own readings and materialisms to this built space. As such, in Chapter 7 I stress the wide array of intertextual factors that do serve effectively to over-determine and nationalize the meaning of inside/out spaces and experiences; intertextual factors that help to lock tropical modern architecture within a semantic register in which Buddhism and Sri Lanka's Sinhala history are centrally implicated. Though Chapter 7 focuses specifically on tropical modern architecture's intertexts, I also stress the importance of intertextual over-determinations that can and must equally be applied to Ruhuna National Park. It also is not a space from which Tamils, Muslims, or other others are actively excluded; neither are there Sinhala nationalist political intentions behind acts as innocent as elephant-, leopard-, or bird-watching. Nevertheless, the park's nature is made to mean in a particular kind of way by the kinds of over-determinations explored in Part I of the book. By teasing just some of these out in relation to tropical modern architecture specifically, Chapter 7 sets forth a more general argument about the host of mechanisms that help form the distributions of the sensible that *sacred modernity* names: the social mechanisms that help comprise what Rancière (2009: 19) refers to as entire 'topographies of the thinkable'.

Thinking both park and architecture together moves from the connected but differential aesthetic registers of landscape, landscape history, fauna, and flora in Part I, through environment and tropicality in Part II, in order to begin to evoke the political contours embedded within, and instantiated through, Sri Lankan nature. Due care and attention, however, must be exercised when mobilizing these nationalizing spatial contours in the Sri Lankan context because, as I have stressed above, this is a politics of what might commonly be regarded as apolitical space. In other words, there are undoubtedly more explicitly and obviously 'political' battles to fight in the context of postcolonial and post-war Sri Lankan nationhood. As I stress in the concluding chapter, however, the effort of this book is precisely to open a new space for thinking about the conditions that enable the constitution of the political sphere in contemporary Sri Lanka. My argument is that those enabling conditions for Sri Lankan politics are the taken-as-given, the apparently apolitical ordinary, that Sri Lankan nature and environment help fashion.

CHAPTER 1

Sacred Modernity:
Nature, Religion,
and the Politics of Aesthetics

Nature, Religion, Modernity

The epithet to the introductory chapter of this book quotes a passage from Michael Ondaatje's novel *Anil's Ghost*: a passage that refers to *The National Atlas of Sri Lanka* (1988), whose very first lines – as I stressed in the last chapter – forcefully assert the historical rootedness of Buddhist monasticism in Sri Lankan stone and soil. It is significant that such bold historical statements about the nativism of (Therevada) Buddhism within Sri Lanka are made within the pages of the country's first national atlas, for national atlases are precisely those kinds of texts that inscribe with cartographic authority the singular and sanctified geographical narratives of the nation state (Huggan 2008: 21–33; Harley 1988). As geographical inscriptions with the full authoritative weight of the state behind them, they are also thoroughly modern instruments. That is to say, they organize the material and environmental fabric of territory in rational, legible ways, deploying scientific and cartographic techniques of measurement, categorization, and taxonomy to articulate, instantiate, and ultimately help naturalize one of the most taken for granted political institutions of the postcolonial world: the nation state. So much so that when the national atlas makes such potent claims about Sri Lanka's pre-modern political and religious origins, there is little that is pre-modern about the articulation of the claim itself. The modern is joined with the interest in knowing and defining the sign of the Sri Lankan national historically, traditionally, and nativistically. Like the two sites I explore in this book, the national atlas then is a typically modernist articulation in as much as it forges complex conjunctures, which, after Perry Anderson, exist at 'the intersection of different historical temporalities' (Anderson 1984: 104; also see Canclini 1995: 41–65).

My argument in this book is that in the context of attempts to understand how the postcolonial Sri Lankan national has been – and continues to be

– forged, nature and religion should not be considered as counterpoints to the modern, but instead as bound integrally to the project and politics of Sri Lankan modernity. Sacred history and modern ecotourism; transcendent environmental experience and architectural modernism; rural idyllicism and cutting-edge architectural innovation; jungle lore and rational spatial technologies of emparkment: all of these apparently oppositional pairs have been used and entwined in the making of Sri Lanka's modernity (see Morris 2000: 1–12) in ways that in turn have had ethnicizing political effects.

To expand, modernity, religion, and nature speak an unfamiliar, almost oxymoronic triangulation in the EuroAmerican academy. Indeed, the very words 'modernity' and 'modernization' often imply society's temporal movement away from the regressive mire of the sanctities of tradition, kinship, and enchanted sacred life (Berman 1983). They imply 'the consciousness of an age that imagines itself to have made the transition from the old to the new' (Gaonkar 2001: 6). Geographically also, modernity and modernization imply spatial movements from the rural, or the natural, to the urban, or the cultural, from spaces of feudal communality to the increasingly mechanized, industrialized space of metropolitan life where, as Marx and Engels (1972: 338–39) put it, 'all fixed, fast-frozen relationships, with their train of venerable ideas and opinions' are swept away. However, the natural (that is to say, human relationships with the environment), and the religious, have never been disconnected from that most modern of political projects in Sri Lanka: nation-building. As I show through the course of this book, both have been amongst those most powerful 'strategies for entering and leaving modernity' (Canclini 1995); nature and religion have been key vehicles for articulating a Sri Lankan modernity whose nation-defining trajectories are necessarily temporally hybrid, looking at once outward towards the internationalism of a postcolonial global stage, forward to Sri Lanka's own national self-determination upon that stage, and backwards to its own historiographical sense of itself.

All of this is to stress that nature and religion are part of modernity's dialectic. It is to assert that Sri Lankan environmental experience, including its sacred Buddhist dimensions, *is* modern, and that modernity itself is a useful concept through which to explore human relationships with the natural world. In this sense, following Fred Jameson (2002), modernity (capitalist and colonial) must be understood as singular, yet at the same time geographically uneven, variegated, and contextual in its force, effects, and inflections. As such, this book is an effort to map Sri Lankan modernity, specifically by identifying two types of commodification of the Sri Lankan environment, both of which mark the kinds of spatial rationality and production that emerged with colonial and postcolonial modernity. Emparkment, and national emparkment, for example, were themselves the preferred spatial tools for the control and regulation of unruly and uncivilized nature (Jazeel 2005; MacKenzie 1988; Neumann 2002) that have not only achieved something of a sedimentation of the nature/ culture binary, but also an articulation of 'the originating landscape of every nation state' (Cosgrove 2008: 71). And of course it is no more than axiomatic that *modern* architecture is explicitly fashioned as a core expression of the artistic and cultural modernism associated with nation-building (see Pieris 2007b; Bozodgan 2001). The postcolonial appropriation of these kinds of spatial rationalities, not to mention the effects of globalization on both Sri Lankan national emparkment and tropical modern architecture, do not imply homogenization or adherence to global standards. As I stress, both park and architecture offer sites – locations – for viewing the operation of Sinhala-Buddhist nationalism through both the cultural articulation and consumption of environment and nature. Park and architecture in this book therefore do not just provide windows onto modernity because of the spatial rationalities they articulate, they are also intricately implicated in the very modern project of Sri Lankan nation-building.

Provincializing 'Nature' and 'Religion'

There is, however, an important sense that to be able effectively to uncover the ways that nature and religion have been implicated in a very modern politics of Sri Lankan nationhood, we must also work hard to think both beyond their conceptual domains and into their own erasures in the Sri Lankan context; that is, we must work hard to provincialize them as modern concept-metaphors, whilst leaving their traces visible as part of Sri Lankan modernity. Though, as Jameson (2002) forcefully asserts, modernity is singular yet geographically uneven, the ability to read Sri Lankan modernity in and through the scripts it is written requires some work. Indeed, it is because of modernity's uneven nature that a degree of postcolonial effort is required to get to grips with the variegated politics of Sri Lankan modernity.

Enlightenment rationality has sedimented both the reality and presence of nature and religion in most of our lives. Both concepts have been foundational amongst the entourage of binaries and categorizations comprising the universal taxonomies of Western thought that confidently describe the world. And, as such, both have also helped render the world comparable through the abstraction that Adorno and Horkheimer (1997 [1972]: 13) famously argued has been Enlightenment rationality's stock in trade. At the same time, however, both concepts have also undergone considerable scrutiny, deconstruction, and reconstruction within the critical social sciences and humanities over the last few decades.

For example, at least since Raymond Williams (1976: 219) declared the word 'nature' to be one of the most complex in the English language, it has become *de jour* to regard the concept as in some sense a construction. A variety of work straddling Marxist, poststructuralist, and environmental historical concerns has developed the key insight, and implication, of questioning the idea that nature names a realm external to society (for examples, see Cronon 1995; Derrida 2002; 2003; Smith 1984; Soper 1995). Much of this work has sought to account for the ways that our ideas and experiences of nature are made present by a suite of representational practices (Braun 2008: 668). At the same time, recent post-humanist- and Actor Network Theory (ANT)-inspired scholarship has promulgated a return and recuperation of the undeniable biophysical materiality of things in the world that comprise networks of the social (see Bingham 2006; Clark 2010; Hinchliffe 2007; Whatmore 2002; 2006). In this rather urgent imperative to allow the world's agency to speak back to our understandings of life, we end up with a world comprised of so many hybrid, networked, 'socio-natures' (see Latour 2005).

For its part, though the word 'religion' less easily names a cluster of material *things* in the world, sociological and geographical scholarship on the concept has long noted its role as ideology in the production of social and spatial meaning (see Holloway and Valins 2002; Kong 1990; Park 1994; 2004; Sopher 1967; Yorgason and Della Dora 2009). This kind of interest in religion has derived valuable insights into some of the most dominant political languages of our time (see Agnew 2006), just as it has probed religion's presence in the 'more-than-rational' aspects of everyday life and (personal and social) ethics (Yorgason and Della Dora 2009: 631). Some of this work has also usefully sought to show how spirituality is not incidental to a secular everyday life but instead integral to it (Dewsbury and Cloke 2009).

This too brief description of a rich, diverse, and important array of scholarship on nature and religion means to establish one simple fact: both concepts remain key to the contemporary research imagination. Nature and religion are concept-domains that are part of modern theory culture. If they have both in different ways been subject to deconstructive and critical modes of thought, it is also fair to say that both nature and religion have never gone away. In this very sense, an Enlightenment rationality born in Europe is still stickily with us, over-determining the ways that we are able to frame engagements with times and places beyond the scene of the Enlightenment's rationalizations. Empirically and conceptually – that is, as categorizations and deconstructive engagements – both nature and religion continue to pervade a research imagination that for better or worse is a continuation of high modernization; that is to say, both concepts form part of a corpus of theory and method that have been seen as naturally metropolitan, modern, Western, as the rest of the world is seen 'in the idiom of cases, examples, and test sites' for this confident theory culture (Appadurai 2000: 4; also see Connell 2008; Jazeel 2009a; Spivak 2011). As the Subaltern Studies Collective amongst others have tirelessly reminded us (see Chakrabarty 2002), the intellectual implications of this for South Asian contexts located miles apart from the European factories of Enlightenment knowledge production are manifold.

What is at stake here, as Talal Asad has reasoned in his creatively subversive attempt to turn the mirror back on religion by tracing an anthropology of its other, secularism, are the colonial continuities buried within this kind of research imagination. The essentialization of the sacred as an external power emerged as European encounters with the non-European world began increasingly to deploy 'religion' and 'nature' as universal categories through which the West could identify and map different variations on those things that both concepts were thought to name (Asad 2003: 35). In terms of 'religion', specifically, such manoeuvres within critical cultural anthropology have effectively questioned and historically situated the concept *as* a colonial essentialization (see Cohn 1996) and an emergent result of orientalist knowledge production (Abeysekara 2002; Scott 1999). For example, David Scott's (1999: 53–69) work on Buddhism in colonial Ceylon has effectively shown us how its emergence *as* a formal religion in early nineteenth-century colonial Ceylon had everything to do with a 'comparative science of religion' driven by orientalist scholars whose obsession was to identify, classify, and interpret the existence of other – that is to say non-Christian – religions in the world. Religions came to be – explicitly at first, then tacitly – understood as textualized systems of doctrines-scriptures-beliefs for which the operation of Christianity provided a template of recognition. Once other religions were identified in the elsewheres of empire, their truth statuses could be investigated, compared, and disputed (Scott 1999: 58). As Scott (ibid.) puts it, 'the emergence of the modern concept of "religion" and its plural, "the religions," occurred pari passu with the emergence of the comparative science of religion. Each was, so to speak, the condition of the other's possibility'.

What this work reveals reaches beyond just the history of religious Buddhist orthodoxy in Sri Lanka. In terms of a history of concepts it also reveals religion's contemporary force as an 'authoritative categor[y] through which the histories of the colonial and postcolonial worlds have been constituted as so many variations on a common and presupposed theme' (Scott 1999: 54). In this sense, precisely because of progressive critical theoretical engagements that seek to examine religion's role in social life, what is often overlooked are the ways that the very categorization religion remains in place, conceived as external and universal force/object to-be-deconstructed. Similarly, if we can locate religion, thought this way as an identifiable system of doctrines-scriptures-beliefs, a *thing*, then it follows that its constitutive outside, the secular, will not be far away. Thus religion is revealed as one more iteration of a fundamentally dualistic 'unthinking Eurocentrism' (Shohat and Stam 1994).

In the Sri Lankan context, if Scott's work emphasizes that colonial encounter helped bring into existence something that could be called a 'Buddhist religion', it also reminds that each time we seek to understand the role that Buddhism plays in Sri Lanka's political present we risk re-essentializing the existence of Buddhism *as* religion that sits *in* particular Sri Lankan spaces. As Ananda Abeyesekara (2002: 30–66) has argued with exceptional clarity, recent critical scholarship has accordingly helped to consolidate a sense that the cause of ethnic fratricide can be traced to the corruption of an authentic Buddhist religion existent in Sri Lanka whose principles have been betrayed in modern times (for example, see Tambiah 1992). The logical conclusion of this line of thought is that if only religious orthodoxy were restored, the cessation of ethnic fratricide would ensue.

A similar critical engagement with the critical nature scholarship also reveals how even constructivist approaches re-essentialize the concept at the very moment of its undoing. Such approaches to nature in all their manifold incarnations may refute the actuality of nature as a domain separate to humankind and society by choosing to trace the myriad of social, cultural, and linguistic work that goes into producing varied and often contradictory understandings of what nature is across different times and spaces. However, by doing so nature itself is ultimately left intact as a presupposed public knowledge both at the outset and end of this work. Like religion's inescapable dualism, this is a universalizing impulse sustained by nature's own implicit dualistic relationship with culture. To unmask nature as social construction is, as Patrick Curry has recently put it, for

> culturalists [to] assume that a nature/culture distinction is a given, despite the fact that members of hunter-gatherer societies do not subscribe to it and even reject it. ... [S]uch accounts present the latter's view as involving a particular social and cultural construction of nature, thereby universalising the very dualism that is also plainly recognisable as 'Western'. (Curry 2008: 52)

Similarly, and as I have stressed above, recent posthumanist work that has sought to theorize the assemblage of the social through various actor networks or hybridities invariably do so by reverting to a Latourian language of 'socio-natures' that inadvertently leaves nature itself in tact.

This is unsurprising given both the linguistic and actual presence of the fundamentally dualistic conception nature – whatever that term may designate to each of us – in most of our everyday worldlings. In its most fundamental sense, quite simply: 'Thus "nature" is opposed to "culture"' (Soper 1995: 15). It names a specific dualism, whilst linguistically and metaphysically it parses the 'cultural' from its domain. It implicitly affirms Cartesian ontologies that distinguish a knowing human subject from a non-human object world out there. In this way, and like religion, nature's presence in the contemporary research imagination shapes what Howitt and Suchet-Pearson (2006: 326) refer to as an inescapable 'hall of mirrors', where Eurocentric ontology becomes another colonizing knowledge; like religion, another mode of 'unthinking Eurocentrism' (Shohat and Stam 1994).

Aamir Mufti has recently cast this kind of bind on the contemporary research imagination as a mode of 'global comparativism' (Mufti 2005). To do so, he employs a powerful motif in the Sudanese author Tayeb Salih's novel *Season of Migration to the North* (1969). The passage that concerns him is set in Sudan towards the end of the novel, in a remote village on the banks of the river Nile, where the narrator – a native of the village, who has recently returned from England with a PhD in English poetry – encounters a locked room in the house of the novel's main character. For Mufti, 'it is the jarring juxtaposition of what [the narrator] ... discovers in this room, in this mud house on the banks of the river Nile in the heart of Africa' that speaks directly to the epistemological problematic that comparativism poses (Mufti 2005: 479). For in this locked room is a perfect replica of an English study and sitting room, with books, books everywhere. Books ranging on astronomy through zoology, reference works like the *Encyclopaedia Britannica*, authors from Hardy to Woolf, philosophers from More through Wittgenstein, even the Qur'an and Bible in English. But not a single Arabic book. And, as the narrator remarks, the room was at once 'A prison. A huge joke. A treasure Chamber' (ibid.: 480).

What we see here is the face of an unevenly globalizing knowledge economy that structures the habitus of a knowledge production and theory culture that remain deeply Eurocentric. Knowledge of the non-West is available only through this painfully out-of-place library, in English, as Mufti writes '*in translation*, assigned its place as Oriental text-object within the architecture of the Western library' (ibid.). In the context of Sri Lanka, and in the context of this book, the methodological problems posed by implicit modes of global comparativism are significant. To search for a 'religiously Buddhist nature' is to evoke the omnipresent prison house of implicit comparativism to which Eurocentric colonial and anti-colonial knowledge confine us. To put this differently, the supplementation of the noun 'nature' with the prefix 'Buddhist' merely provides adjectival modification to the otherwise universal pretensions of nature and religion as concept-metaphors. This risks being performative in the most stultifying of ways in as much as it instantiates Western rationality as acultural and unproblematic discovery; the inevitable forward movement of theory culture's modernity (Taylor 2001; also see Chakrabarty 2000).

Spatial Formations beyond Nature and Religion: Modernity's Inflections

The subtitle of this book should make it clear that I do not seek to avoid using the terms 'nature' and 'religion'. However, a key part of my argument is that to labour with the aim of delineating a 'religiously Buddhist nature' in Sri Lanka is a task unable to make visible spatial formations and their predications of difference produced through modes of discourse and practice that contain their own non-dualistic Buddhist philosophies, ontologies, and ultimately cultural realities. Much more than this as well, I argue that to strive to locate 'religiously Buddhist nature' is in fact actively to dissimulate those non-dualistic Buddhist ontologies and more importantly their marginalizing political effects. In the chapters that follow, therefore, I am concerned with discursive and metaphysical contexts in Sri Lanka and their resulting spatial and affectual productions for which the concepts nature and religion exist only as inadequate cultural translations, or out of place – that is to say (post) colonial – ideas. As I outline, by focusing instead on the aesthetic dimensions of dominant modes of non-dualistic – that is to say, neither sacred nor secular, and neither natural nor cultural – environmental knowledge and experience, this book thinks beyond the conceptual incommensurabilities of implicitly comparative research imagination and theory culture. This kind of work is an attempt to move analysis into the space of the contextual kinds of modernity and metaphysics at play in Sri Lanka, and hence into their cascading political implications. It is to mobilize a postcolonial effort to engage a differently inflected (Sri Lankan) modernity on terms true to the singularity of its difference; a conceptual labour that Gayatri Spivak (2012) refers to as aesthetic learning.

To be clear though, this is not to try to grasp some anterior Buddhist essence or authentic Sinhala-Buddhist culture. Neither is it to claim the very existence of such Sinhala and Buddhist cultural essence as if it were some kind of object that is as yet undiscovered by the West. To do so is to mobilize something of a 'critical regionalist' argument (Frampton 1983) about the autonomy and cultural coherence of a geographical zone in tension with the standardizing world system as a whole (Jameson 1997: 248–49). Indeed, it is precisely this kind of argument that Part II of the book critically engages in order to reveal the political instantiations of those very same claims. In this sense, I should be explicit that I reject a culturalist notion of 'culture' that names certain things. I also reject any nativist assertion about Sri Lankan modernity's wholly 'alternative' essence; an essence that warrants 'cultural preservation'. Gesturing instead towards a differently inflected modernity is to mobilize an adjectival sense of 'the cultural' which moves us to regard difference, inflection, comparison, and incomparability, and 'which builds on the context-sensitive, contrast-centred heart of Saussurean linguistics' (Appadurai 1996: 12). In other words, I argue that common and modern environmental and spatial knowledge, experience, and materiality in the Sri Lankan context are themselves produced through human relations and dispositions to the world that are *written* through Buddhist, and Sinhala, discursive formations. I aim then to describe in two very particular and modern spatial contexts – park and architecture – the instantiation of *another* library of knowledge, that unlike that contained within Tayeb Salih's study (see Mufti 2005) is written in Sinhala, instantiating its own forms of Buddhist hegemony, and must therefore be read accordingly.

It is these spatial rationalities – these geographical instantiations of Sri Lankan modernity – that do the work of hegemony, helping to secure the primacy of ethnicized Sinhala identities as well as the otherness of Tamils, Muslims, and Burghers in the Sri Lankan context. In short, the work of trying to articulate those modern Sri Lankan spatial and environmental formations situated beyond nature and religion reveals the ethnicized spatial and political dimensions of everyday, ordinary life in the Sri Lankan context. To this extent, part of the challenge of this book is what Arjun Appadurai (1996: 17) refers to as the 'deep study of specific geographies [and] histories' that he rightly insists is requisite to gauge the means by which different societies appropriate the materials of modernity, and not least to gauge the political effects of those appropriations. To put this differently, geographically contextual engagements are required to grasp the political effects of modernity's singular yet uneven nature.

Whereas the book looks to spatial formations positioned beyond the descriptive powers of nature and religion, neither does it claim that nature and religion do not exist in Sri Lanka. As the very first line of this book stresses, nature *is* something of an obsession in the country. Though I explore Sri Lankan nature's articulations through different registers that might imperfectly be delineated as landscape, conservation, fauna, and flora in Part I, and environment and 'tropicality' in Part II, it is important to stress that even as a modern, theoretical abstraction, 'nature' has a strong presence in contemporary Sri Lanka. There is, for example, a sizeable industry that has grown up around 'nature tourism'. And through a significant culture of scientific research, Sri Lanka's biodiversity and wildlife management institutions have developed sophisticated engagements with the country's biophysical flora and fauna, both domestically and through international collaborations and funding. Indeed, the country's most prominent non-governmental environmental protection organization has the fundamental duality of nature/culture written into its title: 'The Wildlife and Nature Protection Society'. We can stress all this as part of the 'strategies for entering and leaving modernity' (Canclini 1995) that Sri Lankan nature presents.

Similarly, organized religion in the form of Buddhism also has considerable presence in Sri Lanka; a point that should be reasserted here. As a set of doctrines-scriptures-beliefs, consolidated by monastic institutions such as the *sangha* as well as by frequent fusions of the state with religious practice, Buddhism has a considerable and hegemonic existence in contemporary Sri Lankan society. The current constitution affords the foremost protection to Buddhism and thus to the Sinhalese people. Indeed, it is precisely the existence of a normative religious – that is to say Buddhist – orthodoxy that structures a particular kind of debate about its place in modern Sri Lankan society and in the public sphere. Normative conceptions of religion in contemporary Sri Lanka not only assume that religion/Buddhism is prior to the secular/the modern (Abeysekara 2002: 40), but they also assume that society and the sacred are two separate things. What results from such normative assumptions are a set of discussions about the placing of that religious orthodoxy *in* society and space. Hence a discussion on the relationships between politics and religion is able to proceed along the lines of whether or not religion has any place in modern public and political space. Buddhism thought this way can readily carry anti-colonial political ferment by staking a pure and simple claim to pre-coloniality and cultural authenticity (as indeed it has). However, the state can just as easily claim rational political modernity by claiming that it has excised religion and religious historiography from political and public space. For example, such claims are made that Geoffrey Bawa's parliament building is ostensibly 'secular', or that Ruhuna National Park is a public space of normative nature, wildlife, and biodiversity conservation. My point here is that identifying religion as a normative, essential object is precisely what facilitates the illusion that Buddhism *can* be parsed from everyday life and space in Sri Lanka, held separate from space and the just as pure domain of nature. As I show in this book, however, this claim is a dangerous illusion, dangerous because it actively dissimulates the political effects of Buddhism's more pervasive spatial instantiations and presence in and through modern society.

To recap on where we are so far then, my contention is quite simply that in the Sri Lankan context there are political formations situated and spatially produced beyond the normative objects that both nature and religion name. This is a sacred politics of nature situated beyond nature and religion, so to speak. And as I show in the next section, this politics is best evoked through the common and dominant non-dualistic *aesthetic* formations that produce always already ethnically striated environmental spaces in the Sri Lankan context. We can call these subaltern formations in as much as the modern theoretical rationalizations 'nature' and 'religion' do not make them visible; instead they actively dissimulate alterity, posing the considerable problem of how we can engage the particularity, specificity, and historicity of temporal and spatial contexts, without at the same time reproducing discourses of native authenticity (Birla 2010: 89). Indeed, it should be evident by now that this book is considerably influenced by the Subaltern Studies Collectives' efforts to think and work against the grain not just of historiography (see Guha 1999 [1983]) and world history (Guha 2002), but moreover categories and taxonomies of Enlightenment rationality and modernity (Chakrabarty 2002; and 2000). In this sense, I use subalternity as a trope that traffics in the considerable problematics of intimate translations of ordinariness, everydayness, and rationality located beyond Eurocentrism's familiar coordinates (Johnson 2007).

Sacred Modernity works through the considerable problem posed by the cultural translation of different and variable environmental meanings and value. And doing so, it aims to make visible a suite of non-dualistic human relationships with the natural world that in this context are at once 'aesthetic, poetic, social' (West 2005: 633). Perhaps most of all though, and paraphrasing Henri Lefebvre (1991), these kinds of cultural translations aim to make visible *productions* of space achieved through idioms situated beyond a Eurocentric metaphysics of nature and religion (also see West 2005).

Retaining the analogy of translation, and at the same time developing Arjun Appadurai's invitation to think cultural difference through Saussurean linguistics, it is worth briefly pausing over vernacular approximations of the word 'nature' in the Sinhala language in so far as these speak to the non-dualistic aesthetic formations this book attempts to tease out. In Sinhala, the word *swarbhawadharmaya* is used commonly to refer to the bio-physical world, and its use concords two semantic prosodies. The noun *swabhawaya* refers to the nature of a thing (where *swa* denotes thing), but that 'nature' is perhaps best understood as qualities, like hardness, coldness, smoothness, for example. In this sense *swabhawaya* alone might represent the closest literal equivalent to the Latin *nāturā*, or English 'nature', which, as Raymond Williams writes, used in its earliest sense refers to the essential quality of something (1983 [1976]: 219), but has come to connote a bio-physical object world exterior to the human. But *swabhawaya* is never used alone. It is commonly used in conjunction with *dharmaya*, which comes from dharma, and so connects the etymology back into a notion of Buddhist principles or philosophy (also see de Silva 1998: 29–53). As I discuss in Chapter 6, dharma is the energy that comprises a universe that, thought through Buddhist realist perspectives, cannot be divided into subjects and objects. For Buddhists then, objective materiality only emerges into existence through the cravings that at the same time constitute the self. Naturalistic reality therefore, that is to say a Buddhist metaphysical realism, is grasped intuitively – not object-ively – as the self is sensually undone to rejoin a universe of *dharma*.

This kind of abstract linguistic analysis of the Sinhala language is not necessarily amenable to grasping the grounded, lived aesthetics that produce space and thereby a politics; an aesthetics upon which this book focuses. However, it is useful if only to suggest that *swabhawadharmaya* is by no means a simple equivalent to nature. Idiomatically, its literal use mobilizes an encompassment of metaphysical principles about the (Buddhist) world itself. The point being that moving from nature to *swabhawadharmaya* is no straight-forward trade in equivalence. It requires an epistemic and metaphysical movement of sorts, a transportation and/or rupture of the imagination that makes cultural difference apparent. Equally, however, I do not pose that a Sinhala-Buddhist spatial formation, and thus a spatial politics, is instan-tiated through language or linguistics alone. Rather, the production of Sri Lankan space and all its inclusions and exclusions is constituted within discursive contexts that may themselves include elements of the linguistic and non-linguistic (Curry 2008: 58), but importantly within a particular idiom.

Aesthetics and the Production of Space

In order to begin to develop the strategies and tools to read these different idioms, I turn now to the aesthetic constitution of Sri Lankan spatiality and its politics. *Sacred Modernity* is a book about aesthetic formations embedded in commonplace understandings and experiences of the natural world in Sri Lanka; particularly in two kinds of sites through which nature is commodified and consumed: Ruhuna National Park and tropical modern architecture. It makes an argument about the spatial politics and productions instantiated by those aesthetic formations. I use aesthetics in this context not to signal any specific alignment with aesthetic theory's focus on artistic production and sensibility (Adorno 2004 [1997]). Instead, and as I have set out above, I use aesthetics to denote a suite of environmental knowledges, textualities, and experiences situated beyond the dualistic rationalities of the words 'nature' and 'religion'.

In this sense, the book resonates with recent strands within environmental philosophy that have recuperated aesthetics to suggest how human relationships with the environment are always sensory and perceptual, or, after Alexander Baumgarten, ways of 'sensitive knowing' (Berleant 1992; Brady 2003: 6–28; Kemal and Gaskell 1996). There is an important qualification, however. In his book *The Aesthetics of Environment*, Arnold Berleant writes that there is 'an aesthetic aspect to our experience of every environment' (Berleant 1992: 11), thus reminding us that this kind of environmental philosophy works hard to emphasize how all environmental experience is sensory and perceptual. In other words, there is little that is *an*aesthetic about dualistic experiences of nature/culture or the sacred/secular; nature itself is always a participatory space for sensory engagement (Carrol 1996). Rather than denying an aesthetics of 'nature', however dualistic those aesthetics may be, my approach is to use the term in the Sri Lankan environmental context as a useful shorthand for sensory and perceptive knowledges positioned beyond the domains of the dualisms nature implicates.

Aesthetics, as I use it, is not opposed to dualistic ways of being and knowing. Rather, it provides a strategy for bringing into the research imagination registers of being and knowing that the words 'nature' and 'religion' cannot. It offers a language for naming particular environmental knowledges, textualities, and worldings, and thereby politics, that are historically and culturally located in the Sri Lankan context; it offers a language able to retain the singularity of those differences, and thereby resist 'mere appropriation by the dominant' (Spivak 2003: 11; also see Mcfarlane 2006). Following Jacques Rancière, aesthetics thought this way is 'not the theory of the beautiful or of art; nor is it the theory of sensibility. Aesthetics is an historically determined concept which designates a specific regime of visibility and intelligibility' (Rancière 2006: 1). It is those specific regimes of visibility, intelligibility, and perceptive knowing that this book works hard to tease out in a context where, as I argue, sensory environmental knowledge is written by Buddhist discursive formations that instantiate their own hegemony. In Rancière's terms, it is the 'distributions of the sensible', or *a priori* spatializations, in which both park and architecture participate, that I suggest constitute a politics of Sri Lankan nature:

> I call the distribution of the sensible the system of self-evident facts of sense perception that simultaneously discloses the existence of something in common and the delimitations that define the respective parts and positions within it. A distribution of the sensible therefore establishes at one and the same time something common that is shared and [its] exclusive parts. This apportionment of parts and positions is based on a distribution of spaces, times and forms of activity that determines the very manner in which something in common lends itself to participation and in what way various individuals have a part in this distribution. (Rancière 2004: 11)

If the distribution of the sensible is an a priori consensus of sorts, for Rancière the work of the political is in the perturbation of a distribution of the sensible that the formations of political communities precipitate; the 'dissensus' (Rancière 2009). However, my own interest in this book lies more in delineating the political effects of the distribution of the sensible itself. This is to attend to the politics and hegemonic power of the coercively constituted consensus, and in doing so not to cleave the political from the social; what Rancière himself refers to as the 'police order'. In this sense, my engagement with the formative effects of a domain of environmental aesthetics in the Sri Lankan context also resonates with what Raymond Williams famously referred to as 'structures of feeling'. What I attend to are the political inscriptions and implications of 'meanings and values as they are actively lived and felt' (Williams 1977: 132). Such ways of engaging social life offer important methods for considering the politics located in constitutions and apprehensions of the normal, the taken-for-granted, and the fabric of the ordinary, but specifically through textually located registers subject to their own internal and external dynamisms.

Attending to the aesthetic constitutions of the political has considerable geographical implications. To be clear, my argument is not that thinking a non-dualistic poetics of environmental knowledge reveals particular types of aesthetic formations *in* space, as if space and aesthetics are two separate domains. As I have implied in the previous section, to do so is to frame an always politically neutral space-as-container in which the political – or the religious – can subsequently be lodged or dislodged. My argument instead is that environmental aesthetics performatively produce space in particular kinds of ways, on ethnicized and thereby political terms: these are the sacred modernities I explore in what follows. *Sacred modernity* then is an inherently spatial formation. In the context of Sri Lanka's Sinhala-Buddhist hegemony, locating *sacred modernity* attends to 'the particular spatial organization perceived to be naturally given [that] provides a locus of enunciation' (Dikeç 2005: 173; also see Dixon 2009). Space and aesthetics are coexistent in this sense, together producing forms of power and governmental frameworks for politics; that is, forms of power whose political effect resides in their very taken-for-grantedness.

In an important sense then this book regards space itself as that which is produced through the aesthetic registers that comprise environmental knowledge. Space is both the 'social text' (Lefebvre 2002: 306–11) of particular kinds of 'nature' that Sri Lankans, and others, navigate at the most basic perceptual level of daily life prior to having reflectively to formulate concepts (Edwards 2009: 232), and at the same time it is that which is continuously (re) produced through those navigations. Ruhuna National Park and the genre of tropical modern architecture are, in this sense, both spatial productions that participate in hegemony. In large part, I argue, this is precisely because they afford experiences of a reality commonly deemed pre-social, ordinary, and in some sense natural, albeit ontologically Buddhist and therefore in the Sri Lankan context positioned within the domain of the Sinhala ethnos.

Cosmopolitan Sinhala-Buddhist Nationalism

Ruhuna (Yala) National Park and tropical modern architecture are unquestionably two very different sites through which to begin to explore the commodification of Sri Lankan nature. But I want to stress that across their differences the aesthetic formations that *sacred modernity* names comprise a common plateau for understanding how the environment participates in the ethnicized production of identity and difference in the Sri Lankan context. It is important to stress once again, however, that both sites are somewhat dislocated from the epicentre of ethnicized political discourse and the formally political sphere in contemporary Sri Lanka. That is to say, commonly they are neither seen as political spaces, nor as spaces with much proximity at all to contemporary debates about the politics of identity, territorialization, or the devolution and redistribution of powers, rights, and belonging in post-war Sri Lanka. Their very overlooked-ness within the political sphere is indeed justified. Parks are just parks. Architecture is just architecture.

However, this does not mean that park and architecture – and the politics of nature more broadly – should not comprise a locus for explorations of the spatiality of politics in Sri Lanka. As spatial productions located in close proximity to the realities that natural aesthetics and environments are commonly perceived to name, both, as I have stressed, participate in productions of the ordinary, the everyday, and the taken-for-granted. In this sense, and as I make clear through this book, the *sacred modernity* I tease from both park and architecture participate in what, following Pradeep Jeganathan (2004), I refer to as a 'cosmopolitan mode of Sinhala-Buddhist nationalism'. To be clear here, I do not use the word 'cosmopolitan' to celebrate park and architecture as in any sense progressive or successful spaces of Sri Lankan multiculture. Instead, I join a growing chorus of scholars who point to the political closures in avowedly cosmopolitan hospitality narratives and performances (see Brennan 1997; 2003; Dikeç 2002; Dikeç, Clark, and Barnett 2009; Jazeel 2007; 2011). Rather than placing the production or use of Ruhuna National Park and tropical modern architecture alike anywhere near the centre of militant Sinhala nationalism, or within its mainstream political variants, it is within its 'critical, cosmopolitan margin' (Jeganathan 2004: 195) that this book locates them. That is to say, though we should be careful not to confuse the politics of nature with nationalist political violence in the Sri Lankan context, it is my claim that the politics of nature is that which legitimates nationalist violence. A cosmopolitan mode of Sinhala-Buddhist nationalism seeks neither *explicitly* physically nor politically to marginalize Tamils, Muslims, or any other others within the national polity. Indeed, part of its very cosmopolitanism is its capacity to create space for difference; to welcome the stranger in here. Like any mode of cosmopolitanism, it is worldly in its outlook and articulations, even universalist in ambit. A cosmopolitan nationalism, however, retains its hegemony precisely through its self-perpetuating capacity *to* create space for difference within a pre-constituted majority. Not only does it welcome difference into its domain, it creates what it construes as difference through its own taxonomies of thought and rationality; through the 'distributions of the sensible' that it proscribes; through *its* capacity to do the including and excluding, the tolerating and policing. A crucial dimension of cosmopolitan Sinhala-Buddhist nationalism then is its self certain retention of its own particularity – its Sinhala-Buddhist-ness as it were – that simultaneously claims for that particularity a universal place within the sign of the national (Jeganathan 2004: 195).

Both Ruhuna National Park and various articulations of tropical modern architecture spatially instantiate this kind of cosmopolitan Sinhala-Buddhist nationalism, and in doing so both also participate in a classically Derridean hospitality narrative that curates space for difference to emerge, to be welcomed and tolerated, but only by consolidating and hegemonizing its own sovereign and majoritarian speaking position (see Derrida 2001 [1997]; Derrida and Dufourmantelle 2000). It is the a priori spatializations and naturalizations of Sinhala and Buddhist primacy and rootedness that park and architecture achieve that constitute their spatial politics. They help instantiate the sovereignty of Buddhist and Sinhala thought, tradition, and aesthetics within the fabric of an everyday ordinariness that Sri Lankan nature anchors. In themselves, park and architecture make no political claims, yet they help shape the parameters through which difference can be recognized and tolerated. That is their politics.

In his work on cosmopolitan Sinhala-Buddhist nationalism, Pradeep Jeganathan (2004: 195) also returns us to modernity by stressing how such formations must unmistakably be regarded as thoroughly modern. What he means to emphasize, as I have stressed throughout this chapter, is that this kind of nationalism's sacred content is no counterpoint to the modern; religion thought this way is no regressive antithesis of a disenchanted modernity, as Enlightenment rationality might construe it to be. Rather, this sacred tradition is born of a universalism that has a sense of its own *becoming modern*, and to think as such is to jettison any lingering preconception that the West remains the clearing-house of modernity. This configuration of Buddhism as constituent of its own inflections of modernity is part and parcel of that broader challenge to think beyond the strictures of an enlightenment rationality that will readily assume Buddhism/religion is prior to the secular/ the modern (Abeysekara 2002: 40). Indeed, it is precisely the oxymoronic implication of the phrase *sacred modernity* that I use to force an engagement with the political modernities of nature and religion in contemporary Sri Lanka.

Sacred modernity is therefore a 'site-specific' study, that works from the premise that, as Dilip Parameshwar Gaonkar puts it, 'modernity always unfolds within a specific cultural or civilizational context' that lead, as he suggests, to 'different outcomes' (Gaonkar 2001: 17). Of particular importance to this study is not just the kind of deep study of specific geographies and histories for the study of modernity at large (Appadurai 1996: 17), it is also those 'different outcomes' that Gaonkar (2001: 17) implicates. In fact, the method and hard work required to make this *sacred modernity* visible is only useful in so far as it enables an engagement with the specific political outcomes contingent upon the sacred modern spatial formations I evoke in this book: that is, the spatial instantiation of Buddhist, and Sinhala, hegemony and nationalism.

Sacred Modernity as Strategy

The manoeuvre to displace – not replace – nature and religion in the Sri Lankan context with aesthetics could easily be read as just another mode of unthinking Eurocentrism. After all, aesthetics itself is yet another spoke of theory culture's modernity. To read my argument as such, however, is to mistake this book's methodological effort for theoretical assertion. What I mean by this is simply that this book is intended as a strategic and conjunctural intervention rather than any kind of theoretical treatise. Provincializing nature and religion, that is displacing them with aesthetic understandings of the centrality of non-dualistic *sacred modernity* within human relationships with the environment, is only useful in so far as it intends to make visible spatial formations that participate in a cosmopolitan Sinhala-Buddhist nationalism. Strategy mobilized this way distinguishes itself from any notion of theory conceived as dogmatic, exalted, and relatively immovable object. Instead, strategy is best conceived as an ambivalent cluster of tools chosen to work together conjuncturally as means of achieving social and political ends (see Spivak 1993: 3–5).

The fashioning of more ethnically and historically democratic spaces of nature in particular contexts in Sri Lanka then is the trajectory on which I set the chapters that follow. I do so in the hope that the broadly postcolonial methodologies and industry the book sets forth work in the Sri Lankan context to initiate a conversation about the politics of spatialities rarely regarded as political. In this sense, I do not suggest that the book offers any kind of privileged access to truth; that is, the truth about Sri Lankan nature. It is, rather, an intervention that seeks 'an immanent politics of openings' precisely by thinking about Sri Lankan nature in ways that open out for discussion its politics (Gidwani 2006: 17; also see Massey 2008). And, more than this, by seeking to intervene, the book is not just interpretation, conceived simply as 'mediat[ion] between the object and its understanding' (Ismail 2005: xxxix). It is also a participation in Sri Lankan nature in as much as the intervention it offers in turn offers possibilities for thinking and thus producing nature differently. As much as this book locates aesthetic constitutions of the Sri Lankan political, it also offers political openings through the potential that aesthetic reconfigurations might pose.

Part I

Ruhuna (Yala) National Park

CHAPTER 2

Landscape, Nature, Nationhood:
A Historical Geography
of Ruhuna (Yala) National Park

Deep in Sri Lanka's arid southeastern coastal fringes, some 309 miles from Colombo, is Ruhuna National Park, or 'Yala' as it is more commonly known. The park itself has five 'blocks', although the area known as 'Yala' comprises a contiguous system of nine National Reserves (Map 1) covering 377 square miles. Because of the civil war and the security threats posed by the LTTE, between the late 1980s and early 2000s only Blocks I and II were open to the public. Through the late 2000s, in a bid to protect wildlife from the disturbances of tourism, only Block I was open to the public. Since its designation as a National Park in 1938, Ruhuna has remained one of the most popular of a nationwide network of National Reserves in Sri Lanka, attracting hundreds of thousands of nature lovers annually. In 1995, for example, there were approximately 245,000 visitors to the park, most of whom were classified as domestic (Sri Lankan) tourists, though a significant number were foreign tourists (Panwar and Wickeramasinghe 1997). The park itself has thorn bush landscapes interspersed with pockets of fairly dense secondary forest comprising its 'jungles'. It is dotted with plains where animals can be observed at ease, and water holes as well as rocky outcrops where leopards and bears can be seen. With over thirty-five leopards spotted in Block I alone, Ruhuna claims one of the world's densest leopard populations. The Park is also replete with elephants, sambhur, buffalo, deer, wild boar, snakes, lizards, crocodiles, and an abundance of bird life.

National Parks in Sri Lanka are designated areas reserved for wildlife into which people may enter on permits issued by the Department of Wildlife Conservation (DWC). They appeal to tourists, weekend trippers, and wildlife enthusiasts alike. Visitors travel to the Park either having booked permits from the DWC in advance or with the intention of purchasing them at the Warden's bungalow. Accommodation is available in a handful of bungalows situated inside Block I, each sleeping between five and ten adults, though

Figure 2.1   Wildlife-spotting in Ruhuna National Park (author's photograph).

these must be booked in advance. Alternative accommodation is available either in campsites within the Park or in small hotels and guesthouses close by. The thriving town of Tissamaharama, twelve kilometres away, is where visitors stock up on provisions: water, meat, vegetables, coconut milk, kerosene, mosquito repellent, beer, arak, or vehicle spares, for example. Visitors to Ruhuna will usually go on early morning and/or afternoon tours of the Park, accompanied by a DWC trekker who assists with wildlife observation across a network of tracks navigable by four-wheel-drive vehicles (Figure 2.1). The DWC organizes tours in its own vehicles for those tourists who do not have their own transport. When touring, visitors must stay inside the vehicle at all times. Indeed, except when in bungalows, campsites, and a few other designated spots, visitors are not allowed to walk in the park.

Ruhuna's roots as a National Park lie in colonial cultures of the hunt and associated efforts to civilize unruly and regressive nature that were central to European drives to emparkment, a spatial history outlined in more depth later in this chapter. But today its landscapes are redolent with another kind of history and aesthetics that, I suggest, implicate the park in Sri Lanka's ethnicized politics of nationhood. This part of the book specifically delineates the ways that Ruhuna's landscape histories and aesthetics interpellate visitor experiences in ways that can be located within the contested politics of the postcolonial Sri Lankan national. Central to this argument is the fact that Ruhuna does not merely contain biophysical flora and fauna. Archaeological ruins are also woven into the park's landscapes and these ruin sites are amongst the only designated spots where visitors may alight from their vehicles when inside Ruhuna. Archaeological remains have been 'excavated' and restored by the colonial and nation state selectively over the last 150 or so years in ways that I suggest have signified the area's religio-historical resonance within popular and hegemonic narratives concerning Sri Lanka's national origins. Foundational myths instantiating a particular articulation of the postcolonial Sri Lankan national have become woven into the park's landscape materialities and connected seamlessly to an aesthetics of the natural environment in what I suggest in the next chapter have been politically charged, if quiescent, acts of semiotic and material purification. These include historical articulations of the nation state as principally Sinhala and Buddhist in constitutionally non-secular and majoritarian democratic terms.

Ruhuna today attracts large numbers of Sinhala-Buddhist pilgrims to the restored shrine of Situlpahuwa, located within Block I, and both Tamil-Hindu and Sinhala-Buddhist pilgrims to the adjoining Kataragama Sanctuary. Additionally, within Block I are the restored Sinhala-Buddhist ruin sites Akasa Chetiya and Magul Maha vihara. But in addition to these pilgrimage and archaeological sites the entire park is said to overlie the former Ruhuna kingdom, a vast irrigated, hydraulic civilization that predominated in the southeast of the island between the fifth and thirteenth centuries BCE. Ruhuna has become popularly known in Sri Lanka as the former Sinhalese kingdom that became a jungle refuge to the Sinhalese hero-king Dutthugemenu in the second century BCE. Foundational histories authorized by one of Sri Lanka's foundational, sacred texts, the *Mahavamsa*, suggest that during this period the South Indian Tamil, Elara, 'invaded' and conquered Anuradhapura, the capital of the northern Sinhala kingdom to which the Sinhala king Dutthugemenu was the rightful dynastic heir. Fleeing south, Dutthugemenu took refuge in the wealthy, irrigated Ruhuna kingdom, using its thick jungles at the very edge of the island as a home in exile that nurtured and protected him and his entourage, preparing them to wage a fifteen-year war with the Tamil Elara, which Dutthugemenu eventually won to regain control of the Anuradhapura kingdom (de Lanerole 1999: 41–48). In Sri Lanka's ethnicized postcolonial present, this narration of the nation marks the positivist historical actuality of a modern nation state foundationally written as Sinhala and Buddhist. In popular and sanctioned historical imagination, the Sinhala king Dutthugemenu's deposition of the South Indian Tamil invader Elara simply – if heroically – restored the rightful order of things within (not yet) national space. Importantly, these events are dramatized as central themes in the final chapters of the *Mahavamsa*, whose English translation from Pali by orientalist scholar George Turnour in 1837 quickly became the authoritative history of the colonial state, its poetics and imagery still very much pervading contemporary narratives of national history and memory (I expand upon this in Chapter 3).

In this respect Ruhuna National Park is inscribed with quite particular environmental and landscape histories; it is, I suggest, over-determined in ways that can mark apparently innocent practices of nature tourism as complicit in a contested politics of nationhood. Furthermore, the Yala Protected Area complex straddles three of Sri Lanka's administrative Provinces. It contains within it the Kumbukkan river, the border between the Southern and Eastern Provinces, which variously from 1983 to 2009 marked the southern most extent of Eelam (see Map 1). As a consequence, during the war, and particularly during the 1990s, the Park has been geopolitically fraught terrain within the context of the contested national. At the same time, however, Ruhuna participates in a very modern internationalism by virtue of its designation *as* a national park and biodiversity hotspot. It is Ruhuna's semiotically and materially purified articulation of the national within and through the sphere of the international that, I suggest, places its nature within the realm of the political.

Landscape Geography and National Emparkment

Central to the spatial politics evoked in this part of the book is consideration of Ruhuna's landscape geographies. Landscape has long figured as a critical locus for enquiry into the power and politics of 'ways of seeing' space, as well as for explorations of more grounded modes of experience and embodiment. Across a range of disciplines, including cultural geography (see Cosgrove 1998; Cosgrove and Daniels 1988; Daniels 1994; Duncan 1990; Matless 1998), art history (Barrell 1983; Kemal and Gaskell 1996; Mitchell 2002; Schama 1995), anthropology (Bender 1993; Hirsch and O'Hanlon 1995; Tilley 1994), architectural studies (Foster 2008; Leatherbarrow 2004), and environmental history (Cronon, Miles, and Gitlin 1992; Cronon 1995), landscape has figured as an enormously productive terrain through which modes of power, presence, and the political can be traced.

Recent decades have witnessed a retreat from purely materialist approaches conceiving landscape atheoretically simply as 'areal classification' (after Sauer 1925), towards approaches more sensitized to landscape's textual production. Borrowing from art history and literary theory in particular, early poststructural approaches to landscape geography (see Barnes and Duncan 1992; Daniels and Cosgrove 1988; Duncan 1990) productively regarded the manifold meanings of any given landscape as structured discursively through the dynamic representational processes of everyday, artistic, and intellectual life. Landscapes thought this way, textually that is, are always becoming, and in turn they are both products and signifiers of power relations and exclusions. The emphasis on landscape's textuality has also witnessed a necessary introspection regarding the term itself, especially its cultural demarcation as a concept-metaphor indissoluble from the register of the visual. Landscape has thereby been conceived not simply as area. As Daniels and Cosgrove wrote 'A landscape is a cultural image, a pictorial way of representing, structuring or symbolising surroundings' (1988: 1). Above all else, this work has transformed the study of landscape by casting it first and foremost as 'a way of seeing' though which class and power relations take shape. And it is in this vein that I consider the textual and imaginative fields within which one might critically locate Ruhuna National Park.

Landscape's cultural turn, however, has been critiqued because of the distanciation implied through such a pervasive focus on the visual (see Wylie 2007: chap. 5). The troubling couplet sight/site captures well concerns that foregrounding the visuality of land*scape* masks a more mundane human immersion in spaces that are better thought of as sites of habitation. In short, such interventions – within disciplines such as cultural geography – have asked why landscape has to circulate around the purely visual? These concerns must also be seen in the context of broader critiques of what some have regarded as a dematerialization that followed in the wake of attempts to regard landscape, like culture, as a text or as representation. Such critiques emerged variously from Marxist (Mitchell 2000), feminist (Rose 1993), and materialist (Hinchliffe 2003) concerns about construing the fabric of space in artistic and textual hues, lest this lead to the circulation of dangerously elite or immaterial spatialities. One recent response in landscape terms has turned to a post-phenomenological *sense* of the body in the world, where bodies and worlds are thought as co-emergent (see Wylie and Rose 2006; Wylie 2005). The primary concern has been to recuperate an embodied landscape experience, and landscape *as* embodied experience, in which that confluence of subject and materiality is centrally placed. Another response within critical approaches to nature more generally has attempted to recuperate the material and the bodily by drawing specifically upon science studies and Actor Network Theory (ANT) scholarship that looks to the pulling together of life as we know it through animated networks and assemblages of things and people (see Whatmore 2002; Clark 2005a; Hinchliffe 2007). This also has seen a return to a concern with nature's undeniable materiality. Both approaches – the post-phenomenological and the ANT/science studies – irreducibly conceive of landscape and nature as ground, organic, obstinately there, and material in some sense.

These emphases on embodiment and materiality are vital for considering the spatial politics of embodied nature tourism in Ruhuna National Park. However, that rejection of textualization in favour of embodiment and materiality has troubling implications for understanding Ruhuna's own spatial politics. To return to some of the comparativist concerns addressed in Chapter 1, conceiving landscape, nature, and experience as uniformly emergent across time and space, unwittingly universalizes particular understandings not just of the fabric of space itself, but also of a particular kind of emergent subject. With regards to Ruhuna National Park, when it comes to reading human experiences of its natural landscapes in the present, we can all too easily be coaxed into jettisoning textualizations of landscape meaning for fear of their dematerialization, and having to choose instead to conceive of the non-representational emergence of an unproblematically given material object world and perceiving subject (and subjectivity). Politically, the problem here is that this choice instantiates an implicitly Eurocentric understanding of a body/self/subject upon which just as implicitly Eurocentric biophysical materiality acts. Despite the useful emphasis on emergence and materiality in such configurations, we end up with the emergence of a human and human body that must ontologically be configured in a Eurocentrically individuated way; the vital, individual, and liberal subject/ivity, either with which the world emerges, or upon which the world acts. Either way, this is reductive in as much as it reinstantiates a confidently liberal subject secure in its own self-awareness that it will emerge in a particular kind of way. This precludes a more fluid conception of difference; particularly the emergence of ontologically different bodies, materialities, and, most importantly, subjectivities, that may be written in unfamiliar scripts and thereby infused from the outset with a singularity elusive for EuroAmerican landscape paradigms at least. As the work of tracing Ruhuna's landscape formations, experiences, and environmental histories reveals, materialities and the affective register are themselves written through various aesthetic practices and encounters that must be contextualized and understood through Sinhala-Buddhist philosophy and its hegemony. Emergence in Ruhuna is often about the undoing of liberal subjectivity; as I show, the becoming of a sacred, yet simultaneously modern, (non)self.

But, given these critical engagements with the term 'landscape', why persist with landscape itself as an intervention into Ruhuna's spatial politics? To be sure, Ruhuna is not easily or immediately conceived as a landscape. Its topology – all 377 square miles of it – exceeds any simple and single pictorial framing via traditional landscape conventions. Indeed, no one landscape view can be said metonymically to stand for the park as a whole. Its visual field is, in fact, arguably dominated by the taxonomic scale of species-specific wildlife photography. As I also have stressed, the Park is humanly experienced primarily via the four-wheel-drive vehicle that navigates a maze of criss-crossing tracks, offering only fleeting views amidst wafts of diesel and the incessant clunking of engine noise. Only the bungalows, camp and archaeological sites, and pilgrim routes offer the opportunity for more direct somatic connections with ground. Ruhuna National Park is better described as a vast formerly colonial park, graspable as a whole only in the imagination.

But in other ways the landscape concept-metaphor works well to evoke Ruhuna's spatial politics precisely because of landscape's connections to the textual fields in and through which it circulates as an object both of imagination *and* experience. Landscape more than any other spatial metaphor offers a sense of an environment or space that is narratologically marked, and it is the over-determined inscription and contestation of meaning by colonial encounter and religio-historical narrative that marks Ruhuna National Park *as* a landscape in the imagination. The imagination *can* grasp Ruhuna as an entity, an object, a topological whole. The imagination frames Ruhuna as a landscape within particular historiographical and aesthetic fields as well as circulatory regimes that I expand upon over the next couple of chapters. And this framing is inseparable from a number of colonial and anti-colonial encounters and practices that have, first, set Ruhuna aside as a space of modern, material, emparked nature, whilst secondly, textualized an experiential register where the natural and the cultural cannot ontologically exist as binary opposites. Ruhuna then is humanly experienced, both physically and imaginatively, in ways that instantiate an ethnicized and contested politics of identity and difference that has resonance way beyond the confines of the Park itself. Its dominant landscape histories and dominant landscape experiences, I argue, have come to hold particular salience within a Sinhala-Buddhist and national imagination, which in a non-secular, modern nation state constitutes a politics of space.

National Parks and Nationhood

National emparkment is a worldwide protocol that effectively sets aside space for a nation state's nature. Unsurprisingly, given its modern roots in British imperialism, national emparkment's very internationalism universalizes one of enlightenment thought's primary binaries, that of nature/culture, and in this sense as a process itself it participates in a violent effacement of non-binary worldings and ontologies. The nature/culture binary's pre-eminent authority to discredit the magical, supernatural, and monstrous means that national parks play a role in domesticating other kinds of ontologies, precisely by translating non-binary worldings into the reductive categorizations of either nature, or culture. As I show in the chapters that follow, Ruhuna National Park instantiates modern aesthetic terrains that conceptually and materially are not easily squeezed into post-enlightenment thought's nature/culture binary. It is a space through which bodies and environment often merge through a materialization of Buddhist precepts. That is a crucial part of its politics. But, as a modern and international national park, Ruhuna is at the same time a space set aside for the enclosure of nature, and here I want to stress the salience of the continued bifurcation of nature from culture that national emparkment and its associated environmental industries achieve. The universalizing equation of nature with the real, the essential, the pre-social, is significant in this respect.

It is often in a nation state's nature, in its 'natural landscapes', that quintessentially national virtues are thought to reside. Sri Lanka is no exception here. In a recent newspaper article archived at Sri Lanka's DWC, one Sri Lankan journalist wrote how 'Our breath-taking range of birds, animals and insects is woven into the fabric of our national life' (Buczaki 2000). Such innocuous declarations effectively naturalize social relations and identities deemed commonly 'national' simply by equating the natural with the immutable 'fabric of … national life'. In such ways identities and national templates become tied to stone and soil. Like the national, nature thought this way becomes irreducibly biophysical, material, and pre-social; apparently not humanly written. But if nature can be regarded as 'national fabric', then in the case of Ruhuna at least those fabrics have been – and continue to be – made, inscribed, and written, just as they are consumed, or read, thereby enjoining an imagined national community.

This approach invests Ruhuna's nature and its landscapes with considerable political purchase and social power. It suggests how the politics of identity and nationhood can be powerfully signified through national trajectories apparently deeply embedded in some*thing* as immutable as the nation state's nature. Part of the work of this part of the book is to suggest how social relations inscribed in place and nature, and legitimated through such a place's national emparkment, can be seen as part of the spatial production of the national (see Kaufman 1998; Zimmer 1998); a circulation of governmental power through articulations of nature. These processes inevitably also marginalize alternative claims to representation within the modern nation state by virtue of their exclusion from the natural order of things. This is true of the power and politics of the historical and aesthetic resonance of Ruhuna National Park.

No space then is more representative of a nation state's nature than the national park (Cosgrove 1995; 2008: 68–84; Cosgrove, Roscoe, and Rycroft 1996; Jazeel 2005). Whilst they overwhelmingly attempt to encapsulate national ideologues of the natural world, however understood, we cannot overlook that the cultural dimensions of national parks have also become increasingly relevant to management policies, with some international conservation organizations (the International Union for Conservation of Nature (IUCN), for example) demanding the recognition of parks' cultural components (Carruthers 2003: 257). There are two critical points to stress here: first, such demands participate in that universalizing, too certain, Eurocentric confidence in enlightenment thought's nature/culture binary. Second, because of this spatialization of a reductive nature/culture binary, human/social/historical components of a park easily become fixed either as residues of culture, or naturalized as part of that fabric of national life. Either way, if human/social/historical components are not written out of a national park, they all too often become ossified under signs like nature, culture, or tradition. Furthermore, those fragments or components become valorized; they return in an unexpected way, via a synecdochic function whereby the fragment comes to stand for the local – that is to say the national – culture more generally (Jameson 1997: 250).

In Sri Lanka, this has opened the door for state-sponsored naturalizations and ossifications of exclusivist Sinhala historiography, materially attested to in archaeological remains, or fragments, that subsequently find voice in an international arena precisely because they are now woven into Ruhuna National Park's fabric (see Chapter 3). It is through this modern internationalism, on the global stage of national emparkment, that the postcolonial Sri Lankan national is powerfully authorized and legitimated in a particular and exclusive way. The selection of whose interests are 'local', which 'traditional' components will be sanctioned within national space, and how the 'history' of place is told, embeds these social relations in nature and landscape, authorizing and assigning to them the hue of the real and the immutable. For all these reasons, Ruhuna National Park can be seen as a 'space of "nature"' through which one can read Sri Lankan nationhood. But, of course, hegemonic natures, narratives of nationhood, and social relations are also contested. Debates around security, wildlife conservation, and various pilgrim routes and practices in Ruhuna suggest deeper social and political anxieties over the production and interpellation of identities, 'race', and Sri Lankan nationhood (see Chapter 4). Similarly, contemporary experiential registers within the park, public debates surrounding the Park's landscapes, and the course of its often contested modern history, have all played a role in signifying struggles over ethnicity, belonging, and the definition of the modern Sri Lankan nation state, which feed Sri Lanka's civil unrest in the present.

Since its inception as a hunting park in late nineteenth-century colonial Ceylon, Ruhuna's nature has become gradually but very powerfully inscribed with the Sinhalese religio-historical narratives alluded to above. Dutthugemenu's legendary conquest of the Tamil Elara is regarded in popular renditions of Sri Lankan history as one of the most important episodes and foundational myths of the Sinhala people. The power of myths of origin to draw together imagined ethnicized communities is well known (see Bhabha 1990), and the Dutthugemenu narrative has lent authority to Sinhala claims of rooted belonging *in* the island space of Sri Lanka. It has done so precisely by configuring Tamils as foreigners; historically invaders of a pre-modern island polity and therefore always to-be-tolerated in a modern cosmopolitan, yet essentially historiographically Sinhala-Buddhist, nation state. Indeed that trope of tolerance, or better put the hospitality of the cosmopolitan Sinhala-Buddhist national, is a thread that I argue in this book is more deeply woven into the aesthetic terrain of Sri Lankan nature whether experienced in Ruhuna or through habitation of Sri Lanka's tropical modern architecture. Ruhuna National Park's religio-historically narrativized landscapes are hospitable only in this conspicuously cosmopolitan tradition that does violence by imposing translation on the guest who remains at the gates to-be-tolerated, always other. And it does so precisely because of the Park's strong association with the Dutthugemenu narrative. Ruhuna, and the poetics of nature tourism through its landscapes, are infused with ethnicized forms of memory and meaning that circulate around its heroic past. Yi-Fu Tuan points to the power of such landscape stories in producing the common understandings that both underpin and fracture society:

> At a more affective level, storytelling converts mere objects 'out there' into real presences. Myths have this power to an outstanding degree because they are not just any story but are foundational stories that provide support and glimmers of understanding for the basic institutions of society; at the same time, by weaving in observable features in the landscape (a tree here, a rock there), they strengthen a people's bond to place. (Tuan 1991: 686)

In what follows, I explore the various ways these foundational narratives have been so powerfully inscribed within Ruhuna National Park through colonial and anti-colonial archaeological praxis and modes of wildlife conservation and management (Chapter 3). I explore the contestation and militarization of the park's landscapes since July 1983 (Chapter 4), and I tease out aesthetic practices and experiential registers – distributions of the sensible (Rancière 2004) – within the park that reveal an ongoing production of ethnicized landscape politics (Chapter 3). Through this work there are two points to emphasize. First, the emphasis on experience speaks to a broader attempt through this book to reconcile aesthetic practice with spatial politics in ways sufficiently sensitized to the idioms of Sri Lankan nature. Second, if nature's materiality is textually and idiomatically inscribed, then, as I stress in Chapter 4, the ways that it circulates within and through society become central to the meanings it develops.

Beforehand, however, it is important to outline the emergence and inception of Ruhuna, or Yala, as Sri Lanka's most popular national park.

Ruhuna National Park's Historical Geographies

Following British conquest of the Kandyan Kingdom in 1815, and the subsequent birth of a single socio-political island colony under one centralized administration, there were few political barriers to what Nihal Perera (1998: 71) has suggested was the homogenization of Ceylonese space within a single schema that produced new differentiations and nodes within it. The British re-mapping of Ceylonese space brought the entire island under one imaginative framework rendered through imperial cartography. It represented Ceylonese space as a homogenous surface, organized within a grid of longitudes and latitudes that sought to erase all other signatures and inscriptions in its way, transforming extant space into *tabula rasa*. This Euclidean recasting of space laid the foundations for colonial ways of knowing and valuing Ceylonese land, that is, which parts of the colony derived importance, use-value and, ultimately, development potential under the colonial gaze. And this gaze was, of course, structured around notions of rationality and reason, teleological progress and the potential for improvement, and, not least, economic value: moral and commercial justifications for imperial expansion in the colonies themselves. As a consequence, positivist classical economic thought and its mercantilist manifestations were central to British ways of framing and inscribing landscape meanings in nineteenth-century Ceylon (for more on imperial cartography, see Barrow 2008).

Land in the southeast perimeters of the Ceylonese island held little economic value or potential for the British in the early to mid-nineteenth century. It was inconsequential within the economistic gaze of British administrators who were faced by its unproductive soil, dry heat, and entangled growth. Such land fell into the ubiquitous category of unproductive 'jungle', which right from the very highest level of British Ceylon's administration, the Governor, was deemed an impediment to the progressive potential of industry:

The question is one, not of ease, or convenience, but of life. You must go on, or you must go back ... Hence, the general conviction, that a great effort must be made to accomplish a common object, or the jungle suffered to encroach anew upon Districts which are now a model of thriving industry. (Ward 1855)

For the British administration, the 'jungle' was unhealthy and threatening. Its unchecked and regressive wildness stood in the way of human progress, and it therefore signified both a backwardness and modernizing challenge that taken together ideologically justified the very effort of imperialism. Above all else, the 'jungle' perennially threatened to overcome and subsume potentially productive space. Just one year after his remarks, the Governor, Sir Henry Ward, warned that parts of Ceylon's Eastern Province would soon succumb to 'beasts of the field' who, if not stopped, would become 'the lords of the soil' (Ward 1856: unpag.). His concern was that 'the most lovely country that I have ever seen, rich in all elements of successful industry, bids fair to become, before long, the domain of the elephant, and the Bear, without a single human competitor' (ibid.). As much as this was a warning, it also marked a challenge for imperial ferment.

In contradistinction to jungle, forest and shrub-land had modernizing, economic potential. Forest in particular was healthy, open, controlled, and unfettered from the shackles of extreme wildness or aridity; its aesthetic value derived from its economic potential as timber. But as material as the distinctions were between forest and jungle, they were also textual in as much as it was the very adjudication on whether or not an area had economic potential that determined its designation as either forest or jungle. In the late nineteenth century, the colonial government sought to develop more of the island's environmental resources, undertaking economic assessment of the potential of much of the island's territorially marginal space. Peripheral island-space was thus brought more squarely into the utilitarian colonial imagination because of its potential or not for forestry and plantation agriculture. From around 1870 onwards, previously overlooked areas were surveyed and assessed. As part of this process, the colonial administration published reports researched and written by forestry experts seconded to the island-colony from elsewhere in the empire.[1] They drew on land-use surveys that identified areas suitable for commercial timber industry. The concern was with converting 'jungle' to its more economically productive counterpart 'forest'; a land-use transformation cognate with a progression through colonial teleology, from wild space through to civilized, modern, and economically productive timber plantations.

The Hambantota district in Ceylon's Southern Province, the area now

---

1 For example, reports such as the 100 plus-page *Forest Administration of Ceylon, Report on the Conservation and Administration of the Crown Forests in Ceylon* (written in 1883 by F. D'A. Vincent of the Indian Forest Service), that suggested the most effective ways to manage Ceylon's potential timber resources.

occupied by Ruhuna National Park, harboured particularly poor forestry potential because of the combination of its seasonal extremes of alternate aridity and monsoonal overgrowth. However, F. D'A. Vincent's forestry reports revealed the ruins of abandoned reservoirs, or 'tanks', which amongst other things testified to the region's former agricultural prosperity. The importance of colonial archaeological 'discoveries' are explored in more depth in the next chapter, but here it is important to stress that in the late nineteenth century these alerted the British to the potential of paddy cultivation in and around Hambantota. Given the restoration of tanks and watercourses, colonial administrators believed they could effectively put to use some of the more open jungle expanses with their infertile soils in this previously neglected southeast corner of the island. This nurtured a rapidly reforming landscape aesthetic in southeast Ceylon. Some of the more accessible, forgiving, and less overgrown land around the Hambantota region was transformed into irrigated agricultural land, but the encroachment of 'jungles' nearby now became a more urgent practical as well as symbolic problem.

Effectively, the emerging economic potential of land in the southeast heightened ideological conflicts between the progressive march of civilization marked by the industry of agriculture and the threat of unchecked wild nature. Early in that period during which the Hambantota region was beginning to be re-imagined, a colonial Administrative Report for the Southern Province (Anon. 1874), referred to leopards, alligators, venomous snakes, and bears as 'noxious' because of the threat they posed to sedentary agriculturists. In that same year, an investigation into the working of a Game Ordinance described the land that became the Yala Protected Area Complex as 'mostly forest and low jungle, infested by wild animals and fever haunted' (Fisher 1874: unpag.). These kind of colonial spatial imaginations suggest a moral contest played out across the terrain of landscape, and it is here that the inception of Yala as regulated space of nature must be conceptually and historically located.

Where agriculture or forestry was not possible the British looked to hunting to bring practically and symbolically wild space under their control; to civilize the savagery that inhered in 'jungle' as word and space. The subjugation of unruly nature at some considerable risk to the huntsman was not only affirmation of colonial masculinities, it also held the potential to open up the 'jungle', liberating it from the clutches of what Sir Henry Ward referred to back in 1856 as the 'beasts of the field' and 'lords of the soil'. Furthermore, civilizing the very periphery of a peripheral colony through hunting was not just an appropriately noble, gentleman's leisure pursuit, it also affirmed the power and scope of colonialism itself. By the last decades of the twentieth-century hunting had become a popular gentleman's pursuit in the 'jungles' and plains just beyond Hambantota.

John MacKenzie's work on the relationships between empire and hunting (1988: 12) has suggested how Britain's classically educated elite working in the colonies were influenced by ancient Roman and classical Greek tales of the spread of civilization through man's heroic subjugation of nature. He points to assertions that these fables and the 'spirit of the chase' were equally responsible for the adventures and enterprises that led to the exploration and settlement of 'unknown and pagan lands' (ibid.: 37; also see Lorimer and Whatmore 2009). In late nineteenth- and early-twentieth-century Ceylon, there was an abundance of literature that testified to the romance and virtues of 'the hunt' in Ceylon's peripheral rural areas, including, for example, Samuel Baker's *The Rifle and Hound of Ceylon* (1882), 'Snaffle's', *Gun, Rifle and Hound* (1894), and Harry Storey's *Hunting and Shooting in Ceylon* (1907). The literature made explicit the links between nobility, masculinity, and 'the hunt's' performative capacity to spread civilization across peripheral Ceylon. As Samuel Baker wrote in 1882:

> sport is an amusement worthy of man, and this noble taste has been extensively developed since the opportunities of travelling have of late years been so wonderfully improved. The facility with which the most remote regions are now reached, renders a tour over some portion of the globe a necessary adjunct to a man's education; a sportsman naturally directs his path to some land where civilization has not yet been banished. (Baker 1882: xvii)

Owing to the popularity of this morally virtuous sport in these last decades of the nineteenth century there emerged a genuine concern that fauna in Ceylon's southeast was being hunted to extinction. Pressure to protect fauna, simply to preserve the sport for colonial administrators and the emergent indigenous 'colonial bourgeoisie', came from the Game Protection Society of Ceylon; a quasi-independent group who lobbied the colonial government making full use of their own privileged status and connections to the colonial administration (see Uragoda 1994). For the Game Protection Society, preserving Ceylon's fauna meant preserving 'the hunt' itself, and for members of the Society, many of whom were from the indigenous Ceylonese elite,[2] participation in 'the hunt' placed them inside colonialism's teleology of trusteeship. 'The hunt' was a noble and respectable sport which intended the regulation of noxious and dangerous wild beasts; it was a controlled, rule-bound, and civilizing activity. As Baker quipped, in terms that asserted 'the hunt's' imperial and very British virtues:

> The character of a nation is beautifully displayed in all our rules for hunting, shooting, fishing etc.; a feeling of fair play pervades every amusement. Who would shoot a hare in form? who would net a trout in stream? who would hit a man when down? A Frenchman would do all of these things, and might be no bad fellow at all. It would be *his way* of doing it. (Baker 1882: xvii)

---

2 From the 1930s onwards, following the Donoughmore constitutional reforms, the colonial administration pursued a deliberate policy to 'indigenize' the colonial government.

And so, to ensure the preservation of fauna for regulated and 'fair' hunts activities, pressure from the Game Protection Society led to the enclosure of the Yala Game Sanctuary and adjacent Resident Sportsmen's Reserve in 1898. The Game Sanctuary was roughly correspondent with what is now the Yala Strict Natural Reserve. It was 150 square miles in extent, comprising what administrators referred to as 'absolutely uninhabited forest land' in the Eastern Magam Pattu (Wace 1898: unpag.). It lay between the Yala and Kumbukkan rivers, the latter of which was the designated border between the Southern and Eastern Provinces, and its northern extremity lay at the border of the Southern and Uva Provinces. Absolutely no shooting was allowed in the Sanctuary. It was intended as a game replenishment zone for the next door Resident Sportsmen's Reserve, which was situated to the west of the Game Sanctuary comprising what is now Block I of Ruhuna National Park. The Game Sanctuary included what are now the Kataragama and Katagamuwa Sanctuaries, and was delimited by the Menik river. Here shooting was allowed, although strictly under licences issued mainly to moderately wealthy colonial administrators and the emergent indigenous elite that included members of the Game Protection Society. Administration of the Game Sanctuary and Resident Sportsmen's Reserve fell to the locally based Assistant Government Agent for the Hambantota District, whose reports from the late nineteenth and early twentieth century suggest that the enclosures proved instantly successful in terms of replenishing animal numbers in the region. Furthermore, remissions for shooting licences proved a valuable revenue stream.

Yala Game Sanctuary and the Resident Sportsmen's Reserve grew quickly early in the twentieth century, mainly due to the threat that local poachers posed to the colonial hunt. The nobility of 'the hunt', of course, was to be distinguished from the more morally reprehensible activity of poaching (Mackenzie 1988: 10), so boundaries physically demarcating the Yala Game Sanctuary were designed to keep poachers out. Parts of the northern and eastern boundaries were pathed and widened making them easier to patrol, and in 1914 a report suggested that the Resident Sportsmen's Reserve should be extended to include a portion of the Uva Province to its north, as well as a portion of the Eastern Province (Millington 1914). The thinking behind these extension plans was to surround the Sanctuary on all sides with the Sportsmen's Reserve thus effectively precluding the ability of poachers to enter. But the extension of space designated for licensed hunting activities would also allay real fears that the Sanctuary was becoming so successful in replenishing animal numbers that the outbreak of disease was imminent. In 1914, the size of the Resident Sportsmen's Reserve was accordingly increased.

The 1898 enclosure of the Yala Game Sanctuary and Resident Sportsmen's Reserve was made possible by the discursively violent Waste Lands Ordinance, which was pushed through one year earlier in 1897. The Ordinance allowed the colonial government to declare as Crown property any land not 'legally' owned by any person, native or otherwise. In the southeast, after the Sanctuary and Reserves were declared, some provision was made for locals to pursue native title claims, but the violence of this legislation was that it inscribed the language and bureaucratic machinery of proprietorship onto space otherwise managed through communal understandings and agreements that if documented were done so in scripts that the empire did/could not recognize. In this sense, the absence of title claims in the Colonial Office archives does not adequately convey a sense of just how many people's livelihoods were altered by the Game Sanctuary and Sportsmen's Reserve enclosures. If we can be sure that 'proprietorship' claims could not be effectively demonstrated through the native title claims procedure, we cannot be certain how many local people depended on the land for shifting cultivation and hunting that had been reclassified as 'poaching'. High levels of illiteracy in English and unfamiliarity with the well-oiled colonial judiciary and proprietorship laws would have ensured that the responsible local Government Agent did not hear even a small percentage of local grievances regarding the enclosure's impact on their land use rights.[3]

Tracing Yala's early history shows its inception to be a far cry from its status today as a landscape held in trust for the nation state. Its early enclosure as a Game Sanctuary and licensed hunting Reserve, access to which was restricted to a suitably respectable and masculine elite, served to hasten dispossession of this land from its resident population. The early history of Yala's emparkment was as much about the colonial state's power to restrict a colonized Ceylonese population's access to land and natural resources, as it was about the preservation of fauna. From its inception, Yala fixed in space the relationships of power, proprietorship, and morality that were central to colonialism's civilizing zeal; central to the very operation of colonial modernity in Ceylon. But this is not to overlook another dimension of post-enlightenment modernity that Yala's emparkment also spatialized: a super-organic *cultural* mastery over *nature* that fixed in space an understanding of the binary relations between the human and non-human. In pre- and post-enlightenment western Europe, the 'park' was a space where horsemanship and martial skills were practised and perfected: a visceral space of muscular challenge and violence (Cosgrove 2008: 73–76); it was where hierarchies of culture over nature were performed. On the margins of aristocratic country estates, where landed nobility positioned their cultural selves in Edenic allusions to pastoral life, lay the wildness beyond the garden; a space where hunting and military parties could satisfy their voracious appetites for civilizing nature. These ideological and imaginative templates

---

3 Claims that did make it to the Government Agent and then to court were usually rejected out of hand: for example, a claim was made in 1898 on a significant portion of land in the Yala areas by a Mr Le Messurier on behalf of a number of local residents. The courts swiftly rejected this de facto native title claim, and it was understood by the Provincial agents that Le Messurier had no interest in the land in question, but took up the case on the understanding that he would receive one-third of the land if the claim was successful (Lewis 1898).

have been central to Ruhuna National Park's emergence as Sri Lanka's quintessential space for nature.

In his work on colonial spatial history, Paul Carter (1987: xxi) has written that treating space as simply 'natural', passive, objectively 'there', has the effect of draining what is most characteristic about any place – its historical content, its litany of repetitions, reinscriptions, and re-articulations. Ruhuna's nature, that is to say the fauna and flora it contains and is now deemed woven into the fabric of the nation state Sri Lanka, seems so apparently non-discursive, objectively there, material. But its very setting aside as nature emerges from this colonial history. Outlining the colonial modernities that effectively created the park provides an important context for what follows. Colonialism's entourage of hierarchies and binaries, its elitist and exclusionary practices, gave birth to an enduring spatial structure and landscape element that, though suffused with this colonial modernity, nonetheless lays claim today to alternative Sinhala-Buddhist narrativizations and aesthetics. At Ruhuna it was colonial encounter that 'provide[d] the agreed points of reference, the maps which define the architecture of "here" and "there"' (Jacobs 1996: 21).

From Yala to Ruhuna

In Ruhuna today, a host of practices such as wildlife photography, biodiversity conservation, environmental management plans, and scientific research projects all continue to produce the National Park as a modern and secular environmental hotspot; the (inter)national park *par excellence*, a modern enclosure where Sri Lankan nature is set aside as biophysical object and articulated internationally. But through the 1930s the collection of reserves at Yala began to be re-narrativized with apparently different temporalities: the pre-colonial Sinhala-Buddhist historiographical inscriptions that today are also synonymous with the Park. In Ruhuna National Park, Sri Lankan nature is now pervaded by the sacredness of Sinhala history and Buddhist aesthetics. Furthermore, as Chapter 1 has argued, these kinds of sacred environmental aesthetics and their concordant political configurations of difference cannot be seen as pre-modern in any way. Instead, the sacred and its pre-colonial history may more usefully be conceived as part of the very fabric of modern national life in this South Asian context. Paraphrasing Ashis Nandy, in such contexts mythic and godly histories are part of the modern by virtue of the ways they 'enter and exit the lives of citizens likes so many impossible, unpredictable, troublesome house guests' (Nandy 2002: 9). The twentieth-century anti-colonial reinscription of meaning in Sri Lanka's most popular national park is an important chapter in the spatialization of sacred modernity.

New perceptions and the reinscription of Yala are traced through the colonial archaeological and historiographical formations addressed in the next chapter. However, such reinscriptions were enabled by the Fauna and Flora Protection Ordinance of 1938, which was drafted from recommendations made in a 1934 report by an ad hoc Fauna and Flora Protection Committee established to enquire into the measures required for the further protection of Ceylon's wildlife. Even though members of the pro-hunt Game Protection Society served on this Committee, the report was instrumental in initiating a tide change in Ceylon that saw the decline of perceptions of Ceylon's fauna as 'game'. The 1934 report declared that the word 'game' was inappropriate for future discussions about the preservation of fauna in Ceylon because it implied that animals should be preserved solely for the purposes of blood sport (Brayne, et al. 1934). In this sense, it was consistent with a wider shift in international opinion through the first half of the twentieth century regarding the status of hunting in relation to emergent concerns over wildlife conservation. In framing a policy for the future, the most significant recommendation made in Ceylon's Report concerned the dedication of parts of the country to wildlife so it might live and breed with the minimum of human interference. In doing so, the report drew upon the findings of an international committee that sat in London some years earlier and recommended the constitution of three distinct categories. First, there were to be Strict Natural Reserves, to be entirely dedicated to wildlife with entry strictly prohibited except where absolutely necessary. Second, National Parks conceived as parts of the country where wildlife should be protected but into which the public can enter subject to restrictions to study and enjoy the wildlife. And thirdly, Intermediate Zones where game sports were permitted under strict control. Crucially, however, Ceylon's Fauna and Flora Protection Committee advised on the addition of a fourth category peculiar to Ceylon because of its rich seam of nineteenth- and early-twentieth-century archaeological 'discoveries' and the emergent indigenous interest in the religio-historical stories to which these ruins were pointing (see Chapter 3):

> We consider that three classes are suitable to Ceylon, but we also feel that wildlife cannot be adequately protected without the addition of a fourth. There are a number of places in which it would be of great advantage to prevent altogether the useless destruction of wildlife. We would include in such places several of the localities held especially sacred by Buddhists. In and around these places we feel that public sentiment would strongly favour the protection of wildlife. We cannot, however, constitute such areas as National Parks as a considerable part of the land is already in private hands. We, therefore, propose that a special law should run in such areas prohibiting except under definite conditions, the destruction of wildlife. We propose to term these Sanctuaries. (Brayne, et al. 1934)

These recommendations and their implementation in the 1938 Ordinance can be seen as part of the continued governmentalization of colonial power in Ceylon. As David Scott has shown, the transition in colonial power from the 'rule of force' to the 'rule of law' was central to ushering in Ceylonese modernity (Scott 1995: 208). Colonial circulations of knowledge, legislative procedure, and political rationality powerfully secured the colony as a state precisely by marking the emergence of social and political rationalities that secured appropriate forms of conduct amongst Ceylon's colonized.[4]

The 1934 Flora and Fauna Protection Committee Report can be read as the rational discourse of an indigenizing bureaucracy articulating and anticipating the independent nation state in an emergent, yet compliant, anti-colonial idiom. Ceylon's path to independence was marked by a heavy investment in colonial trusteeship and its teleological political narratives (see Madden and Darwin 1994: 175), and the 1931 Donoughmore Constitutional reforms were testament to the colonial administration's desire for a 'gentlemanly' transfer of power (ibid.). It was the emergence of such a terrain of colonialized political rationality that enabled the Fauna and Flora Protection Committee to recommend 'Sanctuaries' as an addition to the three other categories. The very contours of colonial political and spatial rationality were used to articulate emerging autochthonous myths of origin and nativeness. And in this respect, the precise wording of the recommendation is significant. Although national Sanctuaries have been used in Sri Lanka to protect a plurality of religious sites (including Kataragama at Yala), the recommendation itself makes no mention of places held sacred by the colony's religious minorities: Hindus, Christians, and Muslims specifically, whose emergence as religious and racialized minority groups was itself a biopolitical achievement of colonial governmentality (see Angell 1998; Scott 1999). The recommendation and subsequent legislation proved a way of recognizing Buddhism and its majority ethnicized correlate, Sinhala, within the framework of imperial national emparkment legislature. Even though the category 'Sanctuary' was suggested for private land, the recommendation set in motion state-sponsored recognition of the confluence between wildlife and Buddhism, because the Ordinance's reference to religion was quite obviously a byword for Buddhism.

The 1938 Fauna and Flora Protection legislation enabled the connections between late colonial archaeological 'discoveries' of Ceylon's Sinhala-Buddhist historiography and wildlife conservation to pervade Ruhuna National Park's landscape histories and aesthetics. As a result of the recommendations, archaeological ruins that were being restored selectively by the Archaeological Survey Department could now be embedded in Ceylon's Nature. Given the intense activity around Ceylon's archaeological formation and the incorporation of material discoveries into an emergent 'national' historiographical formation (see next chapter), the recommendation of a network of national Sanctuaries to protect Ceylon's wildlife lay the foundations for equating 'national' fauna and flora with the material traces of the 'indigenous religion',

---

4 Though Scott's argument about 'colonial governmentality' is made with reference to the emergence of Ceylon's Colebrooke Cameron constitutional reforms that occurred some 100 years prior to the Fauna and Flora Protection Ordinance, his argument that the emergence of political rationality in the colonies shaped Ceylonese/Sri Lankan modernity and political power is relevant for understanding this period.

Buddhism, and its associated 'history'. Three powerful domains of colonial public culture were thus being brought together under the anticipated sign of 'the national': nature, Sinhala history, Buddhist religion. The 1930s was a pivotal time in this powerful confluence. At a time in colonial Ceylon when D. S. Senanayake's pro-independence movement was being forged upon multiracial and secular constitutional principles based on the Westminster model, the spatialities and aesthetics of nature and wildlife in Ceylon were being shaped through much more exclusive and non-secular idioms.

It was on 1 March 1938 that the Fauna and Flora Protection Ordinance was passed by the State Council and assented to by the Governor. Immediately, the Yala Game Sanctuary was redesignated as the Yala Strict Nature Reserve (incorporating what is now Block II of the National Park; see Map 1 to follow the changes to the Park). What had been the Resident Sportsmen's Reserve (now Block I of the National Park) became Yala National Park, and the village of Kumana, the pilgrimage sites at Kataragama, were all declared as Sanctuaries. Although all the newly drawn National Reserves were to come under the management of the Department of Forestry, a Fauna and Flora Advisory Committee was appointed to report on the measures needed to bring the Ordinance into operation and to frame regulations. Two years later the Yala North Intermediate Zone (now Block III) and the Yala East Intermediate Zone (now Yala East National Park) were settled and declared.

Perhaps more significantly in terms of that equation of Ceylon's wildlife and nature with the emergent national religion and its racialized historiography, in 1943, Yala's name was changed to Ruhuna National Park. This was an attempt to increase the park's popularity, but it did so by turning this landscape into a public palimpsest recalling a 'glorious' and 'heroic' past civilization and kingdom, that, as I show in Chapter 3, was emerging through intense archaeological and historiographical work as a crucible of Sinhala spirit and Buddhist rootedness. If the renaming proved a successful method of increasing the park's popularity it also irreversibly reoriented the textual and aesthetic field in which the Park is now positioned. As Catherine Nash has argued, postcolonial renaming strategies draw on a repertoire of 'cultural re-appropriation, resistance, recovery and reclamation', but in so doing they can unproblematically spatialize exclusivist assumptions regarding a 'pure homogenous, pre-colonial culture suppressed by colonialism' (Nash 1999: 463; also see Varma 2004).

In 1949, the newly formed Department of Wildlife Conservation took over the responsibility of managing the group of Reserves, and in 1954, the coastal strip of Yala Strict Natural Reserve was redesignated as Block II of the National Park, thereby opening up this strip of land to the increasing numbers of wildlife enthusiasts visiting the park. The coastal strip also contained an old Dutch road that had served as a pilgrim route for East Coast, mainly Tamil, pilgrims travelling to Kataragama, even though it was formerly part of the Strict Natural Reserve and thus intended to be inviolate from human activity (Coombe 1955). Its excision seemed the logical management decision, but I argue in Chapter 4 that it had a significance regarding the ability of the state to regulate and manage the movements of Tamil pilgrims through the park. Yala North Intermediate Zone and Yala East Intermediate Zone were also incorporated as Block III (in 1967) and Yala East National Park (in 1969), respectively. Block IV was added in 1969 and Block V in 1973. The effect of these boundary changes has been today's Ruhuna National Park (Map 1).

From its enclosure as a National Park in 1938, Yala's popularity steadily increased year after year. Following the improvement of roads in the Southern Province in the early 1940s and enthusiastic promotion of the park, the number of visitors continued to grow: in 1946, there were 488 recorded visits; in 1947, 1,001; in 1948, 1,518; in 1949, 1,839; and in 1950, 3,252 (de Silva 1951). In the following chapters, I take this historical geography forward to analyse the inscription of meaning and the subsequent poetics and politics of landscape experience in the Park (Chapter 3), as well as the more contested geopolitical debates and discourses that have pervaded Ruhuna National Park in recent years (Chapter 4). In both of the following chapters the central concern is with evoking and reading the often occluded political contours of what has emerged in Sri Lankan public culture as the nation state's most famous National Park. As with Part II of this book, however, it is not just the politics of those more explicitly symbolic dimensions of the park that concern me – the iconography of its wildlife or historically charged archaeo-logical ruins, for example – it is also the less tangible, but equally symbolic, registers of non-binary environmental experience and aesthetic practice that I am concerned to bring into representation in this work. These sacred modernities suggest a pervasive spatial and environmental politics that the broader argument of this book contends has echoes across spaces of nature in Sri Lanka.

CHAPTER 3

Inscription and Experience: The Politics and Aesthetics of Nature Tourism

> The silhouette of an elephant-black
> Against the darkening gray.
> The mongoose crawls along the road
> At a leisurely pace.
> Still calmness stands alongside the trees.
> The sky darkens.
> Darkness envelopes all around.
> All is still.
> One with the universe.
>
> Kusum Disanayaka, 'Dusk at Yala',
> *The Island*, 8 August 1992

Upon entering Block I of Ruhuna National Park, visitors pass through a gate upon which is a portal inscription. Yellow letters painted on a dark green board announce that:

> Through these gates you enter a Protected area. The animals, birds, trees, the water, the breeze on your face and every grain of sand, are gifts that nature has passed on to you through your ancestors so that you may survive. These gifts are sacred and should be protected. Whisper a silent prayer as you pass through for the protection of wilderness around you and ensure that what you see and feel is passed on to the unborn generations to come.

From hereon in, the expectation and excitement of encountering at any moment a wild elephant, leopard, or sambhur emerging from its natural habitat becomes somehow indissoluble from the feeling that one has stepped into a sacred place, rich in history. Encounters with wild animals (Figure 2.1) are savoured, photographed. Animal behaviour is keenly observed, later explained by the trekker. Throughout tours of the park, visitors are struck by the tranquil aesthetics that seem to seep from its succession of different natural landscapes: flat plains dotted with grazing buffalo; thick, boggy scrub jungle; sand dunes and rocky outcrops where leopards bask; or glassy green lakes dotted with cormorants.

Most visitors will also stop to visit some of the Park's rich archaeological landscapes: Situlpahuwa, Magulmahavihara, or Akasachetiya, for example. At the rock outcrop Akasachetiya, the summit is reachable by a short, steep twenty-minute climb. Here there is a small pool in which Lotus flowers bloom next to the ruins of a Buddhist dagoba just a few metres high, dating back to the second century BCE, and there are breathtaking views, the elevation offering a sense of Ruhuna National Park's territory. In the distance, the gleaming white towers of the restored Situlpahuwa temple complex, which receives some 50,000 Buddhist pilgrims each year, are clearly visible. On one of my visits to Ruhuna National Park, my friends and guides, Anil and Dharshenie (both Buddhist, and both Sinhalese), were keen to show me this view. Staring across Ruhuna's expanse, I could not help but think that all that territory between here and there was somehow just as sacred. The Sinhala-Buddhist resonance of these two places, Akasachetiya and Situlpahuwa, seemed to pervade the landscape stretching before me. As Ruhuna's portal inscription implies, there is something about this place. There was also something very normal about my experiences on top of Akasachetiya; an awareness of how the poetics of that moment were indissoluble from this place's Sinhala history and its concordant Buddhist aesthetics, part of its nature.

As I show in this chapter, my experiences were not unique. It is to these relatively common, yet palpably evocative, senses of history and aesthetics that this chapter pays particular attention. First, to the ways they have in some senses been over-determined through the park's colonial and anti-colonial trajectories, and second to what they continue to signify in terms of Sri Lanka's troubled postcolonial present. If, for the author of the poem with which this chapter began, in Yala one finds moments where '*All is still. One with the universe*', then the second half of this chapter works to read the dominant register through which that indivisible oneness is marked. Both aesthetically and politically, I ask what it means to be at one with the universe in Ruhuna? This work of reading, however, must begin by unravelling the scripts and inscriptions with which the park has been written. I do so in the first half of this chapter by focusing on Ruhuna National Park's dense complex of archaeo-logical, historiographical, and epigraphical formation.

Archaeology, Epigraphy, and Historiography: Inscribing 'facts on the ground'

In recent years the relationship between archaeology and politics has received growing attention from a range of critical scholars, including anthropol-ogists, historians, and archaeologists themselves (see Abu El-Haj 1998; 2001;

Chatterjee 1995; Schmidt and Patterson 1995; Tilley 1989; Wylie 1993). Much of this work has drawn attention to the powerful ways that archaeological practice and its scientific truth claims effectively construct taken-for-granted narrativizations of the past, authorizing particular, often state-sanctioned, historical accounts of place and people. Rejecting the positivist conceit that archaeological science merely excavates taken-as-given buried archaeological records, the work of archaeological 'excavation' has instead been reappraised in recent years as itself a practice that carves particular kinds of meaningful and generative objects out of the earth's depths. Archaeology has come to be critically regarded as a process that produces what Nadia Abu El-Haj (2001: 13; my emphasis) calls '*facts on the ground* that instantiate particular histories and historicities'. Thought this way, archaeological science and praxis can be reconceived as the politically charged inscription of history in space; a practice whose assumed scientific objectivity spatializes historical narrative *as* facts on the ground (ibid.). By authorizing and constructing a common past, and by inscribing it in stone, archaeology produces the historical time of the nation state and the contours of its modern present. In so doing it just as easily defines who 'we' are, as it does who 'they' are, helping to produce a 'national consciousness', and in this sense participating in what Rogers Bruebaker refers to as 'nationness' thought as a category of practice (1996: 7; Abu El-Haj 2001: 6).

Sri Lanka has a strong tradition of state archaeology and associated epigraphical work (the science of deciphering ancient inscriptions), which has played a major role in spatializing Sinhala-Buddhist myths of origin far and wide across the island state (Kemper 1991; Jeganathan 1995). Essential to understanding these processes, however, is recognition of archaeology's role in the complex dynamics of colonial encounter in Ceylon from the nineteenth century onwards. If nineteenth-century archaeological and epigraphical practice led to the inception of what was to become the hugely influential Archaeological Survey Department, it also emerged from an imperial obsession with the Orient's perceived ancientness; an obsession that endures in Sri Lanka today. Colonial archaeology and epigraphy, I argue, must be seen as part of a broader historiographical formation that has pervaded everyday life in Sri Lanka, and today is a dominant aesthetic feature in Ruhuna National Park's contemporary landscape geographies.

Pradeep Jeganathan's (1995) work on the colonial conquest and authorship of 'ancient' Anuradhapura has effectively demonstrated the centrality of archaeological praxis to the colonial state's historiographical formation. As he has shown, the 'ancientness' and Sinhalese historiographical narratives within which Anuradhapura is discursively positioned in contemporary Sri Lankan society, are in fact inseparable from mid- to late nineteenth-century colonial archaeological practices. Anuradhapura's own ancientness in other words, not to mention its authoritative epistemology and pre-eminent position in a national historiographical and public imagination, is a modern – that is to say, colonial – production (Jegenathan 1995: 108).

Tracing the trajectory of Anuradhapura's own colonially inscribed 'ancientness' is instructive for developing a richer, critical understanding of the early twentieth-century emergence of Ruhuna National Park's sacred modernity. The establishment of Ceylon's Archaeological Commission in 1868 was the direct result of colonial fixations and anxieties about what to do with the ruinous remains of old settlements 'discovered' at Anuradhapura (ibid.: 123–4). For a British empire of science obsessed with the Orient's ancientness, Anuradhapura posed a political problem as far as colonial power was concerned: how to author pre-colonial Ceylonese antiquity whilst maintaining Ceylon *as* a British possession? Much more than a specific question over Anuradhapura, this is but one formulation of a more fundamental question that the unfolding of British colonialism continually rubbed up against and confronted through its various encounters: how could the imposition of European history, modernity, and power be justified in space that so evidently had its own pre- and co-existing social formations? In as much as this posed an anxiety, it was allayed, negotiated, even repressed, by the very mechanics of the colonial project in all its complexity. A rich seam of recent scholarship has shown how the governmentalization of colonial power effectively extended the long arm of colonialism through the production of new terrains of social, political, and intellectual rationality (see Duncan 2007; Legg 2007; Prakash 1999; Scott 1995). Ceylon's Archaeological Commission, and the colonial state's rich archaeological formation, must be seen in this respect. It was part of a terrain of scientific-intellectual, geographic, and historical rationality that emerged in the mid- to late nineteenth century, and through which, later in the 1930s, an indigenous elite eventually came to rearticulate the nation state-to-come's geography. Most importantly for our purposes, it was key to inscribing Ruhuna National Park's landscape geographies.

If 1868 marked the inauguration of the colonial Archaeological Commission and its intense activity surrounding Anuradhapura, it also marked the beginning of a broader colony-wide interest in Ceylon's *archaeological record*. It was in the 1870s that the eminent London-trained orientalist Dr P. Goldschmidt led exploratory fieldwork on behalf of the Archaeological Commission (around the same time that F. D.'A. Vincent was conducting his forestry surveys). Goldschmidt's team mapped numerous cave and rock inscriptions in the colony's arid and inhospitable regions. These were photographed and promptly brought back to the administrative centre, Colombo, for painstaking analysis and translation as Goldschmidt hoped to produce a *Corpus Inscriptionum Zeilanicorum* (Gregory 1875). Archaeological artefacts found in the field were also brought back to Colombo for display in the newly constructed museum of 1877, whose Georgian architectural style provided a suitably modern and symbolically apt frame for the 'native' archaeological record. That effort to move artefacts from peripheral field spaces and to do interpretive archaeological and epigraphical work in the colonial metropole Colombo is significant. It articulated the centrifugal technologies of modernity and rationality embedded in colonial archaeological practice itself. It also justified a colonial presence in Ceylon by bringing the colony's backlands under the modernizing power of a scientific gaze whose very claims to authority rested on that notion of the centredness of colonial authority. Significantly, the only other place where interpretive archaeological analysis was being done was in the vast scientifically modern, laboratory-like, Anuradhapura field station: a veritable crucible of colonial modernity (see Jeganathan 1995).

The Pali inscriptions that Goldschmidt translated dated back as far as the fourth century BCE. Engraved on the walls and drip ledges of rock caves and shelters, they indicated that these used to be dwellings inhabited by Buddhist monks (the sangha). Goldschmidt published the first report on his findings in 1876, detailing and translating inscriptions that dedicated land in the North Central Province and Hambantota District to the sangha. His report was ordered chronologically, with findings listed in ascending order of periods of continuous time from the fourth century BCE up to the eleventh century, and geographically, with findings from the various Districts and Provinces discussed in separate parts in each periodic category. History was thus configured as a continuous narrative flowing seamlessly from the past towards the present; a positivist mode of history writing that was essential for empire's claim to be able 'truthfully' to 'excavate' the past of its colonies (Jeganathan 1995: 110). Geographically also, the North Central Province and Hambantota district in the southeast were brought into the imaginative sweep of the singular history of an island-colony. Furthermore, Goldschmidt's work simply sparked a curiosity over the rich archaeological record waiting to be properly excavated in Ceylon's southeast. In 1898, the same year that Yala was enclosed, an Archaeological Survey commission report followed up on Goldschmidt's stimulus by stressing that the Hambantota district and that desolate, wild, and unruly land near Yala required further exploration and survey because of its importance as the site of the former Ruhuna Kingdom.

Historiographical Formations

Important in this story, though, are a broader set of mid-nineteenth-century historiographical and textual formations that precipitated this colonial preoccupation with Ceylon's material archaeological record. In seeking to write, and therefore control, the linear regimes of historical truth regarding their South Asian colonies, imperial historians more generally struggled to find sources they could count on as 'accurate' and 'reliable'. South Asian textual epics contained ahistorical fictions that did not meet the dominant conditions of historical truth required for orthodox colonial historiography (Jeganathan 1995: 111). In Ceylon, this problem was acute with regard to the Pali Vamsa texts whose notions of non-linear and preternatural causality were antithetical to colonial positivist history writing. That is, until George Turnour's 1837 English translation of the Pali text, the *Mahavamsa*. Just as significant as the fact that by 1838 his translation of the *Mahavamsa* becomes *the* authoritative historical text of Ceylon (ibid.), are the violent transformations to the text wrought through the process of translation itself. These enable it to become an authoritatively positivist historical account in imperial eyes. As Pradeep Jeganathan has shown, these transformations were linguistic and stylistic, but, most importantly, they epistemologically transformed the text:

> The dominant regime of [colonial] positivist historiography read out all conceptions of the world and epistemological positions that were contrary to it. That is, notions of incalculable, non-linear time and 'fantastic miracles' that could be regarded as central to the text, were marked in translation as unimportant, biased, 'ahistorical' and 'untrue.' ... [T]hese indigenous fields of knowledge ... became what Foucault calls 'subjugated knowledges.' (Jeganathan 1995: 113)

The crucial effects of all this are twofold. First, we end up with a text that authors a historiographical formation structured through the positivist regimes of historical truth that colonial historians trusted, and in this respect the narrative becomes overwhelmingly dominated by a history of kings, battles, threatened sovereignties, and heroic victories. Second, this narrative formation is, from its 1837 translation, ethnicized. It intersects with nineteenth-century theories of 'race' and historical community. Transactions in the *Journal of the Royal Asiatic Society of Ceylon* were linking a Sinhalese 'race' to North Indian Aryan ancestry, and Tamils to South Indian Dravidian roots (Angell 1998). *The Mahavamsa* 'begins' with North Indians who arrive on the island in 543 BCE and then metamorphose into the 'Sinhalese'. The major narrative then comprises Sinhala kings and peoples who, throughout the period that is the text's terrain, battle with Tamil 'invaders' for control of a nation imaginatively projected backwards through that linear history (Jeganathan 1995: 116). Importantly, if the text is ethnicized, the colonial conception of religion (see Chapter 1) is retro-actively projected onto that narrative simply because the *Mahavamsa* was compiled from the sangha's chronicles by the monk Mahathera Mahanama. If it was emerging as a 'national' text of sorts, it was also 'religious'. Through its orientalizing translation the text *became* a historiographical 'chronicle' that projected the modern (that is to say colonial) 'rightfully Sinhala and Buddhist' nation form back through the previous 2,400 years. The Ruhuna region becomes key to the narrative of Tamil invasion and Sinhala recapture, because one of the *Mahavamsa's* key episodes is the Sinhalese 'hero'-king Duttugemenu's battle with Elara (see Chapter 2).

It is worth emphasizing here just how important the Dutthugemenu episode continues to be to the articulation of the Sri Lankan national. Because of Dutthugemenu's 'heroic' deeds he is often touted as the champion of the Sinhala 'race'. David Scott's own critical take on Sri Lankan public culture's *Dutthugemenu complex* perceptively suggests that, in a certain sense, Dutthugemenu's vanquishing of Elara comes before history, because it participates in a process of imaginative clearing essential for asserting the untrammelled existence of an ethnically Sinhala and religiously Buddhist island (Scott 1999: 98). But this should not mask how, in many other ways, Dutthugemenu lives very much as part of Sri Lanka's mass cultural and historical present, participating in what Sasanka Perera has persuasively referred to as 'the presence of the past in the present' (Perera 1999: 103–34). As K. M. de Silva writes in his still authoritative text, *A History of Sri Lanka*, Dutthugemenu's legend is 'an epoch making confrontation between the Sinhalese and the Tamils, and extolled as a holy war fought in the interests of Buddhism. Duttugamini's triumph was nothing less than the consummation of the island's manifest destiny, its historic role as the bulwark of Buddhism' (de Silva 1981: 15). The simple point – as de Silva's text attests – is that the Dutthugemenu myth is a social text that has continuing force in Sri Lankan public culture.

If Anuradhapura provided the location of Dutthugemenu's battle with Elara, the jungles of Ruhuna were where he gathered his resolve and armies having been expelled from the north. Dr P. Goldschmidt's late nineteenth-century findings in the southeast were helping to fuse these textual historiographical formations with archaeological *facts on the ground*; they hinted at material evidence of the *Mahavamsa* as chronicle. Materially, though, the southeast was still regarded a desolate backland 'infested by wild animals and fever haunted' (Fisher 1874: unpag.), simply because all this interpretive archaeological, epigraphical, and historiographical work was undertaken in Colombo. The seeds of new and ethnicizing pre-colonial historiography, however, had taken root within Ceylonese public culture through the late nineteenth and early twentieth century.

New Archaeological Practices: Reinscribing Ruhuna

The 1933 appointment of Senerat Parnavitarna to Head of the Archaeological Survey Department marks a crucial turning point with regards Yala's reinscription as Ruhuna National Park. This appointment must be seen in the context of a period where colonial governmentalities were gradually but powerfully shaping private desires and rationalities. First, as we have seen, Parnavitarna's passage to the Department came following the mid- to late nineteenth century when the entrenchment of ethnicized 'race' thinking had congealed into persuasive communitarian narratives. Being a practising Buddhist himself, Parnavitarna's spiritual life was influenced by the imperial fashioning of Buddhism as world religion, which process had also contributed to the emergence of protestant modes of Buddhism early in the twentieth century. Second, by the time of Parnavitarna's appointment, Turnour's epistemologically violent translation of the *Mahavamsa* had already become *the* authoritative text of the island-colony-state. That linear historiographical formation of 'Sinhala glory and then Tamil destruction, Sinhala reconquest and Tamil desecration, repeating, recycling' (Jeganathan 2004: 192) was becoming accepted as autochthonous myth of origin. And third, Parnavitarna was appointed Director of the Archaeological Survey Department following the 1931 Donoughmore Commission's recommended 'indigenization' of the colonial government. The semi-autonomous State Council was beginning to argue, in an appropriately gentlemanly manner (see Madden and Darwin 1994: 175), that Ceylon's indigenous elite were sufficiently developed to manage the colony's passage through to independence.

In this context, Parnavitarna's religious and historical convictions convinced him of the need to continue to 'prove' the truth of the *Mahavamsa* through the scientific rationality and method at his disposal. Archaeology and the science of deciphering inscriptions were, for him, learned and modern mechanisms through which to ascertain the historical truth of the *Mahavamsa* as a chronicle of pre-colonial times, and hence to help fashion an independent post-colonial Ceylon. They were ways of proving to the world the text's cosmopolitan Sinhala history, and, perhaps more importantly, to himself. For example, having deciphered one first-century BCE inscription taken from Koravakgala near Situlpahuwa, which was then inside the Yala Resident's Sportsmen's Reserve, he wrote in his 1934 report for the Archaeological Survey Department that 'The inscription, therefore, is very interesting as evidence for the veracity of the *Mahavamsa*' (Parnavitarna 1934: unpag.). In this sense there were important continuities between his archaeological and epigraphical work and Dr. P. Goldschmidt's late nineteenth-century labour, but in another important respect his tenure marked a rupture in prevailing archaeological praxis that had real material effects on Yala.

Parnavitarna initiated new archaeological practices that wrested disciplinary practice away from museum cabinets in the colonial capital, and back into Ceylon's peripheral rural landscapes, where in previous years countless valuable finds had been made only to be removed by archaeologists like Goldschmidt. The shift in praxis was consistent with a broader revalorization of 'the rural' in colonial and elite indigenous culture as well as in Ceylon's anti-colonial politics through the first decades of the twentieth century.[1] State-sponsored archaeological and epigraphical work was yet another way of bringing the island-colony's backlands squarely into the popular imagination. Speaking some thirty-five years after Parnavitarna's appointment, his eventual successor identified the tide change that Parnavitarna's work brought about:

> Many of the old notions about archaeology have been thrown overboard. Time was when most people thought that the functions of Archaeology were limited to the exhibition of objects in museums. The position today is different. Any one with the faintest idea of Archaeology knows today that objects removed from their place of find have lost much of their value. When the people of this country became interested in antiquities for the

---

[1] Leonard Woolf's *The Village in the Jungle* was published in 1913, and D. S. Senanayake's rural resettlement vision, entitled *Agriculture and Patriotism*, was published in 1934.

very first time, finds from various parts of the country were brought to the Colombo National Museum to be accepted there. The accepted principle now is to leave objects in their original places. (Godakumara 1967: unpag.)

Concentrating their praxis beyond Colombo's museum and the Anuradhapura field station, then, Parnavitarna's team embarked upon a colony-wide programme of archaeological restoration and epigraphical translation *in situ*. This included considerable work in the southeast, around the Yala complex, which just decades earlier had been regarded by the colonial administration as 'infested by wild animals and fever haunted' (Fisher ?1874). This new approach effectively breathed new life into dead archaeological artefacts, ruins, and epigraphical inscriptions, charging their corresponding landscapes with profound new senses of time and history.

In his 1934 report for the Archaeological Survey Department, Parnavitarna enthusiastically described the year's fruitful work in the Eastern Maggam Pattu (Yala), which had been undertaken in response to late nineteenth-century recommendations that further exploration be undertaken in Ceylon's southeast. Parnavitarna's work in the southern part of the Uva Province and areas incorporated within the Yala Game Sanctuary, revealed the ruins of dwellings and temples referred to in the Mahavamsa, including Situlpahuwa and Akasachetiya, both of which were in subsequent years excavated and restored. The language used in Parnavitarna's reports is telling, the tone amplifying the ethnicized politics that inhered in translations of the *Mahavamsa*. For example, of one particular inscription found in Yala's Resident's Sportsmen's Reserve, Parnavitarna wrote:

An inscription under the drip ledge of a cave at Koravakgala, near Situlpahuwa in the Maggam Pattu, mentions a general (*senapati*), named Mita, of King Devanampiya Abhaya, *the national hero of the Sinhalese*, and his general Mita with Nanda Mitta, one of ten legendary warriors who *helped Dutthugamini to conquer the Tamils*. (Parnavitarna 1934: unpag.; my emphasis)

His words equated a legendary Sinhala historiography whose textual field was congruent with the *Mahavamsa's* pre-eminence in Ceylon, with the retroactive projection of a pre-modern territorialized Sinhala nation. Through this briefest of passages, we can read a kind of *working out* of history in relation to space; a mapping of historiography that was powerfully striating Yala's colonial landscapes with the purity of heroic, pre-colonial memory. The antiquity of an imagined Sinhala 'national' community, and its perennial struggle to defend its ethnic and territorial borders against a marauding Tamil other, was being inscribed in material landscape as *facts on the ground*. Though the decolonization of the Ceylonese historical imagination can be traced through earlier mid- to late nineteenth-century archaeological industry at Anuradhapura as well as through the violent translations of the Mahavamsa (see Jeganathan 1995), territorially – that is in ways that had more material impact on the peripheral backlands – Parnavitarna's new archaeological approach in the 1930s was directly decolonizing landscape and Ruhuna's nature itself. If the *Mahavamsa*'s refrain was towards a cosmopolitan Sinhala-Buddhist national narratology – Sinhala glory, Tamil destruction, then Sinhala reconquest and accommodation – then Parnavitarna's work was to locate and inscribe those narratives across extant colonial space. More than outright anti-colonial resistance, though, this was an achievement of archaeological modernity that, Parnavitarna believed, simply enabled an igneous history to speak for itself. In the southeast, the stones were attesting that Dutthugemenu and his entourage were once there. 'Discovery' and 'excavation' were the signs under which these new histories were being written.

This new archaeological praxis had other effects as well. Of another inscription found and translated at Koravakgala near Situlpahuwa, Parnavitarna writes in that same 1934 report how it 'mentions that the cave, in which the record is incised, was a gift, to the *sangha*, of the treasurer of Pita Maharaja (the Great Father-King)'.[2] In such ways these inscriptions pointed to native ownership claims that long pre-dated the Crown's colonial claims on land at Yala. Though Parnavitarna's work did not lead to legislative title claims made against the Crown, it was more or less proving Crown land at Yala never to have been *terra nullius*, and it was doing so through the very rationalities with which colonial governmentality had furnished Ceylon's indigenous elite. But these traces of indigenous proprietorship also precluded Tamil claims to any sort of rooted attachment to Yala's soil, and in so doing they participated in the very production of ethnicized community narratives rendered in relation to place. If a Sinhalese historical community was now being spatio-temporally rooted in island territory, a relationally produced other – the Tamil community – was narrativized as transient, *routed through* island space, and thereby guests. In such ways, perceptions of Yala's nature were changing. Its materialities and diachronic frameworks were being renamed. No longer 'mostly forest and low jungle, infested with wild animals and fever haunted' as Assistant Government Agent F. C. Fisher had remarked in 1874, it was emerging materially as the former Ruhuna kingdom, with rich connections to a cosmopolitan Sinhala historiography that could not help narrate Tamil presence in the island *as* other.

Just as its textual and historical fields were being rewritten, Yala was also being aesthetically reinscribed through the religious connotations of its new historical narratology. Caves and rock shelters that excavation and epigraphical translation had deduced were inhabited by monks some 2000 years ago, imaginatively mobilized the non-secular registers that were central to early twentieth-century protestant Sinhala-Buddhist consciousness (see Obeyesekere 1970), and Senerat Parnavitarna's own religious consciousness (see Jazeel 2009c). In apparent admiration for what he regarded as the

---

2 This is the same first-century BCE inscription that, as mentioned above, Parnavitarna suggests is interesting for the veracity of the Mahavamsa.

pervasive ascetic precepts and discipline of a bygone era in the southeast, Parnavitarna wrote that even though

> There is very little, at any of these sites, of the developed stonework and sculpture which one notices at Anuradhapura ... The monasteries, of which the remains are seen today in this area, must have been founded at a time when the ideal of world-renunciation, preached by the early Buddhists, had not yet become a formality, and the monks were still willing to live, devoting their time to meditation, in secluded caves and huts away from the din and bustle of towns. (Parnavitarna 1934: unpag.)

Though the area was less abundantly marked by the stone and sculptural work found some one hundred years earlier at the Anuradhupura field station, it was being brought into the same archaeological, historiographical, and aesthetic fields as that most important archaeological site. If Anuradhapura's new – that is to say colonially inscribed – histories (Jeganathan 1995) also marked out new aesthetic fields that fused the modern with a sense of the 'legitimately ancient', then it was Parnavitarna's conviction that part of the Archaeological Survey Department's work was to facilitate the 'excavation' of those same aesthetic and perceptual fields in Yala's landscapes. I pay more attention to the existence of these aesthetics in contemporary nature tourism in Ruhuna in the next section of this chapter, but here I want to stress that in the 1930s, Yala's archaeological record was suggesting to Parnavitarna that restoration and excavation work would merely help re-mobilize an ethnicized aesthetics that once resided in Yala's stone and soil. Aesthetically, as well as materially, then, his archaeological and epigraphical praxis aimed at manifesting the 'presence of the past in the present' (Perera 1999: 102–34).

> Among the archaeological sites of the Magam Pattu inspected during the year, Situlpavuva is perhaps the most important. It is named 'Cittalapabbata Vihara', in the chronicles and Pali commentaries. From the latter it appears that Situlpavu Vihara, in ancient days, had the reputation of being an abode of Buddhist recluses of very advanced spiritual attainments. The site of which has now been given over to the Buddhists for restoration. (Parnavitarna 1934: unpag.)

Parnavitarna is quick here to mark a distinction between his own secular scientific praxis and the religious 'Buddhists' to whom the site is given for restoration. But his own public preoccupation with a bygone era of meditation, asceticism, and spiritual attainment marks an aesthetic field that, I suggest, speaks of that fluid traffic between a very modern, public, and political sphere that maintained pretensions to secularity, and a just as public register of sacredness connected to the emergent Sinhala-Buddhist historiographical formation. Aesthetically, these are the immanent contours of Sri Lanka's own inflections of modernity in which as I have suggested in Chapter 1 the sacred is no counterpoint to habitations of the modern.

Perhaps the semantic tipping point of all the archaeological, epigraphic, and historiographical formations sketched here came with the Game Protection Society's 1943 decision to change Yala's name to Ruhuna National Park in 1943, to 'bring it some of the blessings it so badly missed as Yala' (Anon. 1943: 130). Now the *presence of the past in the present* was spatially and materially irreversible.

From Sinhala History to Sacred Wildlife

In terms of Yala's emergence as sacred modern space, the significance of Parnavitarna's archaeological and epigraphical work was heightened by the 1938 Fauna and Flora Protection Ordinance. As argued in Chapter 2, the Ordinance provided official sanction for equating Ceylon's nature with the emergent historiographical resonances and sacredness of Parnavitarna's various field 'discoveries'. The effects were marked. For example, through 1940s' and 1950s' Archaeological Survey Department reports we can trace a significantly different deployment of the word 'jungle'. No longer unhealthy and threatening as it was for the economistic mid-eighteenth-century British (see Chapter 2), 'jungle' was a sign that marked space culturally and religiously redolent within the Sinhala historiographical formations outlined above. And, just as significantly, in the first reports of newly independent Ceylon's Wildlife Department (founded in 1949, now the Department of Wildlife Conservation), the country's biophysical nature was being linked directly and explicitly to those same Sinhala archaeological and historiographical formations:

> Ceylon is probably unique in its possession of a historical background of Wild Life Protection extending uninterruptedly into the past 2000 years. It was a traditional duty of the Sinhalese Kings, who were Buddhist rulers, to give protection to wild beasts, birds and fishes, and the fulfillment of this duty is recorded in the Chronicles and inscriptions. (Nicholas 1954: unpag.)

Sinhala historiography and national wildlife conservation were now on their way to being well and truly married: both also meeting in a Buddhist aesthetic and formally religious textual field. The archives provide further evidence of the ethnicization of Ruhuna's fauna and flora. For example, a comment in a 1954 Wildlife Department report noted the 'discovery of a herd of *Sinhala* wild cattle in Ruhuna National Park' (Nicholas 1954: unpag.; my emphasis). Slightly less anecdotally, in 1935, just two years prior to the Fauna and Flora Protection Ordinance, permission was granted to issue licences to shoot fifty elephants in the Hambantota district (Hudson 1936: unpag.). Wild elephants were considered a nuisance by local farmers, whose livelihoods were constantly at risk from their peregrinations; an enduring problem even today. However, in the decades following the 1938 Ordinance the archives become peppered with writings that testify to the elephant's position as iconic fauna in the history of a Sinhala nation, the *Mahavamsa* again being invoked in such textual significations. Elephants, of course, would no doubt have long occupied such revered positions within indigenous and local environmental knowledges, but what is notable is that their representational presence in the archive changes post-1938. In this sense, the elephant (as iconic and sacred fauna) can be seen as a kind of subaltern semiotic figure that only comes into representation with the decolonization of the archive from around 1938 onwards.

Through the 1940s and 1950s, it seems that Ceylon's indigenous and elite scholars of antiquity were beginning to read the important presence of fauna, particularly the elephant, from the *Mahavamsa*, a trend that has continued into very recent history. For example, in a 1981 essay on *Fauna of the Mahavamsa* published in Ceylon's journal of state archaeology there are notes about 'numerous references to elephants of war, the most known of which is Dutthugamanu's war elephant playing its heroic part in the battle of Vijitapura' (Adithiya 1981: 4). And in this respect, by the 1950s, the elephant had become *the* major wildlife attraction at Ruhuna National Park, prompting a major scientific research project on elephant behaviour by North America's Smithsonian Institute into the late 1960s. During the late 1990s, the management plan devised for Ruhuna National Park marked out 'Conservation of the elephant as a "flagship species"' as a management objective (Panwar and Wickeramasinghe 1997: iv).

This faunal amalgamation of sacred historiographical resonance with a modern, rational, and scientific gaze is typical of Ruhuna's nature today. It is another example of what marks the park as at one and the same time a modern space, set aside for the rational and secular management of bio-physical material nature, and simultaneously as spatiality framing a sacred, troublingly ethnicized, history and aesthetics. As I have shown so far, this *sacred modernity* is no taken-for-given essential materiality. It has been inscribed through complex and overlapping processes of late nineteenth-/ early twentieth-century archaeological, epigraphical, and historiographical praxis and its emergent connections to wildlife conservation discourse, that have, as this book contends, helped to instantiate that cosmopolitan Sinhala-Buddhist national at the heart of Sri Lankan nature. It is to the experiential and aesthetic effects of Ruhuna National Park's idiomatically marked nature that the second part of this chapter turns in more depth.

Rereading the Poetics of Meaning in Ruhuna National Park

Let me return to Akasachetiya, the rocky outcrop in Block I of Ruhuna National Park, on the summit of which are the remains of a partially restored second-century BCE Buddhist dagoba. At its base there are caves and inscriptions just as old, and chronicles record that there was once a stairway leading to the top of the rock. In his 1934 report, Senerat Parnavitarna wrote how this site is 'connected with the legends of Dutthugamini, which state that in his previous birth as a *samaneri*, he acquired a store of religious merit by constructing flights of steps ascending to the courtyard of the *dagoba* at this place'. Akasachetiya is one of the most popular of a number of ruin sites within the park, perhaps because its elevation offers fantastic views across the park's landscapes. All in all, it is an outstanding example of how ethnicized facts on the ground have been inscribed through the late nineteenth- and twentieth-century epigraphical, archaeological, and historiographical formations described above. But, as textual as any process of inscription is, Akasachetiya still exists *as* ground, *as* materiality, to be experienced corporeally. Given these colonial and anti-colonial histories, how can we reread nature tourism at Ruhuna National Park? What are the political connotations of those very evocative aesthetic registers frequent in the park experiences with which this chapter began?

In his book *The Presence of the Past* (1991) the anthropologist Steven Kemper explores the powerful ways by which the archaeological restoration of Sinhala ruins across Sri Lanka has contributed to what he refers to as 'enacting Sinhala nationalism'. He suggests how the careful, scientific practice of restoring ancient piles of rubble to what archaeologists believe was once their original state makes it difficult to separate what is 'legitimately ancient' from what is a modern reconstruction. This infuses the present, thought as a moment in space and time, with an architectural and historical past, rendering landscape experience not just visible, but importantly open to the realm of human experience. There is a troubling tension in Kemper's work that too easily confuses the modern (colonial) *production* of ancientness (discussed above) with a notion of the 'legitimately ancient' recovered through careful restorations of place. Kemper's implication is that Sinhala-Buddhist sacredness does reside in ruins, and, under the sign and effort of 'restoration' (or, as Nadia Abu El-Haj suggests, though 'excavation' (Abu El-Haj 2001)), archaeological praxis has the capacity to unlock positivist histories (for a fuller critique, see Jeganathan 1995: 107–08). In other words, the modern formation of 'ancientness' itself is not interrogated.

Despite this, Kemper usefully opens a space for thinking about the confluence of material geography and human experience in the spatial politics of nationalism. His work gestures towards the importance of the aesthetic register for bringing the political into view. In his own words, in the experiential moment the 'blurring of the past and present is what gives sacred places the palpable sense of their sacredness' (Kemper 1991: 136). It is, I suggest, this palpable sense of the sacred within a common and quite particular historiographical framework that forms what I have suggested in Chapter 1 can be considered a distribution of the sensible (Rancière 2004).

Akasachetiya is one of a number of ruined sites within Blocks I and II of Ruhuna that have been excavated and restored to varying degrees, and where visitors are encouraged to alight from their vehicles. Here visitors feel palpable connections with the Sinhala history that seems embedded in the stones, the soil, the trees. As, for example, when I stood on Akasachetiya's summit and the landscape stretching before me felt somehow abundant with history, meaning, significance. It is not just that visitors experience that palpable sense of historical resonance here. It is also that these experiences take place in the midst of the park's nature. The aesthetic field of these ruins point to expressions of reality and history located in ground, as historical *facts on the ground*, authored by the nation state and legitimated internationally as the state's very own national nature. Here at Akasachetiya, the poetics of meaning are easily woven into a present, perceptual, spatio-temporal conjunction of self and world understood in a particular way, semiotically and materially purified, so to speak. For there is little doubting the apparent origin of this sacredness.

In the Sinhala language, *Akasachetiya* means 'shrine of the sky'. Most place names in Ruhuna have a Sinhalese meaning that speaks either of Sinhala historiography or of Buddhist precepts. Naming and renaming in the park have been ways of anti-colonially re-territorializing its material landscapes within particular historiographical and aesthetic domains: 'Yala' to 'Ruhuna' being the most obvious example. Up until the early 2000s, name boards and signs in the park were written in Sinhala and English only, never in Tamil: naming strategies that more obviously ethnicized landscape in ways that emerged from and connected to post-independent Ceylon's well-known 1956 programme of anti-colonial, linguistic nationalism. But, like stories, names also construct a pre-established geography telling us what to make of places. In this respect, they are treatments of space that act in our present (de Certeau 1984: 122). Standing atop Akasachetiya with my friends and guides for the day, it was easy to imagine that Dutthugemenu might have stood here in the second century BCE gazing across the thick jungles of Ruhuna, his bastion and southern retreat, what the 1990 IUCN *Directory of South Asian Protected Areas* tells us was 'the twin cradle of Sinhalese culture' (Green 1990: 245). Perhaps he also bowed his head and raised his hands in obeisance to the Lord Buddha, a gestural mantra I witnessed many others do here on Akasachetiya's summit, each performance further blurring an imagined past with the present, fusing horizons into a seamless connection with a history palpably Sinhala. The modernity of this 'ancientness', easy to forget in such instances (as Kemper does), was perhaps brought home to me as my friend Dharshenie took out her cell phone to call her family, struggling with words adequately to share with them these special aesthetics. But they knew what she meant; such is Sri Lankan nature's own distribution of the sensible.

As mentioned above, there are two similar sites in Block I of Ruhuna National Park: Situlpahuwa temple and Magul Maha vihara. The Situlpahuwa temple complex received extensive restoration during the 1960s. Cave inscriptions there date back to the second century BCE, and a six-metre reclining statue of the Lord Buddha as well as two of ten stupas have been carefully renovated. An important place of worship, it attracts thousands of Buddhist pilgrims during the Poson festival in June each year. A small number of monks live at Situlpahuwa today. Magul Maha vihara was also archaeologically 'excavated' during the 1960s. It is a small site dating from the second century BCE,

Figure 3.1 Magul Maha Vihara (author's photograph).

consisting of a small cave dwelling, rock pond, and stone steps (Figure 3.1). Historically, the vihara is known for its order of *bhikkuni* (Buddhist nuns) that lived there until recently. Today, it is looked after by a janitor. On that same trip to Ruhuna, my friends took me to Magul Maha vihara. Dharshenie was keen to show me her favourite spot in Ruhuna: where she liked to come, just sit and be, she told me.

There is plenty of intertextual evidence that these kinds of aesthetic connections with the park's hegemonic landscape histories are both commonplace and far more than just the products of my friends' desires to sate my own wilfully over-eager ethnographic research imagination. A number of articles published in *Loris*, the journal of Sri Lanka's Wildlife and Nature Protection Society (formerly the Game Protection Society), in the late 1960s and 1970s suggest how similar types of national park experiences were quite didactically promoted. From its 1930s' inception, *Loris* carried fairly normative, scholarly, and predominantly scientific articles that, reflecting contemporaneous modern ecological thought, transacted around management strategies and debates concerning wildlife conservation in Ceylon. In the 1960s and 1970s, however, the journal began to print more essays that catered to its growing non-expert and popular readership. A selection of pieces encouraged the increasing numbers of lay visitors to Ruhuna and other reserves physically to connect with the historical aesthetics of the country's nature:

Few people who visit the Yala National Park and delight in its vistas of jungle cover and its fauna and flora realise that in ancient times it was the home of a people pulsating with life, cultivating their paddy fields, growing their crops and living a full life as it then obtained.

Many of the Sinhalese who gave way to the invading forces of the Tamils, gradually sought refuge and settled in Ruhuna where they licked their wounds, reformed their ranks, rehabilitated themselves, and in course of time sallied forth under Dutthugemenu to drive the invader back from the Rajarata. All this took time, many years in fact. Elara, the Tamil king who incidentally was a just man, alone ruled for forty-four [*sic*] years, during which time the restive Sinhalese who would not accept Tamil dominion were quietly building up dominion in the South ... The Yala of today was then part of this prosperous Sinhalese domain. (Samaraweera 1970: 18)

There is much in this passage, not least the over-determination and mapping of a landscape history entirely consistent with the Sinhala historiographical formations that can be traced back through George Turnour's translation of the *Mahavamsa*. If the passage gestures towards these dominant historiographies *in place* it is careful to also adopt a detached, passive, narratorial voice that objectively identifies 'the Sinhalese' and 'the Tamils' as taken-as-given groups. It simply articulates *facts on the ground*; facts and histories, however, which are ethnicized from the start. In his final passage, the author C. Selwyn Samaraweera, encourages readers when they next visit, to 'dwell for a moment in your minds on the thought that you are in an ancient land full of history' (Samaraweera 1970: 20). Once again, however, that history to be consumed by the visitor has been semiotically purified. Similar such pieces in *Loris* have been even more explicit and instructive on how exactly visitors might immerse themselves in, and engage with, Ruhuna's idiomatically inscribed aesthetics:

It is sad that of the many thousands that go to the Ruhuna National Park for the day or a longer stay, very few enjoy the trees, shrubs and other plants of this portion of land that has been left to nature.

No doubt this aspect of one's destination is not so dramatic as the animals, perhaps less colourful than the birds, perhaps less animate, too. But if you were to pause and if you were to look around there is romance, there is beauty, history and science in and among this silent living. (S.K.R. 1970: 76)

If this piece is didactic in fairly obvious ways, it is also suggestive of an aesthetic terrain in which the 'romance' (a romance of which we can reasonably surmise is born of imperial eyes) and sacredness of history comingle with the modernity of 'science'.

'One with the universe':
The Ethnicized Register of Non-binary Aesthetics

Ruhuna's portal inscription makes it clear that its natural landscapes are to-be-felt. From the 'animals, birds, trees, the water' through to 'the breeze on your face and every grain of sand', it is explicit that if the park's nature is 'sacred gift' it is also participatory space meant to be materially engaged. A first glance at the portal inscription suggests the register of this sacredness is open. That it might be experienced equally by any religio-historical community, Buddhist, Hindu, Muslim, or Christian; a prayer whispered to any god, so to speak. But what I want to suggest here, which should be no surprise by now, is that the park's historiographical resonances are suggestive of quite particular and ethnicized aesthetic modes, concordant with Buddhism specifically, that have come to dominate the *idiom* of Ruhuna's sacredness. And in a contemporary Sri Lankan context where Buddhism is so inscribed in the Sinhala ethnos, this politically territorializes Ruhuna's sacredness. The ways in which park experiences are written and narrated locate its 'sacred gifts' in many of the precepts and principles of Buddhist thought, mobilizing a concordant structure of feeling that, as this book argues more broadly, has become dominant in Sri Lankan nature. As I have argued above, Parnavitarna's mid-twentieth-century work archaeologically and epigraphically to 'excavate' buried histories went hand in hand with his desire to 'excavate' what he believed to be the buried aesthetic registers of the *sangha* who formerly inhabited these landscapes. The Archaeological Survey Department's preoccupation with that bygone era of meditation, asceticism, and Buddhist spiritual attainment has helped inscribe these hegemonic structures of feeling in and around Ruhuna National Park, idiomatically overdetermining its sacredness.

In this respect, over the last few decades, newspaper articles, features, and essays in wildlife journals have increasingly written nature and national park experiences in ways that implicate particular kinds of relationships between subject and world. To attend to these kinds of sources in connection with the glimpses of experience laced through this chapter (through the radical imperfections of participant observation) is methodologically to contextualize the notoriously difficult-to-grasp actualities of park experience, placing them in dialogue with cultural intertexts that hint at a distribution of the sensible that does the work of hegemony. This kind of work reveals Buddhism to more often than not be explicit in the domain of the experiential, thus suggesting how human immersion in Ruhuna commonly instantiates the Buddhist worldings and ontological configurations of subjectivity and difference that the introduction to this book addressed in more depth. When Ruhuna's poetics of meaning are located within these idioms, then the park itself can be seen to participate in the emergence of ethnicized, non-liberal, and Buddhist subjectivities, and in this sense I argue its nature must be located in a broader politics of everyday life and practice. This is not by any means to suggest that sacredness can only emerge in an ethnicized Buddhist register at Ruhuna, or anywhere else. Experience and aesthetics manifest themselves corporeally, and to that extent all our bodies are different. But it is to stress a process of semiotic and material purification in terms of how the park circulates in Sri Lankan public culture. And in doing so it is to tease out a political hegemony that takes hold of, and continues to produce, the *dominant* aesthetic field within which Ruhuna National Park must be located.

Take, for example, a 1996 *Loris* essay entitled 'Wildlife in the Jataka', which dealt with concerns over wildlife conservation in Sri Lanka by tracing the link between Sri Lankan fauna and the Jataka tales (birth stories of the Buddha). The essay promulgated Buddhist beliefs that orthodox scientific and evolutionary theories – Darwinism, ecological science, and contemporary environmentalism, for example – are merely independent discoveries of the vast natural truth to which Buddhist thought points. It went further by suggesting that humankind cannot be separated from nature, and grounding a sense of the non-binary and indivisible 'oneness' of nature/culture in the Buddhist antiquity of an unspecified group of 'our forebears' cognate with the Sinhala 'nation'.

> Going back to a literature [the Jataka tales] such as the one I have referred to will ... serve to show how immediate man's relationship with bird and beast had been in our antiquity, and how much familiarity our forbears had with them, then as to have led to the imagining of the many beast-fables as are found in the collection. If anything, it goes to show how truly naturalist, if also spontaneous and unconscious in this, they had been in their villages and cultivations hemmed in by the wild. (Pieris 1996: 46)

This piece does not focus on Ruhuna National Park specifically, but its content concerns the field of Sri Lankan nature and wildlife conservation for which Ruhuna National Park is the most significant reserve in Sri Lanka. It enters the terrain of nature and wildlife conservation *through* assertions drawn from Buddhist precepts and metaphysics, particularly regarding an ontological worlding that cannot cleave the (cultural) human from the (natural) world. That 'spontaneous and unconscious' experiential domain of 'our forebears' is critical in this respect.

Popular newspaper accounts through the 1980s and 1990s also made similar triangulations between Buddhist precepts, nature, and the nation, in turn implicating similar structures of feeling. The *Daily News*, for example, ran a regular series of photo-essays entitled 'My Own Native Land', which provided short accounts of some aspect of Sri Lankan wildlife accompanied by one or two photographs. Unsurprisingly, many were about Ruhuna National Park. Typical of such pieces is that shown in Figure 3.2, an example textually invoking a historical image of the park's landscapes during the times of the Ruhuna kingdom. It is an image littered with Buddhist iconography: monasteries, viharas, monks, devotees, and Brahmi inscriptions. And it is an image that imbues Ruhuna National Park with its own mysterious personality, echoing tropes in early Buddhist literature that characteristically wrote the forest as 'a mysterious presence with its own identity and personality, solemn, majestic, fearsome and attractive' (Gokhale 1979: 137). In ways reminiscent of this iconography, this small *Daily News* piece declares of Ruhuna: 'This vast, desolate plain is interspersed, with scrub jungle and cavernous rock outcrops. History lies buried in its sands and mystery lurks behind its trees.' We are left in little doubt as to the idiom of its history and mystery, just as it is worth noting how the superimposition of the title – 'My Own Native Land' – over a blackened representation of the whole island maps Ruhuna's hegemonic and ethnicized structures of feeling across an island-wide territoriality.

This kind of interpretive work not only delineates the textual and material fields in which Ruhuna must be located, it also attempts to learn how to read the poetics of experience in Ruhuna National Park, to learn how to become attuned to the scripts with which the park is written as well as the ethnicized idiom pervading its aesthetics and poetics of meaning in the present. In terms of reading the politics of space and nature in southern Sri Lanka, this is to develop literacies positioned to bring the political resonances of apparently innocent yet evocative modes of nature tourism squarely into visibility, specifically by paying attention to the ways that the landscape circulates as both text and materiality. Revisiting the final lines of the poem with which this chapter began – *'All is still. One with the universe'* (Disanayake 1992) – I want, therefore, to suggest that this poetic image can effectively be read as an evocation of a worlding consistent with the circulation of those Buddhist precepts, principles, and textualities that circulate around Ruhuna National Park. As I have stressed in Chapter 1, it is difficult to write or talk about 'Buddhist nature' without immediate anthropologizing conceptual contamination. Instantiating the natural and cultural as biophysical and super-organic categorizations respectively is simply inconsistent with a conception of a world comprised instead of non-binary energies, *dhamma*. At the same time, however, in a post-structuralist cultural studies committed to regarding culture itself (and cultures of nature) *as* textual, dynamic, and what Raymond Williams has described as a persistent suturing of dominant, residual, and emergent elements, it is just as naive to suggest a formulaic and deterministic mechanics of Buddhism. Nevertheless, we need to read the idiom of that poetic oneness by learning from such texts, as discussed above, that suggest attendant biorhythms that persistently deconstruct any 'logical' metaphysical opposition between the 'natural' and the 'cultural' (Spivak 1999: 383 n. 97). To do so is, as Gayatri Spivak has written, to begin the impossible task of 'suspending oneself into the text of the other' (Spivak 2008: 23).

Amongst societies in which Buddhist thought and textualities percolate, natural beauty has long been accepted as an aid to spiritual effort; indeed, as the Buddhist studies scholar Martine Batchelor has written, for many, the environment is regarded as the ideal place for cultivating spiritual insights into reality. W. S. Yokoyama, a contributor to Batchelor's anthology on *Buddhism and Ecology*, goes further by suggesting how Tendai Buddhist monks

In the southern eastern sector of the island between the Menik Ganga and the Kumbukkan Oya stretching twenty two miles is a region called Block II on the map. It is part of the Yala National Park.

This vast, desolate plain is interspersed, with scrub jungle and cavernous rock outcrops. History lies buried in its sands and mystery lurks behind its trees.

The enormous grasslands are the beds of the tanks and verdant paddy fields of the once thriving Ruhunu kingdom. The caves were the monasteries and viharas inhabited by monks and frequented by devotees. Inscribed in Brahmi on the rock face of the drip-ledged caves are the names of the honoured patrons. Hidden in the tangled forests are silent stone columns, strange slabs of granite and piles of crumbling masonry.

Today, it is a wild country into which man, rarely ventures. Large herds of animals roam the plains wary of human presence. At the approach of a vehicle, hundreds of panic-stricken boar scamper off, disappearing into the dust in a mass of squiggling tails.

The massive "kulu" buffalo thunder forward challenging the intruder. Through the heat haze can be seen a multitude of deer, heads upraised and watchful. And in the footsteps of that pilgrim of long ago now treads the leopard and the bear as they climb upto their lairs in the stone massif.

...my own, my native land

Block II, Yala National Park

Photograph — Luxshman Nadaraja

Courtesy — Studio Times

Figure 3.2 'My Own Native Land'. *Daily News* (Sri Lankan newspaper), 3 March 1990, Associated Newspapers of Ceylon Ltd archive, Lake House, Colombo, Sri Lanka, from clippings file on 'Yala'.

in Japan conduct 'thousand-day pilgrimages' around Mount Hiei in order to reach a state of 'oneness with nature', thus returning to an unfeeling point of balance within the natural world (1992: 55–64). Once again, there can be no simple formula for Sri Lanka's (Therevada) Buddhist structures of feeling, but learning the possibility of these biorhythms does suggest how Kusum Disanayaka's poetic image evokes a mindful, intuitive comprehension of the vast natural truth of a Buddhist body in particular; that is, a Buddhist subject seeking out an unfeeling anaesthesia, or infinity (see Chapter 6), wherein mind and body are purged of sensuous cravings, along a path to the undoing of (liberal) subjectivity and selfhood. It is worth stressing in this respect that, discursively at least, in its realist formulation the Buddhist body has six senses: sight, sound, touch, taste, smell, as well as mind. If sight, sound, touch, taste, and smell are material sense organs, Buddhism teaches that the mind is a non-material organ that coordinates experience (Gamage 1998: 22; Rodaway 1994: 22). It is also the bodily organ centrally implicated in Buddhist intuitions of *un*feeling. The central point in this context is that insofar as bodies can be understood discursively, there is nothing exceptional or out of the ordinary for Buddhist subjects to become '*One with the universe*' (Disanayake 1992).

Though I expand on the cultural logic of this kind of becoming in Chapter 6, what I am suggesting here is that in Kusum Disanayake's poetic image of 'Dusk at Yala' the relationship between soil and subjectivity is crucial. If it were not for the park's over-determined Sinhala historiography and concordant aesthetics, that oneness might be more open. But a heady mix of historiographical resonance and non-secularity secure and purify the meaning of Disanayake's oneness with the universe. In this very sense, being in Ruhuna National Park is about being on particular terms that instantiate the legitimacy of ground authored as Buddhist and Sinhala. The park's nature has both intuitive meaning that shapes ways of being in place and an expressive character of its own that serves to objectify – to naturalize – its own materiality. As Chris Tilley has written, this is a union of subjectivity and objectivity in landscape that produces loci for existence; although the topology of land remains distinct from thought, the two play into each other, creating an intelligible landscape, a spatialization of being (1994: 14). In these aesthetics, a politics of nationness is to be found; a cosmopolitan Sinhala-Buddhist nationalism that routinely works towards the production of non-liberal, (non)subjectivities and (non)selves.

Modernization and Experience

Ironically, these dominant structures of feeling appear to become more marked in the face of technologies of dwelling within the Park that would seem to cause a kind of physical separation between body and environment. Today there are a number of park rules and regulations that apparently pull the body (Buddhist or otherwise) further from landscape than direct corporeal immersion would otherwise facilitate. Notably, these include rules confining visitors to their vehicles at all times when touring the park's network of dirt tracks, and the provision of circuit bungalows inside Ruhuna in which visitors stay. Both on the one hand suggest a modernization and technologization of park experience that cannot help but cleave the human body from biophysical nature. In fact, they are technologies that participate in that very bifurcation of the world into 'cultural' and 'natural' domains, respectively. But tracing the history of their implementation actually reveals very different habitations of modernity that have been both pervaded by and aimed at a kind of engineering of that same 'oneness with the universe' that I have located within a non-binary semiotically Buddhist textual field.

What becomes evident in attempting to read these kinds of deployments and consumptions of jeeps and bungalows is the importance of attending to how experience and materiality are always representationally marked. Even when landscape experience seems engineered through technologies of modernization, the poetics of that experience are still marked by the aesthetic and textual fields through which experience circulates. To stress this is merely another way of saying that were it not for Ruhuna National Park's over-determined archaeological, epigraphical, and historiographical formations, the idiom of its sacredness might be a little more open. But it is precisely that over-determination of Sri Lankan nature that this book commits to bringing into representation in order to make visible a politics embedded in a certain spectrum of environmental aesthetics. And, indeed, this kind of semiotic purification of technological materiality is something I draw out much more when I consider the aesthetics of Sri Lanka's architectural modernism. Here, however, in the last section of this chapter, I want briefly to consider the habitations of jeeps and circuit bungalows specifically.

Vehicle-bound wildlife experience is of course a highly mediated and regulated human relationship with the non-human world (see Figure 2.1). In such moments, as we crane our necks to peer at fauna from within our cars, we would be forgiven for thinking that '[t]he two concepts, nature and culture, can only exist in dialectical relation to one another' (Cosgrove 1996: 575). However, in Ruhuna National Park such decisions on vehicular confinement were made as it was noted how animals were less afraid of visitors in vehicles than they were of those on foot. These management decisions never intended to create ascetic or sacred forest dwelling experiences, of course; they were in fact adopted in the 1940s from management principles used in the national parks of sub-Saharan Africa, for evidently practical reasons. But that intention to engineer more direct human connections with fauna does connect with a desire to foster an immediacy in terms of bodily relationships to the park, that it is worth stressing is not inconsistent with those engendered in the Jataka tales, or, more importantly, in Pieris's 1996 *Loris* article on 'Wildlife in the Jataka'. Indeed, in current management strategies, an 'Observation *versus* sighting' approach is taken to visitor satisfaction, the intention being to 'enhance satisfaction by observing and correlating with animal behaviour and habitat' whilst maintaining the 'serenity of nature' (Panwar and Wickeramasinghe 1997: 239). Once again, what different human bodies aesthetically make of and do with that confinement in their vehicles is an open question. But such draconian, if well-intentioned, mediations of wildlife experience are far from incompatible with Kusum Disanayake's more poetic and non-secular image of dwelling, of being '*One with the universe*'. For example, on one of my visits to Ruhuna, whilst driving through a fairly dense pocket of secondary forest on a track that had been recently ravaged by monsoonal flooding, my companion Dharsheni told me how this was the type of jungle in which she loved just to *be*. As I jarred my back between potholes, I thought hard about this.

These tensions also reveal themselves in the Park's legacy of colonial 'circuit bungalows', whose presence and form had been repeated in national parks and other colonial landscapes throughout the British Empire (see King 1984). Despite their colonial roots, the circuit bungalows in Ruhuna these days are closer to postcolonial interpretations, architecturally and stylistically the likes of which I explore in much more depth in Part II of this book. They exhibit many of the same design characteristics of Sri Lanka's tropical modernist architecture that is intended simply to create a fluid connection between outside and inside space: open and low walls, verandas, simple and sparse furnishing, open showers, for example, and a more general effort to blend building materials with the site beyond the structure. Though I pay more attention to this architectural production and habitation of such fluid spatialities in Part II, it is worth stressing here how the placing and construction of bungalows has been a constant challenge for the Department of Wildlife Conservation's attempt to build an appropriate aesthetic and experiential terrain within the park. For example, after the completion of the Yala bungalow in 1966, they remarked how:

> At the moment the bungalow appears too prominent located as it is on top of a sandy ridge, but once the trees grow around it and the paint bleaches it will blend with the surrounding vegetation. (de Alwis 1967: unpag.)

Much more, however, than an attempt to create what Simon Schama refers to in landscape terms as an 'uncompromisingly unified *vision*' (1995: 570; my emphasis), this is also an ongoing struggle to produce spatialities appropriately attuned to Ruhuna's poetics of experience, its sacred modernity. As one journalist remarked following the opening of another bungalow some years later, 'The bungalow is meant for total relaxation being in close proximity to the Magul Maha Vihare and Situlpauwa' (*Sunday Observer* 1993: unpag.). And, finally, the words of another journalist who reconciles a bungalow lodging's architectural grammar with the poetics of meaning that this chapter has read from Ruhuna National Park:

> The very location of the bungalow, its very structure – incorporating large tree trunks and wood, the design which seemed so right for jungle living, all this plus the jungle sounds at night, the breeze that rattles through the woven tats, the bliss of 'being – being there to savour it'. (Rodrigo 1996: unpag.)

Conclusion:
Contested Aesthetics, Political Geographies

The piece quoted above is actually a lament for the loss of the Yala bungalow after it was burned to the ground by LTTE cadres in 1996. In this sense, it is instructive. It is not just a lament for the loss of a material property; it is also an elegy to a desecrated poetics. If the physical destruction of the bungalow was part of an ongoing war, its significance is registered through the symbolic resonance of its aesthetics. The loss of the Yala bungalow represented the violation of an aesthetic field that, this chapter has shown, is itself locked into broader historiographical and national narratives that have considerable political resonance in the present.

> The heart is full of anguish when I think that I will never stand at that self same upstair deck, looking out over jungle, scrub and river.
> That I will never stand in that long bedroom shaded by the magnificent trees and look out at the Menik ganga flowing on its peaceful way. (Rodrigo 1996: unpag.)

It is to those more obviously contested political geographies of Ruhuna National Park that I turn next.

This chapter has shuttled between the domains of inscription and experience. It has worked to show, first, how colonial and postcolonial archaeological, epigraphical, and historiographical formations have effectively striated Ruhuna National Park with over-determined historical resonances. In this sense the chapter has shown that the new archaeological practices of Senerat Parnavitarna in particular have participated in a kind of semiotic and material purification of the park's meanings in the present. Second, the chapter has argued that if this inscriptive process has indeed materially and semiotically purified the park's meanings, then those meanings and their politics are secured through a poetics of dwelling and being in and through space. It is the non-secular, Sinhala, and Buddhist aesthetic idioms, or what I have suggested is a hegemonic structure of feeling that pervades contemporary park practice, that politicizes Ruhuna's landscapes and nature. In essence, then, this chapter has committed to developing a literacy simply able effectively to read a spatial politics of Ruhuna National Park that is otherwise often obscured by the sheer evocative poetics of landscape experience at Ruhuna.

As a coda, though, that very separation of inscription and experience – necessary for the architecture of this chapter – must remain somewhat provisional, and must be taken heuristically. I stress this simply because every moment of experience must also be considered a reinscription, and every inscriptive practice also an experience that holds within it the potential for the park's political geography to unfold differently, anew.

CHAPTER 4

Political Geographies:
Promoting, Contesting,
and Purifying Nature

The last two chapters have evoked the historical striations and aesthetic terrains of Ruhuna National Park, stressing how together they constitute a politics of nationness instantiated through landscape and nature. In the next part of the book, I go on to suggest how aesthetic practices in Sri Lanka's contemporary architectural modernism similarly constitute a cosmopolitan Sinhala-Buddhist nationalism. In both instances – park and architecture – the politics of nature lies in the structures of feeling that both sites spatialize. In Ruhuna National Park, however, there is also a more obvious political, and politicized, geography that this chapter works to tease out, because during Sri Lanka's civil war Ruhuna's landscape geographies were not uncontested.

In this Chapter I focus on the contestation and securitization of Ruhuna National Park during the 1990s and early 2000s, tracing some of the public debates, physical struggles, and semiotic slippages surrounding the park. As I show, these connect directly to deeper social and political anxieties regarding struggles over ethnicity, belonging, and quite literally the nature of the national in the context of Sri Lanka's civil war. Despite the park's popularity, complex and fraught issues of popular and practical concern have affected Ruhuna in the last twenty or so years. Through various contestations around wildlife and security particularly, it is possible to see, and indeed feel, some of the many tensions in Sri Lanka's contested contemporary politics of nationness and belonging. In this chapter, I connect practical issues concerning park management and security in the 1990s up to broader political and social anxieties over the fragmentation of the nation state in the face of Tamil separatism, as well as the accommodation of non-Sinhala-Buddhist sacred practice in Ruhuna's semiotically purified national landscapes. Specifically, and in turn, I regard debates about the park's security following LTTE attacks during the 1990s, as well as concerns about the routing of east coast Tamils through Ruhuna on their annual pilgrimages to the adjoining holy site, the Kataragama Sanctuary.

These contestations and struggles over meaning and security must be taken in the context of a continued, quite aggressive promotion of Ruhuna *as* a national space of Sinhala-Buddhist heritage for a particular vision of the national populace through the second half of the last century. Before turning to those contestations and anxieties over the LTTE and Kataragama pilgrims, respectively, therefore, this chapter briefly expands upon this period to highlight the ongoing semiotic purification of Ruhuna in the context of a Sri Lankan public culture that between the late 1950s and 1983 was becoming ever more ethnically exclusive.

Circulating Ruhuna

Yala's name change to Ruhuna National Park in 1943 paved the way for a period of propaganda and promotion of the park and wildlife conservation more generally during the 1950s and 1960s. The newly independent government's strategies aimed at increasing the park's popularity amongst a Ceylonese public, educating them on how best to enjoy their wildlife heritage, and, importantly, making Ruhuna itself accessible to a particularly wide and fairly democratic vision of the Ceylonese people. These strategies of democratizing Ceylonese wildlife helped constitute a period that saw the opening of the post-colony's geography to its citizenry, both imaginatively and physically. As much as this was an opening of the newly independent nation state's nature to the public it also participated in the creation of a new and self-consciously 'post-colonial' public through a kind of performative and benevolent sharing of the country's natural fabric with a particularly wide sweep of *the people*. In this sense it was a cultivation of post-independent citizenship and public formation through the terrain of geography and especially wildlife; a politics whose very performance paved the way for journalists forty or fifty years later to write, as quoted in the previous chapter, that '*Our* breath-taking range of birds, animals and insects is woven into the fabric of *our* national life' (Buczaki 2000; my emphasis). But, if that sweep of the people was broad, then, as I have shown in the previous chapter, wildlife itself, particularly Ruhuna, was being rather more narrowly written. It was wildlife for the nation state, but of the Sinhala-Buddhist nation; a cosmopolitan mode of Sinhala-Buddhist nationalism whose nationalism works precisely by claiming as universal its rather more particular content. And the ways that Ruhuna was made to circulate in post-independent Ceylon helped contribute to the formation of this pervasive disjuncture and banal mode of nationalism at the heart of Sri Lankan nature.

The Department of Wildlife Conservation went to great efforts to target the promotion of Ruhuna National Park to all classes of Ceylonese people, not just the elite.

> National Parks are not established with the sole object of protecting Wild Life, although that is a vital element in their functional purpose. Their educational and recreational aspects are also highly important, and these benefits must be made available to and taken advantage of by all classes of the people and not by certain privileged or by more fortunate sections of the population only. (Nicholas 1956: unpag.)

In this important respect, such efforts marked a significant departure from the elite body politic that formerly saturated the Yala Resident's Sportsmen's Reserve. In the post-independent period, a number of strategies were implemented to encourage working, student, and less affluent visitors to the park. These included the provision of cheap but adequate accommodation for parties of limited financial means, including the opening of circuit bungalows and camping areas, for example, as well as the fixing of affordable entry fees, and, importantly, the improvement of major roads leading to Ruhuna such that it could be serviced by public bus:

> Motorable roads are essential in National Parks to make the Parks accessible to visitors of all classes, the traveller by bus as well as the motorist. Without motorable roads they would be accessible only to a few who own specialised vehicles with 4-wheel drive, and they would not then be national institutions but the pleasuring grounds of the rich and leisured class. (Nicholas 1954: unpag.).

Up until 1966, entry fees were kept as low as fifty cents (around 1p) in order to attract as many visitors as possible. They were five times higher for foreign nationals, and even today foreign nationals pay over thirty times as much as Sri Lankans to enter Ruhuna – a not uncommon price discrimination strategy in Sri Lanka that ensures a healthy revenue stream from foreign tourism whilst not economically denying access to Sri Lankan citizens.

These kinds of Department of Wildlife Conservation management decisions in the mid- to late 1950s enabled a democratization of Ceylonese nature; its fabric was effectively opened up to an emergent, post-independent public. But, as I have stressed, the contours of this now widely available fabric were instantiating a Sinhala-Buddhist particularity. Politically, this was coterminous with the rise of populist Sinhala-Buddhist nationalism in post-independent Ceylon, which was gaining considerable force in the mid- to late 1950s. The Prime Minister D. S. Senanayake's United National Party (UNP) vision of a multi-racial, plural and secular, independent Ceylon, was being overtaken by S. W. R. D. Bandaranaike's breakaway populist and welfarist politics that, in the form of the Sri Lanka Freedom Party (SLFP), was targeting Ceylon's ethnically majoritarian masses by championing Sinhala culture and Buddhist religion. The backbone of the SLFP's populist support comprised Ceylon's villagers, working classes, and students; precisely those groups whom the Department of Wildlife Conservation were targeting. The goal of making Ruhuna accessible to the nation at large can thus be seen as part and parcel of Ceylon's gathering populist Sinhala-Buddhist culture.

One of S. W. R. D. Bandaranaike's first policy mandates upon election to office in 1956 was the passing of the Official Language Act, which installed Sinhala as Ceylon's sole official language thereby relegating English, but more importantly Tamil, to the status of a secondary, or 'other', language within the nation state. This has had a marked and lasting effect all over the post-colony, not least in Ruhuna National Park. The language and diction of the park's promotion from 1956 onwards was overwhelmingly Sinhala. Thus the material ways it circulated in Sri Lankan public culture provided a seeming, and seamless, correlate to its emergent Sinhala historiographical and archaeological formation. The park was becoming a 'culturally' Sinhala space through the channels and idioms of its circulation as much as its own materiality. As Department of Wildlife administration reports record, in 1957 'maps of Ruhuna in Sinhalese were sent to Yala for distribution free to visitors particularly school children' (de Silva 1958: unpag.). Language was emerging as one of the central political issues circulating around the idea of 'the national' at the time, and Ruhuna National Park was both inscribed with a Sinhala historiography registered through its Sinhala place names and historical iconography, and cartographically it was being represented *in Sinhalese* to the youth of the nation as well as every other visitor. To mention these kinds of circulatory regimes is to stress that if we can consider Ruhuna National Park a social text, inscribed and striated with its particular markings as it has been, then its modes and means of circulation were as important to the emergent nature of that text as anything else. As I show in Part II, this argument is also central to reading the aesthetic resonances of Sri Lanka's architectural modernism.

The techniques and technologies of promoting Ruhuna National Park in post-independent Ceylon worked. In 1950, there were 3,252 visits, but by 1959, there 17,673 (de Silva 1960: unpag.). Ruhuna's popularity has steadily increased since the late 1950s as well, with some 245,000 recorded visits in 1995 (Panwar and Wickeramasinghe 1997). However, as I now suggest, over the last few decades the park's promotion as a space enframing the particularities of the sacred modern have not always been easy to achieve, nor have they been uncontested. The modern period has witnessed significant ongoing work to secure Ruhuna's meaning.

Contesting Ruhuna's Nature:
Landscapes of Fear and the LTTE

On 15 June 1996, the Yala and Talgasmankada bungalows in Block I of Ruhuna were attacked and set ablaze by an unidentified group. The ten domestic tourists staying in the Yala bungalow were driven from it eventually escaping unhurt. This was the latest in a series of raids and attacks in the park over the course of the previous decade that had seen all but Block I close to visitors. One month after this latest attack, on Friday, 12 July, thirteen park visitors were abducted and released by suspected terrorists. Department of Wildlife officials soon thereafter confirmed that these abductions were perpetrated by LTTE cadres – not poachers or local gangs as had been speculated – and henceforth they closed the whole of Ruhuna National Park to visitors. It was now public knowledge that Sri Lanka's most popular and most famous national park was occupied by Tamil Tigers who were dwelling under cover of these famous and dense jungles. Government security forces more or less immediately launched an operation to drive the LTTE from the park, and over the next couple of years Block I opened and closed a number of times whilst the other Blocks remained closed.

Following the 1983 riots and the subsequent war, confirmation of the LTTE presence in Ruhuna was neither unexpected nor surprising. Ruhuna National Park contains the border between Sri Lanka's Southern and North Eastern province, a line which also marked the southern most extent of Eelam (see Map 1). Concealed bays and dense jungle cover along Ruhuna's eastern coast provided the perfect cover for arms shipments from southern India to encamped LTTE bases, and Government security forces reasonably believed that LTTE cadres could easily get to Yala from the east coast town of Batticoloa and the rebel-held Amapara district in the east. Though the war was being fought mostly in the far north, the Yala Protected Area complex was geopolitically something of an 'eastern front' marking a transition zone between the occupied east and still 'clear' south.

In this respect, Ruhuna's historiographical connections to a history of Tamil invasion and Sinhala reconquest were not at all insignificant, and, as a consequence, both before and after these attacks in 1996, the security struggles over Ruhuna National Park received ample news coverage. Rather than focusing just on the sequence of events that led to Ruhuna's closure and eventual clearance, what I suggest here is that despite the real security threats of LTTE presence in the park, securing Ruhuna was as much about discursively and textually securing the integrity and resonance of Sri Lankan nature as it was about physically clearing its landscapes. Central to securing Ruhuna's material ground *for* the nation state then, were processes that sought to purge its textual field, as well as its material landscapes, of the presence of non-native iconographies and symbolic impurities. Once again, this is not to underplay the physical threat that the LTTE's presence in Yala posed. It is, however, to draw attention to the ways that material security and safety at Ruhuna were achieved, in part, by recapturing the proper meanings and particularities of Sri Lankan nature's sacred modernity. To this extent, much of the journalistic coverage of the day translated the main political issues raised by the LTTE's occupation of Yala – regarding national identity and the spatial politics of belonging, for example – into the language of wildlife resource management and species endemicity. Two signs in particular marked the semiotic terrain of these struggles: tiger and jungle.

'tigers' and 'Tigers'

Following the 1996 attacks and closure, a number of reports began to play with the LTTE's own iconography, seizing the opportunity to quip about the presence of 'tigers' amidst Ruhuna's natural landscapes. If Ruhuna National Park was now occupied by the LTTE, figuratively 'the tiger' became a potent metaphor for the problems that had beset the park. For the LTTE themselves, the tiger has been an official symbol since 1972 because of its association with bravery, fearlessness, and heroism. During wartime, the pro-LTTE website EelamWeb wrote that Tamil freedom fighters 'should act like a Tiger with its agile and aggression [sic]', further stressing that the Tiger has rich historical associations in Dravidian civilization, making it the perfect symbol for the organization:

> There is a reason why Prabakaran choose 'Tiger' as national symbol. Tiger symbol has historically deep roots into Dravida civilization. It illustrates Tamil's heroism and national upraise of that time. The symbol of Tiger points [to] heroes and their faith. The Cholaz won several historical battles under Tiger flag and held the Tamils as patriots. The Tiger flag always deeply represents as a symbol of national patriotism, national feeling.
>
> The choice of Tiger symbol by our national leader proves to be the most intelligent and historical decision. And that helps to lead armed struggle of our nation which was ruled by colonialists and now by Sinhalese over 500 years [sic]. (EelamWeb)

With Ruhuna's closure, the media stressed how a landscape held in trust for the nation state was now off-limits to its citizenry because an aggressive animal presence had penetrated its folds. In an article published just days after the park was closed, a headline dramatically stated the facts as: 'Tigers Prowling Around Yala'. Writing of a tour by a Department of Wild Life (DOW) official to assess the security of the park following the attacks, the article tells how 'He [the DOW official] stressed that except for some deer and an elephant they did not come across any Tigers …' (Fernando 1996: 1). This rather anxious mode of humour works through a would-be understanding of a simple wildlife fact shared between the newspaper's imagined reader and the journalist: the feline tiger is not, and never has been, a species endemic to Sri Lanka. It is well understood that Sri Lanka's largest endemic and wild feline species is the leopard, and this public knowledge served to hasten the semantic force of the LTTE's violation of Ruhuna, which could now also be regarded as the violation of the rightful order of Sri Lankan biodiversity. The tiger has no space in Sri Lankan nature. Feline or otherwise, it does not belong within the natural composition of the postcolonial Sri Lankan national.

In the coming months, similar kinds of headlines proliferated in the dailies and weekend supplements: 'Massive Search for Tigers in Yala' (Weerawarne and Palihawadane 1996), 'Tigers Stalk Yala Waiting for Weapons Ships?' (Defence Correspondent 1996), 'Tigers Infiltrate Yala Again' (Bulathsinhala 1996), 'The Latest Addition to Wildlife at Yala Appears to be Terrorists' (Wijeratne 1996),

'Army, Police Comb Yala to Track Down Tigers' (Dinapurna and Liyanarchchi 1996), and 'Move to Prevent Tiger Infiltration' (Bulathsinhala 1996). Though all reported facts and the latest developments regarding Ruhuna's occupation and closure, they mobilized public understandings of the incontrovertible exoticness of the tiger in Sri Lankan biodiversity speak to layer their rhetoric, painting at the same time a picture of a helplessly stricken national wildlife resource penetrated by an invading, aggressive, non-native animal other. The historiographical refrain of Tamil invasion, Sinhala reconquest, repeating and recycling, familiar from the *Mahavamsa*'s historiographical formations, was never far from this rhetoric, but it was reframed around the coordinates of a discourse of non-native species belonging.

Symbolically, this kind of rhetoric was also already pervaded by the violently sexualized image of predatory feline LTTE cadres actively terrorizing a more passive natural and feminized national resource such as Ruhuna National Park. If Ruhuna was helpless and stricken in the face of 'Tigers Stalking', so to speak, then this language was layered over a genre that, since 1983, had written Ruhuna as a landscape that required protection by the patriarchal guns of state in the face of an LTTE whose incursions into the park were written as the sexual defilement of national nature. As a *Daily News* piece wrote in 1985: '"Yala East is being raped ... and unless there are guns to help, there is nothing we can do about it," the Director of Wild Life Conservation, Dr Shelton Atapatu, told the "Daily News" yesterday'. The piece's headline read: 'Yala Raped ... but Dept. Helpless'.

Coming back to 1996, newspaper reports further reveal the Department of Wild Life Conservation's public position that stressed the LTTE presence in, and occupation of, Ruhuna was an improper appropriation of the national. In particular, they played on those by-now well-established equations of Ruhuna's public accessibility with citizenship. The *Sunday Leader*, for example, quipped how

> As an added precaution, it is learnt that the department [of Wild Life Conservation] put up several signs on *kumbuk* trees along the Menik Ganga reading, 'LTTE please note: No entry without permit.' (*Sunday Leader* 1996)

Humour again was used to reassert that debt of obligation and responsibility that each of Sri Lanka's citizens has to pay for the right to consume the nation's wildlife resources, however nominal that fee may be. Given that the LTTE's *raison d'être* has been to splinter the very claims and authority of the Sri Lankan national, this humour worked by reminding the nation at large that national park consumption without permit was grounds for excluding the LTTE from the sign of the national. But it is worth stressing how these kinds of tactics hastened a sense that Sri Lankan nature be understood to contain, and be consumed, on particular terms that required vigilant and constant securitization by the state. If there was now an LTTE presence in Sri Lanka's national nature, it had succeeded in inverting its semantic and material stability; nature now required the intervention of the state once again to purify its content. At the time, the government Minister for Labour and Vocational Training, Mahinda Rajapakse (who was to become Prime Minister in 2004, and President in 2005), gave a speech to a concerned audience of Buddhist clergy and ley people at the Situlpahuwa temple complex about the real and symbolic importance of Ruhuna National Park as a national resource, and therefore the necessity of protecting it militarily. He stressed that

> The Yala National Sanctuary is a resource asset and a legacy not only for the people of Ruhuna but also for the entire country. It should be conserved and protected at all cost. (Tissamaharama special correspondent 1996: 7)

The Right Kind of 'Jungle'

If 'the tiger' was employed as metaphor for the politics of belonging within the sign of the contemporary national, then we can also read that destabilization of the semantic purity of Sri Lankan nature through displacements of the meaning of the word 'jungle'. When speculation was rife about the Tamil Tiger presence within Ruhuna National Park, newspaper reports speculated that the LTTE 'had penetrated Yala from the Pottuvil jungles in Ampara district' (Abeywardene and Bulathsinhala 1995: unpag.), referring to those areas of dense secondary growth between Batticoloa and Yala East National Park. Despite the factual accuracy of such speculations, this kind of reporting also reveals an uneasy slippage regarding the meanings circulating around the idea of 'jungle'. Specifically, there was a kind of anxious struggle to retain control of what had emerged as the proud and anti-colonial nationalist semiotics of Sri Lankan 'jungle' (see Chapter 3). If the LTTE posed a threat to the national then a major part of that threat was the way that their very presence in the landscape effectively reinscribed Sri Lankan 'jungle' *as* landscape of fear. It is this kind of 'jungle' anxiety we can read in the national press of the time.

As the previous chapters have stressed, through the park's previous 100 or so years, the term 'jungle' had been significantly transformed from a word that marked physical impediment and challenge to progress in the colonial imagination, to a sign full with the historiographical and aesthetic resonances of Sinhala nationhood secured by the likes of Dutthegemenu. Securing the meaning of the 'jungle' was an anti-colonial discursive battle central to the processes of landscape reinscription that eventually wrested territory back from the British. As Chapter 2 has suggested, the colonial challenge was to open up 'jungle', liberating it from the clutches of what the Governor Sir Henry Ward referred to in 1856 as 'beasts of the field' and the 'lords of the soil'. In this historical context, anti-colonial Ceylonese landscape reinscription effectively resignified 'jungle' by infusing the term with the national historical particularities and aesthetic resonances explored in the previous chapter.

Now, however, the 'jungle' was under threat again. Not just physically, but imaginatively as well. LTTE presence in the Ampara district ceded these 'jungles' back into the possessive grip of other meanings; meanings that threatened the integrity and authenticity of properly national Sri Lankan 'jungle'. As Maureen Sioh has written of the environmental history of Malaysian rainforest in times of insurgency, as fears of political violence become displaced onto landscape, the sign of the 'jungle' is afforded a space to emerge with all its accompanying references to savagery (Sioh 1998: 160). From the early 1980s to the mid-1990s, 'jungle' was becoming dangerously bifurcated imaginative and material terrain in the Sri Lankan context. It rotated from landscape redolent with Sinhala historiography and an idiomatically inscribed national pride, through to landscape of fear, occupied by a savage other and full with the potential of political violence. As journalists at the time hinted, if Yala's meanings were to be protected then its designation as a sanctuary was essential in that struggle to remain the right kind of healthy and semantically pure 'jungle' faced by the alien threats all around:

> Police said that the Tigers had come to Yala Sanctuary from the rebel-infested jungles of Ampara. The Potuvil and Ampara jungles are both unprotected by security forces and resulted in the free movement of rebels between these jungles, they noted. (Bulathsinhala 1995)

What we can read from this moment is an anxiety about the inversions of meaning that LTTE presence in and around Ruhuna was having, precipitating a sense that 'jungle' needed to be reclaimed imaginatively as well as physically. As 'The Island' newspaper wrote in 1986 in terms that betray well this kind of anxiety over the semiotic trajectory of Sri Lankan 'jungle' in the face of suspected LTTE presence:

> Whatever the source of the menace may be, this will contribute greatly to undermining morale among that section of the population which believed that conditions in the country were normal enough to make a holiday at Yala safe. It will also create the conditions for cutting Yala away from the rest of the country thus achieving the objective of whoever may be behind the present exercise.
>
> The authorities must take a very serious view of such attempts because *we cannot allow the law of the jungle to take over the country even though some of the areas thus menaced are in fact jungles.* It is admitted that law enforcement agencies are permitted against complex and sinister forces at a time when the country's territorial integrity is under challenge. (*The Island* 1986: unpag.; my emphasis)

There is an evident sense of confusion as well as unease here about precisely what Ruhuna's jungles were fast becoming in the face of security threats in a civil war that struck at the very core of questions concerning the nature of the national. For many Sri Lankans, to fear this national landscape was to be imaginatively and physically marginalized from the sign of the national. In this sense, the LTTE presence in Ruhuna placed one of the most symbolic markers of a very particular Sinhala historiography and aesthetic terrain, the 'jungle', off limits and out of reach to the Sri Lankan citizen. That was the imaginative force of the LTTE's presence in, and subsequent closure of, Ruhuna National Park between the early 1980s and mid-1990s. The loss of the 'jungle' was the loss of the national, aesthetically and symbolically. The journalist quoted in the conclusion to the last chapter puts this sense of loss best following the destruction of the Yala bungalow in 1996 by the LTTE, when she states that 'The heart is full of anguish when I think that I will never stand at that self same upstair deck, looking out over jungle, scrub and river' (Rodrigo 1996: unpag.). The loss here comes about through a violent LTTE seizure. As another journalist melancholically mused during that same period of closure: 'As the shadows of the Tigers draws its cloak over Yala's wild corridors, we are left with our precious memories and a few enchanted names.' (*The Island* 1996: unpag.). The threat of Ruhuna being lost to the LTTE, and the posed threat to the semiotic purity of its 'jungles', was written in no uncertain terms as an incursion into the national.

> The sword of Damocles hangs threateningly over Sri Lanka's favourite national park. An air of uneasiness spreads over the 'land where the buffaloes roam and the deer and the antelope play,' and whatever the authorities may say, Yala still lies crippled ten days after the torching of the Pattanangala bungalow. (Williams 1996: unpag.)

To stress the relevance of a semiotics of 'jungle' here is again not to de-emphasize the real threats to security that potential visitors to Ruhuna National Park faced during this period. It is, however, to stress once again how the park's implication in ongoing processes of nationness has often revolved around the ways it has been made to circulate as a geographical imagination congruent with and productive of quite particular articulations of the national. In terms of reading the politics of Sri Lankan nature then, contestations to the park's hegemonic geographical imaginations are as telling as the physicality of landscape experience itself.

Militarizing Nature:
Checkpoints and Subjecting Citizenship

Ruhuna National Park was increasingly becoming marked as a potential and actual target, a field of anticipated violence with the 'sword of Damocles' (Williams 1996: unpag.) hanging threateningly over it. As such during the mid-1990s it was fast becoming known as the 'eastern front' to Sri Lanka's civil war. Anxieties were fuelled by the occasional discovery of landmines and arms caches deep in the park's midst. Securing the park became a government objective both because of the strategic importance of making sure the LTTE could not make inroads to the south through Yala, and, as I have suggested above, to safeguard a national historiographical and aesthetic resource that the nation was threatened with losing. As a consequence, it was not long after the LTTE presence was confirmed that the government deployed a significant army presence in Ruhuna. Soldiers were posted around the various Blocks in a very public effort to secure the park militarily as soon as possible. This kind of militarization of threatened national space and meaning is of course not uncommon in Sri Lanka (see de Mel 2007), and accordingly martial presence offered visual and symbolic reassurance that this national landscape was no longer helpless. Soldiers remained conspicuously present to visitors in Block I for a good many years; the appointed guardians of national security, for all intents and purposes fixing Yala's landscapes with the masculine panoptic gaze of the state.

Part of these soldiers' jobs was to perform checkpoint duties within and at the entrance of the park. 'Checkpoint culture' is well developed in Sri Lanka (see Hyndman and de Alwis 2004: 549). If not necessarily an effective method of securing public space, it has evolved as a formalized state inscription of space and society; a very visible and performative attempt at securing society by the impossible and always incomplete regulation of movement through space. As Jeganathan has argued, checkpoints work via a logic of 'possible targets' and 'anticipated violence' (Jeganathan 2002). Their presence in the landscape produces a cartography of violence (ibid.: 360). Such a cartography is not limited to just a mapping of potential terrorist attacks across space, though certainly we can say that Ruhuna was emerging as one such place. A cartography of violence is also a production of *locations* within the space of the nation state where the citizen is subjected, laid bare, made transparent, and dissected by the state's optic. Checkpoints are an active inscription in space of the power of the national, of the hegemony of those who check.

At Ruhuna, the checkpoint efforts of the army worked well to restore some confidence in the park's security following the attacks of 1996. Two journalists enthusiastically reported in 1997 how soldiers had asked them 'cursory, polite but searching' questions when they tried to enter. As the reporters stressed, only after being 'Satisfied with our explanations and having established our identities [did] they let us proceed to the ticketing counter' (*Sunday Times Plus* 1997: unpag.). Of course, restoring confidence in the security of the park this way also further enmeshed the park's landscapes in the very particular contours of the Sri Lankan national. Park visitors were required to have their identities 'checked' before access to this national resource was made available to them. For most visitors, this 'checking' would pose no problem, but, as Jeganathan writes, there is a rather 'precarious nature of this agreement between checker and checked. For each citizen to position his political affiliation in terms of alliance or enmity with the state is also then to work through his own subjection [by the state]' (Jeganathan 2002: 364). As Hyndman and de Alwis have noted, the checkpoint is a constant threat full of fear for those whose own biopolitical striations as marked on their identity cards – place of birth, address, name, even the handwritten language in which the card is completed – mark them as dangerous to the state (Hyndman and de Alwis 2004: 549). If the anti-colonial Sri Lankan national involved sliding the particularities of Sinhala Buddhism over and into the universality of the Sri Lankan national (Jeganathan 2004; 2009), then thought this way the checkpoint reproduces locations where 'identity' as such only registers itself when it emerges as deviation from that now hegemonic universal: as the potentially dangerously non-Sinhala, as the Tamil, for example. Therefore steps taken to secure Ruhuna's nature meant the further instantiation of a normalizing, yet significantly militarized, cosmopolitan Sinhala-Buddhist national at the park.

In July 1998, Ruhuna National Park was declared safe again by the army. The headline of a *Sunday Times* feature on Yala published in August simply read, 'Pronounced Safe' (Fernando 1998: 3). This, together with other newspaper articles from around that period, heaped praise onto the army and its 'competent authority' for 'clearing' the park of the lingering terrorist threat and encouraging wildlife enthusiasts to flock back. In fact, only Block I was fully open again to the public, as it was for brief periods through 1996 and 1997, and the park was heavily and visibly militarized in ways that conveyed a sense of safety to visitors who did choose to venture back. So, although there is no denying that the army's work in the park succeeded in a kind of physical 'clearing', the very public declarations that Ruhuna was now safe for visitors coupled with visible signs of the army's sheer presence also participated in a process of clearing that was as textual and performative as it was material. As I have been suggesting through this section, essential to these more textual dimensions of 'clearing' the park were exercises in conquering spatial imaginaries that themselves threatened the violent loss of Ruhuna as a resource *for* the nation. Together, the discursive and material practices discussed in this and the last section worked to secure once again the ways the park circulated in the 'national' imagination. If, for example, the army's very presence provided physical security for park visitors, then their checkpoint practices and visibility (jungle fatigues aside) offered more performative and symbolic reassurances that the optic of the state was fixed on Ruhuna, working constantly to screen out danger and purify the park once more. Only when discursive and performative purification folded into the park's material geography, could it cease to be the landscape of fear that it had rapidly been becoming.

> At Paranathatupola, where visitors are allowed to alight from their vehicles, a number of foreign visitors were relaxing by the river. 'We are not frightened to come to Yala now because the army is here,' said Amarasiri, a jeep driver employed by Flamingoes Safari. (Fernando 1998: 3)

This same piece even suggested that the army had drawn Ruhuna's disparate publics together around the perceived threat to the national that the LTTE posed. Not only had poachers in Ruhuna surrendered their weapons when offered an amnesty, some had subsequently been recruited for Yala security. In such ways, securing Ruhuna National Park was about reterritorializing and stabilizing once again the quite particular aesthetic and historiographical registers for which the park is so well renowned. Once again to be able to claim that Ruhuna's sacred modernity was available for public consumption was to reinstantiate the claims to nationness embedded within Ruhuna's nature, in its semiotically pure 'jungles', so to speak. As one army officer told the press: 'The LTTE is trying to cripple Yala Park economically ... This is a national treasure. We must look after it so that people of all races can visit and enjoy it' (Fernando 1998: 3). In this sense then, there was perhaps no more telling a headline than that printed by the *Sunday Times* (1997: unpag.) when visitors first started coming back to Yala late in 1997: 'The Jungle Awakes'.

Kataragama Pilgrims: Incorporating Non-Buddhist Sacredness in Ruhuna

Fears about safety in Ruhuna did remain, however. Notable were fears that in order once again to penetrate Block I of the park the LTTE might masquerade as Tamil pilgrims making their way from the east coast, through Yala to the adjoining Kataragama Sanctuary, or as Tamil Hindu pilgrims would call it *Katirkamam*. Indeed, the status, passage, and effects that Tamil pilgrims to Kataragama might have on Block I had been cause for concern to park authorities for most of Ruhuna's colonial and post-independent history.

Under the terms of the 1938 Fauna and Flora Protection Ordinance, Kataragama is designated as a Sanctuary, situated on the western boundary of Block I (see Map 1). A pilgrimage site for Buddhists and Muslims, but perhaps most celebrated amongst Sri Lanka's Hindus, it is one of a few sites in Sri Lanka where pilgrims from three major religions converge around the same sacred space. For Hindu worshippers, the principal edifice in the site is the Katirkamam shrine, devoted to the Lord Katirkamam. The presiding deity is Lord Murugan, or Skanda the son of Siva, who halted to rest here on the hills of this area known as Kataragama on his return to India after defeating the Titans. To be clear in this respect, Hindu pilgrims will make their way to the area called Kataragama in order to visit the Katirkamam temple. The few Muslim pilgrims who travel to Kataragama believe that a being called al-Khidir gave his name to the Islamic shrine within the Muslim quarter of Kataragama, the Khalir Makam. For Buddhist devotees, however, Kataragama is a place name inseparable from the Buddhist deity Kataragama who resides there. Though religious clerics will in fact debate whether the God Kataragama hails from Buddhist or Hindu mythology, the point to stress here is that the common place name to be found on most maps of the area, Kataragama, only indirectly articulates non-Buddhist religio-historical iconography.

Just as significant are precisely those difficulties that religious scholars have in identifying racially and religiously 'pure' origins for what are perhaps better conceived as a maelstrom of different sacred narratives sliding fluidly over one another. It is said, for example, that Dutthugemenu built offerings to Hindu gods here. Place, Kataragama that is, has irreducibly been formed through the conjunctural 'thrown-togetherness' of narratives and trajectories (see Massey 2005; 1994). If we can say that in some sense Kataragama was always-already impure, then the colonial obsession with race-thinking and delineating religious communities helped shape a long history of seeking semiotic, material, and ethnicized purification in place. As far back as 1874, the Assistant Government Agent for the Hambantota District remarked of Kataragama that

> It is remarkable that even the Hindu worshippers who attend the festival, are careful to make offerings on the site of the wihare.
> The temple of Karthikaya is said to have been endowed by Dutthugemenu, king of Magama, about two thousand years ago, as a thank you offering supernatural help in his conquest of the Tamil king, Elara. (T. Steele in Herbert 1874: unpag.)

More telling than the remarkableness of Hindu offerings at the Buddhist vihara is the agent's incredulity at such religiously impure practices. Agent Steele's rather categorical racialized gaze betrays a broader colonial desire to fix unbound and fluid sacred practice amongst historical communities with what Partha Chatterjee has referred to as the 'bound serialities' of colonial modernity (2004: 22–23). As we shall see below, this ethnographic fixing of difference has remained in contemporary observations of the *Pada Yatra*.

Returning to Tamil pilgrims specifically, the pilgrimage route from east coast towns and villages, through Yala to the shrine of Katirkamam, is known as the *Pada Yatra*. Hugging the southeast coast, pilgrims walk through Kudimbigala, Yala East National Park, a small part of Yala Strict Natural Reserve, Ruhuna National Park Block II and then Block I, on their way through to the Katirkamam shrine at the Kataragama Sanctuary (see Map 1). Kataragama has figured strongly in management deliberations and decisions regarding Yala since its early enclosure as a Game Sanctuary and Sportsmen's Reserve late in the nineteenth century. Since before that time, British administrators had become aware of the various pilgrimage traditions through to Kataragama, therefore from the time of Yala's very enclosure the *Pada Yatra* pilgrimage needed to be factored into the modern process of emparkment itself. It was believed that *Pada Yatra* pilgrims, many of whom were 'estate coolies', imported as plantation labourers by the British from South India, were liable to spread disease across plantations upon their returns from Kataragama due to the unhygienic conditions along the route. Pilgrims walked as much as 100 miles, spending days and nights in what the British still thought was 'unhealthy jungle', exposing themselves to what became known as the 'Kataragama fever', or malaria. As a British Malariologist, commissioned to investigate possible causes and measures that could be taken, put it in 1925: 'It has been maintained that in some years the Tamil labour force in Uva is absolutely disorganized after the festival owing to the sickness' (Carter 1925: unpag.).

Such concerns around hygiene remained, and following Yala's reclassification as a network of national reserves in 1938, they were combined with fears that pilgrims caused a significant disturbance to fauna. From around 1953 onwards, plans to build a road skirting the northern boundaries of the whole Protected Area complex, specifically for the *Pada Yatra* pilgrims, were discussed. The main barrier to the materialization of this road was a straightforward lack of funds. Calls for this road were at quite obvious odds with an understanding that the journey on foot through the park's wilderness was an essential component of the *Pada Yatra*. But the road would have excised the pilgrim route from the space of the national park itself, and in this respect it is significant that plans for the road were revisited by the SLFP's Department of Wild Life in September 1958, just three months after Ceylon's 'ethnic riots'. Though the reasons cited in the annual administration report were to 'enable game to be left completely undisturbed' (de Silva 1958: unpag.), as I show below, anxiety over the presence of Tamil *Pada Yatra* pilgrims in the midst of national space has proved an enduring tension. Unsurprisingly, the riots themselves, and the political tensions leading up to them from 1956, severely reduced the number of Tamils who made the pilgrimage: in 1953, there were 2,700 estimated pilgrims (Nicholas 1954: unpag.), in 1957, between 50 and 60, and in July 1958, there were 240 (after tensions had calmed a little) (de Silva 1958: unpag.).

Ethnographic Optics and Distancing the Other

Since 1983, there has been a renewed concern about the annual *Pada Yatra* routing through Ruhuna National Park, which can be connected more directly to concerns about national security. Following the 1996 LTTE attacks, and the subsequent military presence in the park, fears surfaced that the LTTE could try to gain access to Block I by disguising themselves as *Pada Yatra* pilgrims. Security officials were aware that the LTTE could make inroads to the southwest from territories they held in the east by coming through the park, and that by doing so they could attack the Wirawila detention centre which at the time held approximately thirty suspected LTTE terrorists. As a result, through the late 1990s, pilgrimages also came under the watchful eye of the state; once again, checkpoints ensured that pilgrims' movements through the park were monitored, screened, and only allowed by the army.

> When asked about the dangers of infiltration by Tigers, who may come in the guise of pilgrims during this annual 'Paada Yatra' pilgrimage, Maj. Jayakody said that there was a process of screening, conducted first at Pottama by the STF and then by the army at Warhena, which minimizes enemy infiltration. (Amarasekera 1998: unpag.)

As I have stressed above, such screening processes participate in a kind of performative and semiotic purification of Ruhuna as a properly national space. The screening of subjects at checkpoints is a subjection of any citizen's agency to the scrutinizing gaze of the state, but targeting and screening *Pada Yatra* pilgrims specifically also does more. Necessary or not for security reasons, it is an articulation of the state's benevolent tolerance of non-Sinhala-Buddhist sacred practice in national space. In this sense, a tolerating practice like screening specific ethnicized groups reinscribes hegemonic power relationships within the nation state. It instantiates a spatialization that fixes the tolerated at the threshold of the spaces that such checkpoints are designed to curate. The tolerated remain at the gates, to-be-tolerated, always other, and eternally strange.

In the newspaper article quoted above, it is also worth noting how the journalist objectifies the *Pada Yatra*, at the same time distancing himself from it by writing it as ritual of the other; an object of ethnographic knowledge set apart from the modern national self and made transparent by his combination of words and parenthesis, 'this annual "Paada Yatra" pilgrimage ... '. In fact, if screening in this broader figurative and textual sense intends to know a group, to gather data about its characteristics and of individual group members' intentions, then it participates in a work of anthropology of sorts (see Jeganathan 2002: 362), the state writing ethnographies for the strategic aim of securitization. Screening, in this sense, works on a logic that presupposes particular kinds of difference in its construction of the norm.

One particular article published in *Loris* in 1997 offers a quite telling example of these kinds of state ethnographies in practice. It was written by a member of the Wildlife and Nature Protection Society, whose narrative operates under the implied sign of the 'modern' with an affiliation to the 'national'. Some years prior to the essay's publication, and prior to the LTTE attacks in Yala, the author had ventured into Ruhuna to gather knowledge about the *Pada Yatra* pilgrimage rituals, practices, and participants, choosing to follow the route in his four-wheel-drive vehicle. The essay is a journal of adventure that mixes sheer curiosity concerning traditional and unfamiliar non-Buddhist sacred practices into a narrative pitched to readers as strategic need-to-know data in politically tense times. In this respect, it works as ethnography: fixing, screening, and setting the *Pada Yatra* traditions and practices apart from the 'modern' and the 'national'. Though the text itself was not circulated beyond *Loris*'s subscribers, its composition and content offers a sense of the surveillance and anxieties regarding Ruhuna's infusion with a non-Buddhist sacredness and body politic during politically tense times. Early on, the author, Ranil Bibile, makes direct reference to the need for understanding the pilgrimage and the spaces it traverses in the context of recent LTTE incursions into Ruhuna:

> In 1994 I had a window of opportunity to follow the same path as the pilgrims, fortunately in a 4 WD vehicle and not on foot. Even at that time there was some tension on account of previous terrorist activity, but now (in 1996), those areas have once again been swamped by the terrorist and are therefore inaccessible to most citizens of this country. Therefore a

somewhat detailed narrative of our 1994 journey may prove informative to members of the WNPS, most of whom must surely have a desire to venture into those distant parts again some day. (Bibile 1997: 87)

That the article only made it to publication after the 1996 LTTE attacks is indicative of how this narrative became a necessary quasi-ethnography only after Ruhuna's landscapes were breached. Its task was to make the non-national and traditional praxis of an ethnicized other transparent to the ethnographic gaze; in this sense to participate in a practice of state-sponsored surveillance. In fact, Bibile soon anchors his narrative a little more firmly in the professionalized ethnographic formation by making two references – his only two references in this six-page essay – to disciplinary anthropological scholarship on Sri Lanka (to the work of Michael Carrithers and Gananath Obeyesekera). The very act of separating himself, we can say 'the ethnographer', from the *Pada Yatra* pilgrims, 'the subjects', works as a distancing mechanism that is echoed throughout the text. This distancing works at two levels.

First, to distinguish the traditional praxis of Tamil *Pada Yatra* pilgrims from the modernity of his own ethnographic and observational technologies. In this sense, the four-wheel drive becomes a metonym for the author's modernity, as are his instruments and vocabulary for wildlife observation that mark him as a member of the scientific WNPS community: his video recorder (ibid.: 90) for example, or reference to elephants as 'pachyderms' (ibid.: 89). In contrast to his own modernity, Bibile's observed group and their *Pada Yatra* practices quite noticeably only come into representation through his narrative voice and, moreover, his own fear. In such ways Tamil pilgrims remain subaltern, mired in the traditional and unable to articulate their modes of sacred praxis in ways that are not ventriloquized and recanted by Bibile's own ethnographic gaze. There is a lengthy passage that recounts the party's encounter with a Hindu worshipper at a tree shrine as they camped one night.

At around 2 a.m. we are woken up by a strange sound. Someone or something in the depths of murky forest around us is grasping for breath, very loudly in and out, as though ill and at death's door. What's worse, the noise is getting closer and closer to us. Then in the dim lamplight we see a weird, bare-bodied figure emerge from the forest, gasping loudly all the time ... The figure goes to the tree shrine, which is just an old weather-beaten table under a tree with a picture of the goddess, just five feet from us, and makes some seemingly jerky, even violent movements. I think 'perhaps it was not such a good idea to camp here in the first place'. Everyone in our party is sitting up, tongue-tied and frozen to their bedding. Suddenly the figure turns around, runs stopping the loud moans. We watch in amazement as he (or it) returns to the tree-shrine, not taking the slightest notice of us, and repeatedly passes a forearm over a flame lit with something. In the forest's darkness our eyes are riveted on the flame as it wraps itself around the black arm, from wrist to elbow, back and forth. The moaning continues, interspersed with gasps, and then, as suddenly as it appeared, the figure disappears into the forest, still making those ghastly sounds which gradually fade into the dark night ... (Bibile 1997: 88–89)

The next morning the party are told by pilgrims that this was a form of worship practised on the *Pada Yatra*, but Bibile's estrangement from it as ritual and praxis is telling. His text writes the *Pada Yatra* as unenchanted Hindu sacredness, mired in the backward recesses of the traditional. Through Bibile's narrative voice, this non-Buddhist sacred praxis is animalized, and held from his modern self at the significant distance that enlightenment anthropological thought places between the traditional and modern.

The second way that Bibile's distancing works through the text is to distinguish the fabric of Ruhuna's historiographically Sinhala landscapes, over which he feels a sense of communion and connection, from more superficial and ephemeral Tamil and Hindu markings and practices on that fabric. For example, in the first page Bibile describes dispassionately a Hindu tree shrine they arrive at: 'There is a framed picture of Lord Ganesh – a Hindu deity, and a metal trident stuck in the ground' (87). To clarify that Lord Ganesh is a Hindu deity presumes a mostly non-Hindu readership as it seeks to render transparent modes of non-Buddhist sacredness. In just the next paragraph, however, Bibile writes very differently of another spot: 'To our right a stupa on a high rock – historic Kudimbigala, one of *our* oldest cave monasteries dating back to around the second century B.C.' (ibid.: 88; my emphasis). He refers to this spot in the possessive mode, at the same time writing the monastery into history, thereby marrying the landscape and its past to the community of the national to which he belongs. Nowhere does Bibile need to specify to his readership that Kudimbigala is especially resonant for Buddhists. That much can be read by a textual community who accept terms like 'stupa', 'historic', 'cave monasteries', and, later in that paragraph, 'hermitage', 'monks', and 'meditation', as the familiar coordinates of a cosmopolitan Sinhala-Buddhist world shared amongst them. In this way, his words participate in a quite specific distribution of the sensible. His rocks and caves suggest the weighty organicism of that history, unlike those more ephemeral Tamil shrines he encounters. For example, the tree shrine at which his party encountered the Hindu worshipper the previous night, Bibile emphasizes its material superficiality, writing the shrine as impermanent clutter balancing precariously on the landscape, 'just an old weather-beaten table under a tree with a picture of the goddess' (ibid.: 88).

Through such techniques, Bibile renders transparent for ethnographic consumption the non-Buddhist sacred and 'traditional' praxis of the *Pada Yatra* and its ephemeral landscape markings. His narrative also firmly suggests how his own modernity is not in any way antithetical to the sacredness of Ruhuna's historically essential – that is to say, Sinhala and Buddhist – landscape meanings. If not the conscious intention of his piece, then one of its effects was to re-appropriate national space in the midst of very public anxieties over the LTTE presence and the ongoing *Pada Yatra* pilgrimage. It participated in the semiotic purification of Ruhuna following the 1996 attacks by the LTTE that this chapter has concentrated on teasing out.

As a postscript to this section it is worth stressing that as far as anxieties around the LTTE and the *Pada Yatra* go the processes of semiotic and material purification in which texts like Bibile's 'Kumana and the pilgrim path' participated were never entirely successful. In an ethnographic reversal of sorts, there is some suggestion that the LTTE's very presence in the park provided a kind of counter-militarization that inverted senses of attachment, subjection, and belonging that individual park visitors might have felt. For example, in one 1996 feature in *The Island* newspaper two journalists wrote of the LTTE's own makeshift checkpoint and screening process in ways that evoke that kind of poetic reversal for Tamil *Pada Yatra* pilgrims at least:

> In ... [an] encounter on the nineth [*sic*] at Tirrukkovil, three armed cadres had wanted to know where those on the Pada Yathra were going. When told Kataragama the Tigers had allowed them to pass without any harassment. (Abeywardene and Sahabandu 1996: unpag.)

To mention this in closing is merely to stress how much during this period the landscape itself became entangled in ethnicized claims of belonging. Space was not merely a backdrop or stage for the playing out of an identity politics forged in an abstract, baseless political sphere. Instead, struggles over Ruhuna's poetics and purities of meaning, in both imaginative and aesthetic registers, and how these meanings circulated in Sri Lanka played central roles in reducing identity to the uncomplicated, militarized, fraternal articulations of pure sameness. Indeed, the point of this part of the book has been to show how Ruhuna's sacred modernity has participated in the production of a polemic, ethnicized spatial politics in postcolonial Sri Lanka.

Concluding Ruhuna National Park

As I have suggested in this chapter, public and political anxieties that surfaced in the 1990s around the LTTE's presence in Ruhuna National Park and with regards to the *Pada Yatra* pilgrimage, bring into view the broader and ongoing work that maintains the connections between the quite particular content of Ruhuna's nature on the one hand, and its more universal claims on the other. It is this work that positions Ruhuna National Park and its nature within the terrain of nationalism. Ruhuna's dominant historiographical and aesthetic formations together instantiate a powerful spatial politics of identity and nationness in contemporary Sri Lanka. However, precisely because of the evocative nature of the park's poetics, these landscape geographies often slide under the radar of discussions regarding politics and political intervention in the Sri Lankan context. Quite simply, we rarely stop to consider the often-intense poetics of experience in Ruhuna *as* political. Why should we? They are modern moments of nature tourism, secular in the sense of not being formally religious, and historical in an apparently evidentiary way. But they are also political manifestations in as much as they inscribe the hegemony of Sinhala history and Buddhist aesthetics through landscape.

The broader contention of this book is that such political manifestations are common in other spatialities associated with Sri Lankan nature, where similar distributions of the sensible also inflect meaning, the reality of experience, and the ongoing aesthetic production of space. To develop this argument, it is to architectural tropical modernism and its environmental resonances that I turn next; a site that demonstrates how aesthetically similar kinds of Sri Lankan environmental experience not so obviously striated by archaeology and landscape history, nonetheless carry similar political implications. Ruhuna, however, is a good place in which first to bring the spatial politics of Sri Lankan nature into critical focus, because through its landscapes the connection between the historiographical and aesthetic is fairly obviously manifest. As I have shown, intense anti-colonial national and post-independent archaeological, epigraphical, and historiographical work has served to over-determine the park's aesthetic field in ways that effectively suture any gap between otherwise open experience and ethnicized meaning. In this way, at Ruhuna, the poetics and politics of meaning slide over one another in ways that the historical and critical ethnographic research undertaken in this part of the book have demonstrated.

On 26 December 2004, Ruhuna National Park's coastal areas were devastated by the Indian Ocean tsunami that struck the south and east coasts of the island. Some 250 tourists and park personnel lost their lives to the elemental wave on that morning, and the Yala Safari Hotel as well as a number of park bungalows were completely destroyed. Events of such magnitude and tragedy stubbornly serve to remind us of nature's inescapable biophysical materiality, no matter how much we stress the importance of recognizing its aesthetic and imaginative productions. For some, the fractures and fissures caused by the tsunami momentarily opened Sri Lanka's taken-as-given ground to the radical potential of progressive reconstellation (see Clark 2005a). Whilst there was some genuine hope in the wake of disaster that the event itself might lead to openings and dialogues between and across contested political communities, as de Mel and Ruwanpura so astutely put it, 'the tsunami that hit Sri Lanka did not occur in a vacuum but in a space that had a prior history' (de Mel and Ruwanpura 2006: 2). As such, since 2004, many of Ruhuna National Park's pieces have now fallen back into their familiar places, reminding that despite nature's inevitable and powerful materialities it is always also a conceptual object whose meanings are both sticky and pervasive.

Part II
Tropical Modern Architecture

CHAPTER 5

Built Space, Environment, Modernism: (Re)reading 'Tropical Modern' Architecture

In a quiet spot on the banks of Lake Deduwa on Sri Lanka's southwest coast, lies the sprawling estate of Lunuganga, the home and garden of the late Geoffrey Bawa, perhaps the best-known of Sri Lanka's 'tropical modern' architects. Now owned and run as a boutique hotel by the Lunuganga Trust, this twenty-five-acre assortment of stunning landscapes and eclectic architectural experiments (Figures 5.1, 5.2, and 5.3) was Bawa's country retreat from 1948 until his death in 2003. Set amidst a backdrop of unceasing tropical growth in this wettest and most fertile region of Sri Lanka, the estate straddles two hills and juts into the lake. Originally jungle, the land was planted with cinnamon, then rubber and hardwoods up to the early twentieth century. When Bawa bought the estate in 1948, he chose to keep the main house on the northern hill, opening up the landscapes and vistas around it with slow but steady precision, imagination, and purpose. Over the next half-century, the garden and estate evolved in dimension and texture. Today, its open spaces, terraces, and ornamental paddy fields are liberally sprinkled with statues, pavilions, and walls, all of which form part of the estate's careful choreography. Though not always paralleling one another stylistically, the evolution of the estate and the development of the architect's career as perhaps the most well- known proponent of Sri Lanka's emergent tropical modern architectural style are entwined with one another. As one of Bawa's chief commentators, David Robson, has written:

> Here he held court, drawing together a circle of painters, designers and architects and plotting with them to write a new chapter in the history of Sri Lankan art and architecture. Here he also developed and honed new ways to set buildings into their site, to create enclosed and semi-enclosed outdoor spaces, to link interior with exterior. (Robson 2002: 238)

If Lunuganga was the private estate and plaything of Sri Lanka's most famous, and arguably influential, modernist architect, stylistically it is perhaps not the best example of Geoffrey Bawa's proximity to the international modernism for which he is famous. Indeed, the influences of the international style can more readily be seen in many of his other works, some of which I touch upon in the following chapters – the Kandalama, Bentota Beach, and Lighthouse Hotels for example[1] – and they are perhaps more consistently visible in the work of other early pioneers of this style, like Minnette de Silva and Valentine Gunasekera (see Pieris 2007a), as well as current architects like Phillip Weeraratne and Varuna de Silva, who themselves have been heavily influenced by Bawa's work. In fact, apart from the clean lines of a few of the pavilions and extensions that dot Lunuganga, the estate's influences are far more eclectic and historical than just twentieth-century European and international modernism.

The heavily landscaped estate is distinctly Palladian in as much as its planning, purpose, and evolution speak of an urge to improvement and country retreat as praxis (see Cosgrove 1993). The references to Renaissance humanism can also be seen in the Italianate and classical statues that pepper the terraces, and the main house has a distinctly rustic yet Arcadian feel about it, not least because of the ways it has been made to frame views across the estate. The choreography and gentle drama of the garden also owes much to eighteenth-century English landscape architecture by the likes of William Kent and Capability Brown, whilst just a handful of structures and interior designs including the Cinnamon Hill bungalow (Figure 5.2) and the porch extension to the main house (Figure 5.3) hint at Bawa's adaptations of international modernism. But the estate's paddy fields, Chinese urns, and careful planting of regional varieties of vegetation all ornamentally also anchor this garden firmly in Asia. These many and diverse influences are unsurprising. Eight years before Geoffrey Bawa pursued his architectural studies at London's Architectural Association School of Architecture (AA) in 1954, he went on his own eighteen-month grand tour that encompassed the Far East, North America, and Europe (Robson 2002: 22). In 1948, he even flirted with the idea of settling in Italy before returning to Ceylon. In his subsequent work in Sri Lanka, including Lunuganga, the traces of this worldly internationalism are clearly visible.

Geographically, then, Lunuganga is an eclectic and distinctly relational space, and Bawa's unswerving attention to designing and choreographing its eclecticism makes the estate pre-eminently recognizable precisely *for* its artistic qualities. This heterogeneous space is firmly situated in the popular imagination as a testimony to the experimental creativity and internationalism of Sri Lanka's tropical modernism. Lunuganga's artistic modernism in this sense speaks a confidently depoliticized secularism in the contemporary Sri Lankan context. Though the style cohered in the late 1940s and 1950s around a self-conscious 'post-coloniality' (a deliberately fashioned break with

---

1 For an online portfolio of Geoffrey Bawa's work, see the ArchNet Digital Library entry for 'Geoffrey Bawa' <http://archnet.org/library/parties/one-party.jsp?party_id=73>.

Figure 5.1 Landscapes at Lunuganga, by Geoffrey Bawa; terraced ornamental paddy fields and Lake Deduwa (author's photograph).

Figure 5.2 Living room pavilion at Cinnamon Hill bungalow, Lunuganga, by Geoffrery Bawa (author's photograph).

Figure 5.3 Rear porch extension to main house at Lunuganga,
by Geoffrey Bawa (author's photograph).

colonialism), today because of its worldly qualities it is rarely spoken of in the same register as Sri Lanka's contested national question. Indeed, walking across Lunuganga's manicured lawns and gazing upon the European Classical bust and torso statuettes that scatter the various terraces, it seems counter-intuitive to suggest that such an outward-looking space might somehow be implicated in Sri Lanka's own ethnicized politics of nationhood. Aesthetically, Lunuganga exemplifies the broader sweep of Sri Lanka's tropical modernist architecture in this capacity: 'art for art's sake' is how the genre is commonly framed by public discourse. Furthermore, Lunuganga's very careful artistic and architectural composition would suggest at first glance that it has little in common with Ruhuna National Park and the ethnicizing politics I have teased from its landscape's geographies. If Lunuganga and tropical modernism do have a more acknowledged political underside, it is most certainly for their classed exclusions. These are not the kind of spaces that the average working-class Sri Lankan, whether Sinhala, Tamil, or Muslim, would physically experience in capacities other than domestic service or manual labour.

But Lunuganga is also exemplary of Sri Lanka's tropical modern architecture because it is a built space where a particular articulation of the Sri Lankan environment is made present by its author. Indeed, tropical modernism is a style of building largely predicated on the necessity architecturally to negotiate the tropical materialities inherent to elemental Sri Lankan nature. To walk through Lunuganga is to experience the estate's enfoldment in a tropical environmental context that surrounds, engulfs, and extends seamlessly into and out of its humanly fashioned spaces. As I show through this part of the book, tropical modernists work hard to make Sri Lanka's environment present in and through their work. If this kind of architectural disposition has become characteristic of the style, it has emerged out of the perceived necessity to build appropriately in the context of the country's superabundant tropical biophysicality. I focus on built space here because tropical modernism is essentially a form of environmental architecture; one through which the environmental aesthetics I have teased from Ruhuna does, I argue, find strong idiomatic and political echoes.

It is precisely because of commonly held assumptions regarding Lunuganga's environmental resonance, its characteristic tropicality, that I use the estate to begin this part of the book. Its aesthetic modernism is precisely what commonly frames it as an ethnically depoliticized and neutral space; one whose genius is its unfussy simplicity and seamless entwinement with the environment. However, as I suggest in this chapter, Lunuganga can well be reconsidered a deeply political space because of the aesthetic and environmental fabrications it puts in place, and in this sense it stands as an example with which to introduce on the politics of Sri Lanka's tropical modernism. Just as this modernism can be read as secular built space whose environmental resonance retains a stylistic autonomy from statecraft, the kinds of environmental aesthetics it makes present for its users and publics are, as I show over the next three chapters, woven from similar sacred modernities to those teased from Ruhuna National Park. In particular, Lunuganga's environmental timbre speaks of and appeals to the moderate cosmopolitan nationalism that this book evokes; one that can readily declare itself autonomous and irreligious, just as it aesthetically produces space and environmental relations in particular kinds of non-secular, if modern, ways. As I show in this part of the book, at Lunuganga, as in Ruhuna, there is a system of self-evident facts of sense perception that disclose the existence of a 'something in common' (Rancière 2004: 7–42). It is precisely the aesthetic fabric of this 'something in common' that centres a sovereign Sinhala-Buddhist host as it writes non-Sinhala presences as other. As I argue in the chapters that follow, in the ways that meaning circulates through the dominant aesthetic registers of Lunuganga, and Sri Lankan tropical modernism more generally, a cosmopolitan Sinhala-Buddhist nationalism is spatially instantiated. Tropical modernism is another iteration of the same domain of non-binary, non-secular environmental sensibility that I have teased from Ruhuna in Part I of this book.

The politicized productions of space and nature are faintly legible in some of Bawa's own narrativizations of Lunuganga, which through this chapter in particular I tease out. To do so I employ the interpretive process of (re)reading the space such that its politics might be more easily seen through the ether of tropical modernism's ethnically apolitical pretence. But, to be clear, it is not my argument that authorial (architectural) intention alone constitutes the politics of Sri Lankan tropical modern space, nor that reading the traces of sacred modernity in the likes of Bawa's own narrativizations of his spaces marks him out as any kind of nationalist (indeed, ethnically Bawa was a Burgher). Through the following chapters, I stress how an architect's intent regarding his or her work is only one part of the larger equation regarding first, how buildings come to mean certain things, and secondly, the effects buildings have in and through society as people use and inhabit them either corporeally or imaginatively, as well as when political institutions – like the state – bring these buildings and their semiotics into their sights. Indeed, the very term 'built space', as opposed to 'architecture', signals an attempt to de-centre the architect. The architect is just one part of the broader circulations of meaning that built space develops as it pervades daily life and imagination (see Till 2009).

This is an important methodological point, because the range of architects, architecture students, and indeed users I interviewed through the course of this research have varying degrees of involvement and interest in the national question. Most would abhor, perhaps even feel betrayed by, the claim that their work or their buildings are implicated in Sri Lanka's ethnicized politics. Yet, as I have stressed throughout, this book is committed to teasing out a politics of everyday life and space that is not immediately recognizable *as* political. Furthermore, one strand of this book is to suggest that the meanings of nature and space, more importantly the politics of those meanings, develop through a combination of authorial practice, circulation, and use. It is the choreography and praxis of ordinary spaces of nature, the apparently pre-social and naturalized, that I commit to making visible *as* political. Through its environmental resonances, tropical modernism participates in these spatial politics of nature.

Cultural Geographies of Built Space

In the chapters that follow, I draw upon two broad approaches to critically engaging built space in order to tease out the spatial, and spatializing, politics of Sri Lanka's tropical modern architecture. Both emerge from scholarship on architecture that is situated at the intersection of cultural studies and human geography. First, a significant body of work that has attempted in different ways to read the semiotics of architectural space. Akin to interpretive approaches to landscape, this work has stressed the politics of architecture's form and theatricality; in other words, the power embedded in its physical and performative signification. For example, such approaches have variously been used to read the symbolism of skyscrapers and other urban edifices (see Domosh 1988, 1989; McNeill 2005; Woolf 1988) to underscore the sacred, allegorical, and performative dimensions of (non-Western) urban topologies and building practices (Duncan 1990), and postcolonially to allude to the presence of the imperial elsewheres within metropolitan building projects (Driver and Gilbert 1999; Jacobs 1996). Though this work is expansive and diverse, its common concerns are with the representational mechanics through which buildings become signs in a semiotic system of meaning that evidences broader social, cultural, and political contexts (Jacobs 2006: 2). In the context of Sri Lanka, for example, Nihal Perera has usefully employed a similar approach to show how a colonialized elite indigenized the symbolism of late nineteenth-century Colombo's urban topography, therefore alerting us to the performative and symbolic anti-colonial politics of Sri Lankan built space (Perera 2002; also see Pieris 2007b).

Anthony King's work on architecture, global culture, and postcolonialism has proved an influential supplement to these representational approaches by alerting us to architecture's postcolonial and translational geographies. In particular, his work on the 'bungalow' tells the story of a so-called 'global' architectural design that with the travels and translations of empire finds a slightly different enunciation and manifestation in diffuse geographical and historical contexts worldwide (King 1984; also see Jacobs 2006: 2). King's point, that he revisits in his book, *Spaces of Global Cultures* (2004), is that each repetition of the architectural sign of modernity, each skyscraper, high-rise, or modernist house and garden, is different, carrying and conveying different kinds of symbolism that may be specific and legible to their respective interpretive communities; each is specific to its historical, cultural, and professional/technical conditions of enunciation. Architectural modernity in this analysis, like any modernity, is cultural as opposed to acultural or universal (Taylor 2001). And, as King urges, 'attempting to read architectural meanings without the discourses that accompany them is a notoriously ambivalent project' (King 2004: 60). It is for this reason that the job of locating Sri Lanka's tropical modernism is no simple task of ticking off Bawa, de Silva, or Gunasekera's international influences, as if they exist in isolation from their situatedness in a particular moment of Sri Lanka's own relational, colonial, and post-independent history. It requires a finer analysis attuned to the historical and cultural situatedness of the architects' building philosophies and narrativizations *within* their domains of circulation.

However, as Fred Jameson (1997) has argued in his forceful critique of Kenneth Frampton's celebration of Critical Regionalist architecture, there is a certain danger attached to taking at face value tropical modernism's essentially local provenance, or its self-consciously *arrière-garde* articulations amidst a standardizing world system as a whole. As the analysis that follows shows, Sri Lankan tropical modernism emerges within the singular yet globally uneven nature of capitalist modernity. As a style therefore it testifies to the ways that modernity touched down in postcolonial Sri Lanka. The aim of reading the iconography of Sri Lanka's tropical modern architecture then is not to unearth its native quintessence. Rather, it is to begin to tease out how tropical modernism began to mobilize the materials of tradition and nostalgia in order performatively to tell the story of the avowedly 'post-colonial' national within and on the international stage. The aim is to read the articulations of Sri Lanka's tropical modernism and to tease out the political effects of those articulations.

The second critical approach to built space that I draw upon in the following chapters emerges from work that shifts the register of interpretation from built form only, to a more conjunctural analysis of the relationships between built space and people. Much of this work has sought to evoke the voices of building users and occupants in a bid to understand what subjective and social effects buildings have on those who inhabit them (see Jacobs 2006: 2). For the sake of my own attempt to uncover a politics of space, the value of this work is its recognition that buildings mean little without the physical and imaginative contexts in which they are set to work. Locating and reading architecture postcolonially then, must take more than just a description of semiotic meaning as its interpretive task. As Anthony King has also written, an interventionary and postcolonial analysis must also attempt 'to understand the connection between the built environment and the construction of the subject' (King 2004: 61; also see Nalbantoglu and Wong 1997; and Scriver and Prakash 2007).

Whether or not designs are physically realized, built space is always implicated with the people who may, and do, use it. Built space is always also lived space in this analysis, which requires some thought about how its users are implicated in what it comes to mean (see Lees 2006; Lees and Baxter 2011), and how users' bodies and subjectivities are themselves produced as they move through, or indeed imaginatively engage, those spatial forms (see Imrie 1996; Longhurst 1998). Though the distinction between physical and imaginative use requires pinning down on a case-by-case basis, it is worth stressing here that broadly speaking I take use to imply cognitive possession of prominent built forms as much as physical appropriation. For example, just as Ruhuna National Park might occupy a place in one's imagination even if you have never been there, Lunuganga also occupies a place in the imagination of many Sri Lankans and beyond that I would argue could broadly be construed as 'use'. Though this cannot apply to buildings of all scales that I engage (particularly domestic), my central point around building use is a simple one: built space has effects on people, just as people affect the meanings of built space.

Though this kind of approach urges a move towards the materiality of built space, I do not take it to constitute a wholesale move away from semiotics and representation, for the simple fact that materialities also carry the weight of meaning; they come to bear a cultural logic of sorts. Attending to architecture's implication with users like this can be thought of as a kind of 'semiotic materialism' (Jacobs 2006: 2). So, in the analysis of Sri Lanka's tropical modernism that follows, engaging architecture's implication in the lives and experiences of people is certainly not to suggest that architecture might be in any way 'nonrepresentational' (see Lees 2001). Taking the semiotic analyses of architecture together with a recognition of the relationships between buildings and their users is to locate tropical modern built space within the social and cultural contexts within which it is, and has been, implicated. Doing this, I work towards an understanding of what architecture's materialities mean and do in and through those worlds. Evoking the representational/semiotic elements of spaces like Lunuganga in tandem with the register of aesthetics and experience like this, suggests how architecture is both product of, and productive of, society, subjectivity, and the fabric of ordinary spatiality, its semantic delimitations and naturalizations. As with the explorations of the politics of Ruhuna National Park, crucial here is a fluid understanding of how the aesthetic is also semiotic in the way it participates in the production of Rancière's 'distribution of the sensible' (2004), itself a deeply political entanglement.

In the chapters that follow, I approach Sri Lanka's tropical modernist built space in ways attendant not just to the symbolism and semiotic positioning of designs themselves. I am also concerned to draw the lines of connection between tropical modern environments and the mutual construction of subject and society as a way of teasing out what I stress are the political contours of such aestheticized space. This effort requires work properly and contextually to locate the architecture by the likes of Geoffrey Bawa, Minnette de Silva, and the extensive architectural movement that they have been instrumental in forging. As I show in the rest of this chapter, the contextual work to position the built space within its attendant historical, geographical, and social discourses is necessary to begin to read from it the naturalizations the architecture continues to mobilize within contemporary Sri Lankan society. If places like Lunuganga were shaped by Bawa's international influences and thoroughly modern, European training (which itself was common amongst Sri Lanka's early tropical modernists), paying attention to the domestic historical contexts in which they were forged suggests alternative kinds of modernity and aesthetics woven into their spatialities. It is these alternative aesthetics and their political implications that this chapter begins to evoke by working from the example of Lunuganga.

Developing these lines of thought, in Chapter 6 I shift the focus more squarely to the relationships between space and subjectivity. Specifically, drawing upon a series of interviews and conversations with architects, architecture students, and users of tropical modern built space, I argue that one of the predominant experiential registers central to the meaning of tropical modern built space is a kind of living inside/out that itself inscribes non-binary engagements with the natural environment. If this inside/out design and use of space is born from the demands of tropical environments, then the built space's dominant cultural logic has come to reinstantiate what I have been referring to in this book as sacred modernity. As with experiences that I have read from Ruhuna National Park, I suggest how these poetics are commonly subsumed by Sinhala-Buddhist interpretations of a metaphysics not amenable to binary understandings of nature/culture, and the sacred/secular. The politics of Sri Lanka's tropical modern built space, I suggest, lie in its instantiation of these commonly acknowledged and shared sensual, and sensible, domains. If tropical modernism expresses something of the emblematically Sri Lankan, then its experiential domains are ethno-politically marked I argue in Chapter 6.

Both this chapter and the next work hard to stress that this argument should not be taken to suggest some authentic and essential core to Buddhist experience that this architecture somehow deterministically creates, one that is somehow affectively different from Hindu, Christian, or Muslim experience. Accordingly, Chapter 7 works to expand on the contextuality of environmental experience in tropical modern space. Specifically, it pays attention to ways that meaning is in some senses excessive of tropical modern materialities, caught as it is in a complex skein of institutions, discourses, and market pressures that effectively over-determines tropical modernism's semiotic materialisms. The discourses that now circulate around the architecture itself have helped to lock dominant interpretations of its aesthetic registers into a notion of the 'emblematically Sri Lankan' that, I argue, remain constitutive of the political.

Locating Sri Lanka's Tropical Modernism

Describing her first meeting with Le Corbusier in 1947, and their subsequent friendship, Minnette de Silva wrote:

> Le Corbusier was asked how he would talk to me since he refused to speak in English, as it wasn't good. He said, 'She doesn't speak French so I have to [speak English] in order to converse with her.' He was greatly attracted by his first live contact with *l'Inde*. I think he romanticized our meeting. I became the symbolic link with *l'Inde* the idealized symbol. Since then I have been deeply touched by his sympathy and interest in me and my work. His was an enduring, understanding friendship, pure and simple. At the time I hardly realized the great honour. (de Silva 1998: 100)

If Geoffrey Bawa holds a pre-eminent position in Sri Lanka's tropical modernism, it is because, as Anoma Pieris puts it, his well-known portfolio is 'typically used as a measure for evaluating contemporary Sri Lankan architecture' (Pieris 2007a: 10). But Bawa was by no means the first to adapt an international style in Sri Lanka. In 1945, some nine years before his professional training at London's AA, a young woman from Kandy, Minnette de Silva, secured a place at the Royal Institute of British Architects (RIBA) and the AA to further her own architectural training which had begun in Bombay some years previously. Though de Silva's own profile in the history of Sri Lanka's tropical style is somewhat eclipsed by Bawa, she was the first Sri Lankan-born architect to experiment with the modernist style at home. Excavating her own development as a modern architect then, is central to the work of locating Sri Lanka's tropical modernism, just as it is central to the process of (re)reading the aesthetics of tropical modern spaces more generally.

De Silva's own recollections of meeting with Le Corbusier at the Congrès internationaux d'architecture moderne (CIAM) in Bridgwater, near Bristol in 1947, are I think telling. Not just in terms of her role in the development of modernism in Sri Lanka, but also with regards Sri Lankan architectural modernism's iteration of, and relationship to, the international style. If de Silva was indeed Le Corbusier's idealized symbol of *l'Inde*, then their friendship perhaps also sheds light on Le Corbusier's broader, perhaps just as eroticized, fascination with South Asia that culminates in his early 1950s involvement in the Chandigarh project. Irrespective, what is striking from de Silva's recollection quoted above is her own evident situatedness within, and proximity to, the fulcrum of the international style.

De Silva was born in 1918 in Kandy, her progressive Sinhala-Buddhist father being a well-known politician whose reformist work through the Ceylon National Congress (CNC) helped gain universal franchise in Ceylon and secure representation and rights for estate workers and Kandyan villagers. She came from an upwardly mobile middle-class, colonialized family, whose political agitations for independence should not be confused with vitriolic anti-colonial nationalism, but were rather the more gentlemanly negotiation of independence that was trusteeship's own narrative conclusion. Her family's position within the indigenous, yet colonializing middle class afforded her the mobility and enablement to pursue overseas training for her somewhat unconventional career choice. In this very sense, her movement to London in 1945 traced a transnational geography born through the imperial eddies that underpinned Ceylon's late colonial experience; in other words, coming to London for this colonialized elite was, ideologically at least, to arrive in Ceylon's own capital (see Jazeel 2006).

Though de Silva's writings attest to an awareness of her own relative exoticism in the professional spaces of RIBA, the AA, and the CIAM in the late 1940s, they also suggest a confidence in her own locatedness within international modernism. Modernism's applicability to a South Asian context was a challenge that she accepted by embracing that symbolic status of '*l'Inde*' afforded her within the occidental spaces of her chosen profession. For example, writing of the influence of her CIAM colleagues in ways that suggest her fluid translational (King 2004) search for regional architectural sensitivity, she expresses gratitude to a colleague who had first introduced her to the work of the planner Patrick Geddes. It was Geddes's work in India combined with Le Corbusier's formalism that proved invaluable to her own quest for a modern architectural approach appropriate to Sri Lanka:

[Geddes's] Ghandian approach to planning in India was so much common sense and written in 1915! ... This book should be read by all Asians – not only architects. His idea of 'conservative surgery' (instead of the destruction of both community and its life) in the rehabilitation of slums and the old villages and townships is now the latest trend ... It was the perfect counter-balance to the Corbusian classical; the two complementing each other became the foundation for most of my thinking. (de Silva 1998: 100)

Her subsequent emergent ability to bring Ceylon into modern architectural representation on her terms, *as a Ceylonese*, was itself a self-consciously 'post-colonial' departure tethered to the gestation of Ceylon's own political modernity. For de Silva, and architects like Geoffrey Bawa that followed in her wake, the strength of modernism in this avowedly 'post-colonial' and transla-tional sense was its ability to concretize a rupture from colonialism's strategy of representing authority through the 'artifice of the archaic' (Pieris 2007a: 2). But, through Geddes, she also found ways of conserving both the best of colonialism's modernity and those indigenous signatures that colonialism had sought either to erase or appropriate. So, in this sensitively creative rupture, de Silva's appropriation of the international style in Sri Lanka can be thought of less as an ideological challenge to fashion a hybrid style, and more as organic application of modernism's own principles. When de Silva returned to Ceylon and began to practise in 1948, her architecture, like Bawa's from the late 1950s onwards, evidenced an important maxim of the international style: it rejected the ornamentation and paraphernalia associated with colonial building in favour of forms derived from their functionality and appropri-ateness. In doing so, it also articulated the utopian spirit of modernism (see Gold 1997: 2), not to mention its belief in clean uncluttered lines. It was what she considered democratic architecture, liberated from the historical and ornamental impediments of colonial Westernization.

But whilst architects like de Silva and Bawa sought such new beginnings, their relationships with colonialism were a little more complex than the word 'rupture' might at first suggest. It was, after all, colonialism's class structure that had enabled their own passages to the UK as well as their professional training and exposure to the international style. So, despite those breaks with the past that she sought, de Silva – and after her Geoffrey Bawa – also abhorred the more obviously religious Buddhist revivalist trends of architecture framed around cruder modes of anti-colonial nationalism; those that they thought antithetical to the secularity and simplicity of modernism's élan. Their own tacit acceptance of the trusteeship narrative – that Britain was looking after her South Asian colonies until they were developed enough to look after themselves – influenced their propagation of a style of building that looked for a deferential break with colonialism, and as such was able was able to bring Sri Lanka's architecture into modernity on its own terms.

De Silva's commitment to this 'conservative surgical' approach to forging Sri Lankan architectural modernity saw her recuperating the sociological experiences of rural life in the Kandyan region. She sought to frame her structures, inspired by the international style, around a desire to bring traditionally Sri Lankan ways of life back into the modern home: internal courtyards, or *midulas*, and verandahs, for example, open-air bathing spaces, a disdain for heavy walls in favour of transparency and ventilation, and importantly the use of local at-hand materials, and just as local crafts-manship. This was the spatial grammar she deemed appropriate for Sri Lanka's cultural, geographic, and climatic specificities. Those modernist maxims of appropriateness and the simplicity of form married to function were negotiated by de Silva through her interpretation of the traditionally and historically Sri Lankan. But, crucially, as Chapter 3 suggests, it was precisely the same notion of tradition and history that was instantiating the primacy of the national thought retroactively as Sinhala-Buddhist. As de Silva herself put it:

> Much of my work has been based on finding a workable synthesis of traditional and modern architecture. Throughout my childhood I had lived and moved among Kandyan craftsmen and artists. When I was a child my parents, who were greatly influenced by Mr. Ananda Coomaraswamy, used to take us to Anuradhapura, Polonnaruwa and other ancient places. I would gaze at the beautiful columns and sophisticated structures which the master builders of the 'Golden Age' had left for posterity. All this seeped into my unconscious mind, later manifesting itself in my work ...
>
> My parents had kept our roots intact for my generation, but now I had to interpret this in architecture. I decided to live in Kandy, it being the centre of Ceylon and the heart of our national tradition. (de Silva 1998: 114–115)

Her equation of traditional arts and crafts with Kandy, and those with the sign of 'the national' is telling, just as is her reference to the pre-eminent South Asian art historian Ananda Coomaraswamy. Coomaraswamy's seminal 1908 monograph *Medieval Sinhalese Art* was itself enabled by the Sinhalese arts and crafts movement. The monograph called for a modern revival of that tradition (Jeganathan 2004: 194). As an aesthetic manifesto of sorts, it was published at a time when the historical narrative of the national within the colonial was being cemented as Sinhalese and Buddhist through the various archaeological and historiographical formations explored in Chapter 3. Coomaraswamy's text became part of that ideological terrain. Its focus on 'traditional' and 'Sinhala' arts and crafts helped ethnicize a history of arts and crafts in the island. As Pradeep Jeganathan has written, his text therefore stands within the critical, educated, and cosmopolitan margin of Sinhala-Buddhist nationalism because of its contribution to a racializing history of material culture (ibid.). Thus, Minnette de Silva's work to marry elements of the traditional Sinhala crafts movement with the rectilinear lines and simple curves of her iterations of the architectural modern were forged through the idiom of that cosmopolitan equation of the newly independent Ceylonese national with the Sinhala-Buddhist.

There is little doubt that de Silva's family upbringing as a Sinhala-Buddhist in Kandy influenced her understandings of history, tradition, and their Sinhala-Buddhist contents at the national scale. However, they also owe much to her ongoing associations with Sri Lanka's own modernist movement, the so-called '43 Group. In particular, she struck a friendship with the painter George Keyt, whom she met through her mother's cousin Lionel Wendt, himself a founder of the '43 Group. The formation of the group came about as a group of colonialized elite artists sought out their own version of anti-colonialism within the larger picture of national struggles that gained momentum in mid-twentieth-century South Asia (see Weerasinghe 2005). Their work to forge a distinctively Sri Lankan artistic modernism combined European modernist trends (cubist pictorial language and expressionism, in particular) with orientalist themes that spoke to Sri Lanka's particularity. But, once again, that particularity was articulating a sense that the contours of a 'post-colonial' national to come were cognate with a Sinhala-Buddhist tradition and aesthetics whose cultural kernel was the Kandyan kingdom. In de Silva's own book, which is both autobiography and a compilation of her architectural work, she tellingly reproduces an essay by George Keyt on *Folk Culture of Ceylon* that begins with the lines:

> The survival of folk culture in a small country like Ceylon is astonishing when we take into consideration the later history of the Island. The occasional raids and invasions from Southern India in ancient times were not culturally destructive ... because the cultural structure of Ceylon was fundamentally an Indian extension. But destructive forces of an alarming nature made their appearance when ...Ceylon began to stagnate and was finally subjugated by the sweeping domination of three successive powers from Europe ...
>
> Largely responsible for the survival of the Ceylonese folk and classical culture was the Buddhist religion, a faith which was somehow preserved through the centuries since Asokan times. (George Keyt in de Silva 1998: 144)

Keyt's pithy introduction encapsulates a historiographical thinking that has come to pervade the broader sweep of post-war artistic, architectural, and literary modernism in Sri Lanka: foreign contamination of an idealized pre-colonial Sinhala-Buddhist 'national' came, the modernists thought, both from South Indian invasions and European colonialism. Though the latter was deemed more destructive, the former was still marked out as ethnicized difference, coded Tamil. Through such a narrative Sinhala-Buddhism is naturalized under the sign of the national, marked as coming before history, so to speak, precisely so it can be recuperated through modernism. If this sounds familiar, it is because it is exactly the same historiographical refrain that has been inscribed in Ruhuna National Park's environmental aesthetics.

Minnette de Silva was somewhat of a pioneer, her work being described by an international community of scholarly engagement with tropical architecture, as '[t]he earliest, clearest, most critical reformulation of tropical architecture' after the war (Lefaivre and Tzonis 2001: 30). She completed her education at the AA five years before Maxwell Fry and Jane Drew started their Department of Tropical Architecture, and a full ten years before Geoffrey Bawa completed his own studies there in 1957, not to mention the host of other Sri Lankan architects who were either contemporaneous to Bawa at the AA or a few years his junior: Valentine Gunasekera, Roland Silva (himself a former Director General of Archaeology), Shelton Wijeyratne, Nihal Amarasinghe, Christopher de Saram, and Yvette Kahawita, for example. So it is not surprising that Bawa's work, and all Sri Lanka's tropical modernism since, owes much to de Silva's turn towards the Kandyan Sinhala.

For his part, Geoffrey Bawa's iteration of tropical modernism also heavily referenced the vernacular and in so doing reinvented the spatial and material characteristics of what he saw as a timeless tradition (Pieris 2007a: 10). As Lunuganga demonstrates, however, compared with de Silva, his somewhat broader range of historical and European influences helped shape a regionalist vision of the picturesque that could be said to capture something of a pre-colonial Arcadia (Pieris 2007a: 9; 2011). Perhaps this is why Bawa's commentators suggest he never thought of himself as a vanguardist (Robson 2007: 18). But the marriage of his many cosmopolitan international influences with the 'traditionally Sri Lankan' still articulated what I want to suggest is a problematically rooted notion of history that we can begin to read in the aesthetics that have come to pervade his built space. Of his design philosophy, he once wrote in a newspaper interview in 1968:

> In my personal search I have looked into the past for the help that previous answers can give and at the pointers of previous mistakes. By the past I mean all the past, from Anuradhapura to the latest finished building in Colombo, from Polonnaruwa to the present moment. (Bawa 1968)

Bawa's own democratically universal, and secular, configuration of 'all the past' is itself set within a tacit acceptance of historiography that has become accustomed to narrating history *through* the temporal landmarks of the former kingdoms Anuradhapura and Polonnaruwa, spaces that in the popular imagination at least are indissociable from Sinhala sovereignty. Like de Silva's negotiations of the traditional within the modern, the universality he signifies by his phrase 'all the past' is itself situated within a diachronic framework that reiterates a common refrain: Sinhala possession, Tamil invasion, and Sinhala reconquest. Though I would resist making too much of such an innocuous comment, what I do stress here are the ways that the coordinates of this historiography become imaginatively mapped onto tropical modern built space through such discursive proliferations.

Situating both Bawa and de Silva like this is to sketch the contours of the space of global culture (King 2004) within which their fluid iterations of modernism were forged. Despite their recuperations of a Sinhala-Buddhist particularity, both *were* at the same time resolutely modern. They shied away from association with the ethnicized register of politics throughout their careers and built buildings for all Sri Lanka's ethnic groups (if not classes). Though they – de Silva particularly – equated tradition with Sinhala-Buddhism, we can also suggest that they thought their design briefs and practices to be mostly secular, even when they were commissioned to build viharas, churches, or other religious buildings. Indeed, we can even suggest that the designation of their work as secular was a requisite for architecture that purported to be the latest democratic design iterations of modernity on the Sri Lankan market.

Having positioned the emergence of Sri Lanka's tropical modernism like this, the readings and re-readings of tropical modern space I now pursue reveal not only its readily apparent modern and secular characteristics in line with its internationalism, but crucially also the sacred modernity and thus politics simultaneously inscribed in and through spaces marked by this avowedly 'post-colonial' architectural praxis.

(Re)reading Tropical Modern Space, or How to Understand Lunuganga

Returning to Lunuganga, Geoffrey Bawa's estate, a first reading as I have suggested shows the garden to be replete with diverse visual and spatial arrangements that testify to its author's exposure to various modernist and European influences. The geometred simplicity and earthy minimalism of the Cinnamon Hill bungalow (Figure 5.2), for example, as well as the clean white and sharp lines of the main house's porch extension (Figure 5.3) recall the international style's precision and marriage of form with function. And the sheer work that went into choreographing scenic views across and beyond the estate speaks of a privileged single-mindedness reminiscent of that progressive modernist mantra 'art for art's sake'. One view in particular, from the entrance area of the main house south across Cinnamon Hill, stood out as one of the architect's favourites. Standing at the house, looking across the thick lawn and up the gentle hill slope, the view is framed by trees on either side, and in the middle distance, on the crest of Cinnamon Hill, a lone moonamal tree looms over a large jar. The tree points to the gleaming white dome of the Katakuliya temple, a Buddhist dagoba nestled in the verdant vegetation of a hill separated from the estate by a thin sliver of lake. Each day, the temple is visible with the naked eye from the estate (Figure 5.4). Of this landscape composition, Bawa once remarked:

> Over the years moving through the garden as it grew, one saw the potential of various areas which had inherently different atmospheres. For instance, the long view to the south ended with the temple, but in the middle distance was a ridge with a splendid ancient moonamal tree and when I placed a large Chinese jar under it, the hand of man was established in this middle distance. Now the eye stops here, travels to the glimmer of the lake beyond, to the slope across a long stretch of rice fields and to the stupa on the crown of the far hill across the lake. In this view the vision of the lake was too slight to be effective and it soon became obvious that a part of the ridge needed to be lowered a few feet to make this whole composition establish itself with a total finality which has not changed and now looks as if it had been there since the beginning of time. (Bawa, Bon, and Sansoni 1990: 13)

From this description it is easy to read Bawa's modern choreography and spatial planning. As he describes it, the garden is quite obviously a cultivated

Figure 5.4 View of temple at Lunuganga, by Geoffrey Bawa
(taken from the middle distance, author's photograph).

landscape, both spectacle and a series of scenographic images. As a *landscape view* it bears many of the hallmarks of the Eurocentric power relations of which the new cultural geography and landscape studies have made us well aware (see Cosgrove 1998; Daniels 1994). The vista itself implies a classically modern separation of active viewing subject from a passive field of objects gazed upon, toiled over, and possessed, as Western gardens are through the logic of capital and proprietorship. The smoothness of the landscape – its casual lines of sight – conceals and codifies the significant work that has gone · into its artifice. As Bawa stresses, he took great care to sink the access road leading through the estate, just like an eighteenth-century ha-ha, such that it would be invisible to the eye taking in the sweep from the main house. And there is a certain secularizing ornamentalism to the framing of the Buddhist temple that seems at first to bring religious iconography within the apparent realm of surface and artifice: a speculation borne out by Bawa's encounter with the priest at the Katakuliya temple who suggested that Bawa pay for the temple's repainting seeing as he derived so much visual pleasure from it. Bawa's cheeky retort was to offer only half the cost, given that only half the temple was visible from his estate (Robson 2002: 239). And, finally, we might in passing note how in Bawa's own words the labour that inheres in the landscape is explicitly coded masculine. Given Bawa's British architectural training like de Silva's, and his exposure to a wealth of European classical and renaissance styles that so obviously influenced him, these connections to a modernist landscape and design aesthetics are hardly surprising.

However, rereading the view, and the space itself, with an eye for those alternative and self-consciously 'post-colonial' kinds of modernity that architects like Bawa and de Silva were simultaneously weaving through their experimentations with modern Sri Lankan built space reveals much more. Dwelling in the view a little longer, reading Bawa's words in ways more attentive to the turn inward characteristic of 'post-colonial' Sri Lankan modernism, another type of worlding emerges; the trace of another kind of aesthetics. Bawa uses this landscape vista as an example of an 'atmosphere' inherent to an area of the garden, signalling that, evidently, this is more than just a view, and the view itself signifies a more-than-visual aesthetic. Furthermore, the 'temple' to which he refers – and which at first glance seems ornamentally placed – becomes integral to this composition, such that in a particular idiom it becomes key to the creation of the special atmosphere inherent to this environment. In fact, precisely because it is positioned beyond the estate the temple for Bawa signifies a balance that he believes the estate's artifice has attained with its environmental context, or setting. In short, for Bawa the temple signifies a naturalistic reality in which the estate is set. So if, as Bawa stresses, the 'hand of man' is established in the middle distance where he 'placed a large Chinese jar', then the temple is in fact woven into the environment beyond, naturalized, so to speak. In Bawa's description of the landscape then, there is more than a faint outline of an alternative habitation of modernity, a Buddhist aesthetics that a rereading attuned to this different spatial idiom is positioned to tease out.

We know, of course, that Bawa was neither religiously Buddhist, nor was he ethnically Sinhalese. But, as I have suggested in Chapter 1 to this book, the tropic structure of religion, thought as a formal system of doctrine-scriptures-beliefs, has become one of the authoritative categories through which an 'unthinking Eurocentrism' continues to write the universal history of colonial and postcolonial Sri Lanka. This is to stress that despite the presence of powerful religious communities within contemporary Sri Lanka, in southern Sri Lanka a Buddhist aesthetics and philosophy also textualize society in ways that do not announce themselves formally as religion, but rather remain present within an aesthetic realm that cannot be pinned down by the normativity of a sacred/secular binary. At Lunuganga this kind of a priori spatialization is residual as an effective element of the environmental present. It haunts Bawa's description of this view. This is not only to stress that Buddhist textualities dwell here as a form of enchantment that a modernist European landscape architecture could never quite banish. It is more. It is to mobilize religion beyond Eurocentric and enlightenment understandings of the word. It is 'to de-transcendentalize the sacred, to move it toward imagination' (Spivak 2008: 10).

Just as importantly, however, just as Bawa was not religiously Buddhist, we know that Bawa's mobilization of the Katakuliya temple in his description should rightfully be located within the realm of landscape architecture's attention to artifice: the *fashioning* of a space designed, fabricated that is, in a particular way. Nevertheless, it is precisely Bawa's fashioning of this space *in a particular kind of way* that helps to inscribe these kinds of aesthetics in and through place. His own attempts at fashioning a self-consciously 'post-colonial' landscape architecture that reconnected with what he regarded as Sri Lanka's own tradition, history, and culture is precisely what positions the Buddhist temple within the centre of the landscape's compositional balance. The temple – and, by association, all it aesthetically, historically, and ethnically signifies – forms the content of Bawa's 'pre-colonial arcadia' (Pieris 2007a: 9) that his work sought to recuperate within the idiom of a Sri Lankan architectural modern. As I have shown by tracing Minnette de Silva's early architectural trajectory, this turn towards the particularity of a suppressed national tradition and history thought as Buddhist and Sinhala was a common narrative for a Sri Lankan tropical modernism that was trying to forge its own utopian signature. And the allure of Buddhism, though so often figured architecturally as artifice and ornament, was consequently deeply embedded within the early fashioning of a tropical modern disposition and aesthetic. For example, Bawa's hugely influential Danish architectural partner, Ulrik Plesner, stressed in an interview that it was his own 'conviction that Buddhism is the only religion that makes sense' (Plesner 1993: 19) that drew him to Sri Lanka in the first place. He stayed for fourteen years, helping Bawa to conceive and construct a large proportion of his early portfolio. For both Plesner and Bawa, it seems, there was something about Buddhism's rationality and reason that lent itself to their architectural modernity; that enabled them to mobilize its aesthetic terrain ornamentally through their work.

None of this is to suggest that Lunuganga is in any normative sense a religious landscape, nor that religion in any formal sense played a role in the fabrication of this spatiality. Rather, it is to suggest that when Bawa describes his favourite view over Cinnamon Hill, just we know he does not describe a religious landscape as such, neither should we suppose he describes an entirely secular space. Instead, he evokes, and inscribes, a structure of feeling, a narrative conjunction, in which the sacred cannot easily be separated from the modern. And, moreover, his purposeful recuperation and deployment of that structure of feeling under the sign of 'tradition' is precisely what helps to territorialize and naturalize that aesthetic realm *as* foundationally Sri Lankan.

In this sense, we should note that compositionally the Lunuganga estate itself not only blends outside with inside within its boundaries. It also works hard to extend out and into the imagined environment of the nation state. Lunuganga cleverly evokes three key elements of the utopian Sinhala village imagination that Sinhala nationalists were articulating though populist post-independence rhetoric: the *wewa* (lake/reservoir), *dagoba* (temple), and *kumbhara* (paddy fields). One journalist writing of Bawa recently remarked how:

> In the '70s, the distinguished architect Geoffrey Bawa threw a big garden party at his sprawling and celebrated home, Lunuganga. Taking his guests on a tour of his home and garden, he made an expensive gesture that

seemed to suggest the surrounding countryside was an extension of his own grand property. (Prins 2008: unpag.)

In another section of the illustrated book dedicated to Lunuganga in which Bawa formulated those landscape descriptions I have been (re)reading in this section, he himself stressed how 'Lunuganga from the start was to be an extension of the surroundings – *a garden within a garden*' (in Bawa, Bon, and Sansoni 1990: 11; my emphasis). It is precisely this formulation that speaks of the territorialization and naturalization of the Sinhala tradition and Buddhist aesthetics that this book stresses is a common component of Sri Lankan nature. If this is indeed a garden within a garden, then Bawa's hard work to make the temple central within his landscape composition, such that as he wrote, it 'now looks as if it had been there since the beginning of time', leaves us under no illusion that the idiom of the larger garden – the garden of the post-independent nation state, so to speak – is aesthetically Buddhist, and therefore in the Sri Lankan context ethnically striated as Sinhalese.

There is little room in this kind of territorialization of the architectural modern for any simultaneous naturalization of otherness: Tamil-Hindu, Muslim, or Christian. In fact, it is precisely this territorialization of the architectural modern that writes the Tamil-Hindu, Muslim, and Christian as other. It is also the temporal dimension, the anchoring of Buddhism to 'the beginning of time', that effectively inscribes Bawa's tropical modern built space this way. The point of grasping this is to force us into a slow, uncertain descent into the fabric of this space's ordinary dimensions, wherein the ordinary's political effects can be revealed. My aim in this kind of rereading then is to bring into representation the habitations of modernity at Lunuganga (and similarly tropical modern Sri Lankan built spaces) such that we can begin to discern a spatial politics implicated in their otherwise apparently benign modernism. As I show in the next chapter, this has implications for the ways that tropical modern spaces help shape subjectivities as well, but here I want to stress the political contours of the authorization of those spaces.

The Idiom of the Ordinary

I was first taken to Lunuganga by two architectural interns who agreed to let me shadow them whilst they completed some minor renovations across the estate. I return in more depth to the time I spent with them in the next chapter, but when we returned to Colombo they took me to the office of the metropolitan practice in which they both worked. The practice itself is medium sized, well established, and well known today for its devotion to distinctly tropical modern architecture. Both senior partners collaborated with Geoffrey Bawa from the 1980s onwards: a professional history that to many cements the practice's reputation as a trustworthy heir to Bawa's architectural heritage. The practice's office building itself is a characteristically earthen, minimalist, and extremely stylish tropical modern bungalow that blends outside space with the office and waiting areas. It was designed by one of the senior partners and built on a plot of land that connects through to a residential property designed by Bawa. Throughout, the office is sparsely yet thoughtfully furnished adding to the space's uncluttered and organic feel. Amongst the very few ornaments is a large stone Buddha's head, perhaps one and a half feet tall, that sits on a table in the computer-aided design (CAD) room gazing across computers and architects alike. As young architects come and go, electronically modelling, discussing, and re-modelling their designs, the statue is routinely ignored. It just sits there.

Like Bawa's practices, and like most contemporary tropical modern architectural practices in Sri Lanka, this particular practice is not a religiously aligned institution. In fact, as I have been stressing of the tropical modern style more generally, the practice's position within Sri Lankan architectural modernity rather depends on a certain distancing from the many institutionalized forms of Sinhala-Buddhist religious practice in the Sri Lankan context. This commercial space, preoccupied with the business of space itself, pretends to a secularity consistent with the transnational modernity of modern architecture and design. However, as I have also been stressing, to conceive of Buddhist aesthetics beyond a Eurocentric understanding of the word 'religion' requires taking the statue's very present-absence seriously. For the statue speaks a pervasive Buddhist textuality in southern and central Sri Lanka that is symptomatic of Buddhism's symbolic, aesthetic, and textual presence at every stage of modern life. The statue participates in precisely those sacred modern formations that it is the aim of this book to tease out; a distribution of the sensible that Pradeep Jeganathan stresses emerges from 'a tradition that has a sense of its own conditions of becoming, a tradition that is not a counterpoint to the modern but is part of the modern' (Jeganathan 2004: 195).

Iconographically, it is certainly true that the sculptural Buddha's head does not carry the same religious symbolism associated with the three predominant forms of seated Buddha in narrative Buddhist sculpture.[2] In fact, it is precisely the sculptural Buddha head's more decorative connotations that enable it to be used by a modern and secular practice as an ornament, even a relic. Crucial here is the statue's invisibility, its present-absence. It is its unseen taken-for-grantedness that cements its place in the choreography of the ordinary. For the ornamentalism of the statue idiomatically speaks a particularity, Buddhism, but it simultaneously claims a universal place for this particularity by virtue of its overlooked-ness. This is its powerful choreography of the ordinary, its

---

2 Those three predominant narrative sculptural forms of a seated Buddha being (1) *dhyāna mudrā*, the highest station of ecstasy through meditation, in which the hands are crossed in the lap, (2) *bhumisparsa mudrā*, in which the right hand is moved forward across the right knee, and (3) *dharmacakra mudrā*, with hands raised before the chest (Coomaraswamy 1964 [1916]: 330–32).

cosmopolitanism actually. In itself, the statue makes no political claims, but it shapes the parameters within which difference can be articulated.

Returning briefly then to Geoffrey Bawa's description of his view over Cinnamon Hill at Lunuganga, I want to suggest that it is this same grammar of ordinary thought that he articulates when he stresses that 'the long view to the south ended with the *temple*' (my emphasis). Though a couple of lines below, Bawa is more specific in his reference to the temple as a 'stupa', thus designating the ornamental structure *as* Buddhist, here he does not need to specify that he refers to a Buddhist 'temple' rather than Hindu. That much would be taken-for-granted by an implied readership well aware that in this tropical modern mobilization of the quintessentially Sri Lankan picturesque, this is a spatial idiom that writes 'temple' as Buddhist from the outset. The temple is woven into the fabric of this tropical modern space, metaphysically naturalized, so to speak, whereas the architect's non-Buddhist intervention must be announced as '*Chinese* jar'. In other words, this is a space whose purview is idiomatically – that is to say ordinarily – Buddhist and Sinhalese despite its architectural modernism. In this sense, not dissimilar to the checkpoints in Ruhuna National Park through the late 1990s, this is a space where Tamil, Muslim, or any other can only arrive as guest, marked as Tamil, as Muslim, named as other.

If these kinds of tropical modern spaces are plural then, that is to say ethnically hospitable (despite their more obvious striations of class and privilege), they are so in that conspicuously cosmopolitan tradition that like Jacques Derrida's impossible ethics of unconditional hospitality (Derrida and Dufourmantelle 2000) does violence by imposing translation on the guest. Indeed, as the introduction to this book has suggested, the trope of translation is important here for precisely the type of spatial rereading that this chapter has been moving towards. The work to locate the emergence of Sri Lanka's tropical modern built space within those transnational eddies spun between a worldly and modern architectural training on the one hand, and on the other a turning inward towards a recuperation of history and tradition thought as Buddhist and thus Sinhala, aims at critical readings sensitized to the idiom of another textuality: a textuality that as this book suggests is not immediately available to an unthinkingly Eurocentric gaze that insists first on the universality of the sacred/secular binary, and second, and as I push it further in the next chapter, the nature/culture – and subject/object – binaries as well. If Sri Lanka's tropical modern built space is a social text of sorts, then reading its politics requires developing a literacy able to tease out the idioms and scripts through which it is written.

As if to emphasize this methodo-philosophical point, in the very last line of the epilogue to his book on Lunuganga, Bawa defers to the reaction of a visiting lorry driver who once took the opportunity to walk around the garden. His words, it seems, were of great compliment to Bawa, who writes: 'when his bricks were being unloaded – [the lorry driver] said to me 'මේක නො හරි සීදේ'ව තැනක්'' [but this is a very blessed place]' (Bawa, Bon, and Sansoni

1990: 219). In this glossy coffee-table book, whose high production value is reflected in the thoughtful text, drawings, and high-quality black and white prints throughout, it is significant first that Bawa chooses to leave the final endorsement of his garden to a working-class Sinhalese delivery driver. It suggests something of his own perception that despite his work's classed exclusions the Sri Lankan public have taken his modernist and picturesque built space to its collective heart. For Bawa, this may have been something like an endorsement of the immersion in Sinhala folk culture that he and de Silva – after the '43 group – sought in their self-consciously 'post-colonial' recuperations of Sri Lankan tradition. Secondly, however, and perhaps moreover, it is significant that Bawa chooses to publish the compliment in the Sinhala script with which it was uttered by the driver. For Bawa, it seems the richness of the compliment itself inheres precisely in its linguistic and cultural idiom; its apparent untranslatability, so to speak. By retaining the Sinhala script, Bawa implies that the literal English translation cannot quite capture the essence of the compliment, therein perhaps the essence of the place, in quite the same way that the lorry driver's Sinhala expression does. And it is perhaps worth stressing here the significance of the English word blessed in the context of understandings of the Lord Buddha himself as the 'blessed one'. (Though it does not matter for my reading here that a more faithful literal translation would suggest the driver said either 'but this is a very beautiful/serene place' or 'but this is a place of much prosperity', where 'prosperity' is associated with the Sanskrit term 'Shriya Devi' meaning the goddess of prosperity.)

By stressing the idiomatic importance of this particular remark, once again I do not mean to suggest there is some authentic spatial essence that the lorry driver correctly puts his finger on. Rather, what interests me is the distribution of the sensible that Bawa himself takes to disclose the 'existence of something in common' (Rancière 2004: 12) between him and his lorry driver. Whether or not Bawa actually interprets the comment as the lorry driver intended is less important than stressing that it is Bawa's perception of a something in common that acts, in effect, as but one consecrated moment in the place's ongoing inscription as idiomatically Sinhala and Buddhist. This kind of fashioning of an aesthetic state, paraphrasing Rancière, is a pure instance of suspension, a moment when form is experienced for itself. It is the moment of the formation and education of a specific type of humanity (ibid.: 24).

In the next chapter, I explore in more depth the spatialized politics of the national instantiated through the materialities of this kind of tropical modern built space as it is conceived, experienced, and made to mean. But, for now, I want merely to stress that the production of the kinds of experiential registers and aesthetic terrains I proceed to explore have emerged from tropical modernism's attempt to recuperate and fashion a spatial idiom, or particularity, deemed by its influential authors as somehow quintessentially Sri Lankan.

Bawa, Grand Designs, and the National

Despite the idiomatic turns to a Sinhala tradition and Buddhist aesthetics in the likes of Bawa's and de Silva's work, there is also much flexibility in their architecture: a flexibility that others have rightly argued enables open and plural interpretations of, and identifications with, their work (see Perera 2005; Vale 1992). In this very sense, there is a certain danger of confusing tropical modern architecture with modes of conservative and militant Sinhala-Buddhist nationalism that have played a more conspicuous role in fanning the flames of ethnicized politics and civil war in Sri Lanka over the last half century. As I have been stressing, de Silva, Bawa, and other tropical modernists should not be thought of as militant Sinhala-Buddhist nationalists, but rather located within a pervasive and at times banal spatial politics of everyday life. In this sense the question of modernism's meaning, as well as the question of a politics of modernism, are always conditioned by the relationship between the market and cultural production. In other words, and as I explore in much more depth in Chapter 7, whether or not there is a sufficiently developed market for modernism dictates the extent to which a cultural field can retain autonomy over its own utopian aspirations and intent (Canclini 1995: 47).

However, in the interest and industry of (re)reading Geoffrey Bawa's work to which this chapter has committed, there is a significant additional component to the locatedness of his architecture, and that is the role of the state. From the late 1970s, Geoffrey Bawa's emergent position and growing international reputation as one of the most innovative modern Sri Lankan architects on the market did not go unnoticed by the Sri Lankan government. Early in 1979, Bawa was commissioned by the United National Party (UNP) President, J. R. Jayawardene, to design the new Parliament building in Kotte, a fifteenth-century Lankan capital, just outside the Colombo Municipal Council limits. Though practically motivated (the old colonial parliament building was far too small), President Jayawardene's choice to relocate the parliament from the colonial capital Colombo can itself be seen as an anti-colonial national manoeuvre. Jayawardene's tenure as prime minister and president was also marked by a performative self-styling in the fashion of pre-colonial, Sinhala and Kandyan royalty. For example, he was the first modern political leader in Sri Lanka to deliver speeches from the octagonal pavilion (pattirippuwa) of Kandy's Temple of the Tooth (Dalada Maligawa): a ceremonial political performance more associated with the historical Kandyan dynasty (Perera 2005: 247). Likewise, the construction and political conception of the new parliament building was itself a project not wholly unconnected to a conscious process of nation building during the early 1980s, where the government promulgated the image of a *dharmishta* society following, or recuperating, Sinhala-Buddhist principles (ibid.: 255).

Bawa's design for the parliament building has rather generously been described as 'ambivalent' as regards the expression of ethnicity through its symbolic architectural fashioning of the national (see ibid.). Characteristically, it employs diverse architectural and political references – for example, with its deployment of a symmetrical debating chamber based on a Westminster model and, as David Robson notes, an 'asymmetrical arrangement of pavilions that recalls Mogul lake palaces, South Indian temples, Chinese palaces' (Robson 2002: 148). It is easy to see how; this 'inauthentic and nonunified character of Bawa's representation is precisely its strength' (Perera 2005: 261). However, the design itself does exhibit some notable allusions to various Sinhala expressions of a retroactively imagined pre-colonial national symbolism. For example, the terracing of the parliamentary complex with its overarching double-pitched roof is a direct reference to Kandyan spatial configurations and building, just as the terracing of the broader landscape of the parliamentary island in the image of paddy fields makes a symbolic connection to Sri Lanka's two millennia of tank-building and hydraulic civilization that have also been written as Sinhala. Furthermore, Bawa himself remarked that the look of the complex is meant to reflect 'the visual formalities of the old Sinhalese buildings' (Bawa, quoted in Robson 2002: 148).

However, these iconographical readings are hardly the point. Whether or not Bawa himself wrote into the parliament complex any kind of iconographic references to Sinhala-Buddhist historiography, the more important point I want to stress in closing this chapter is simply that his choice to accept such a notable commission from the state has irrevocably located him within the terrain of 1980s' state-led Sinhala-Buddhist nation-building. Similarly, when the state became his patron, they accelerated a purification of meaning that has subsumed any autonomy that Bawa's work – and the tropical modern style more generally – might otherwise be able to claim. If, as Nihal Perera writes of the parliament commission, the '1980s was the first time a government in Sri Lanka employed architectural representation on a national scale' (Perera 2005: 258), it is also when the question of tropical modernism's meanings became political rather than just artistic.

Soon after the parliament commission, in 1980, Bawa was commissioned by the state to build the new Ruhunu University in Matara, on the south coast. Another grand design, this commission was another very visible endorsement by the state of the tropical modern style that in effect helped bring the style itself, and its best-known proponent, under the sign of the 'national'. And, in 1991, Bawa was hired by the country's largest hotel corporation and the most important spoke within the Sri Lankan tourist industry, Aitken Spence, to build the landmark 150-room Kandalama Hotel in the country's 'cultural triangle', not far from the site of the historic Sigiriya rock. This project enjoyed the backing and facilitation of the then President Premadasa owing to Aitken Spence's pre-eminent position and proximity to the government. The hotel remains one of Sri Lanka's most bespoke and unusual design statements to this day, and was recently featured in the travel supplement of the English broadsheet newspaper the *Observer* as one of their 'Magnificent Seven' of modern hotel design icons around the world.

These three grand designs all have one thing in common: they have all been hugely emblematic in the context of the 'post-colonial Sri Lankan national', through a period when the content of that 'national' has been increasingly historiographically and ethnically purified. Though Chapter 7 pays more attention to the complex networks and institutional assemblages that over-determine tropical modern architecture, there is a simple but important point to make that bears upon this chapter's efforts to locate and (re)read the built space. Bawa and tropical modernism more generally have developed a relationship to the 'national', via the state in part, that has had some considerable influence on the ways that its materialities are made to mean, as well as on what those meaningful materialities do politically in and through society.

CHAPTER 6

Architecting One-ness:
Fluid Spaces/Sacred Modernity

Reading the politics of nature from Sri Lanka's tropical modern architecture is not just a question of situating the effort and inscriptions of its authors. It also requires considerable work to tease out the built space's semiotic materialisms; that is, the combination of the building techniques that characterize the style, and, importantly, the common structural and narrative qualities of the environmental experiences those building techniques afford users. The task of this chapter then is to delineate the entwinedness of tropical modern style with dominant structures of feeling and being. By considering the work of architecture, and how architecture works, the chapter traces the relationships between 'doing, making, being, seeing and saying' (Rancière 2004: 45). In the context of Sri Lanka's ethnicized politics of difference, it excavates the social and political contours of tropical modern built space *as it* is physically and imaginatively inhabited.

In this respect, there are three movements to this chapter. First, I sketch a range of common building techniques and ideologies developed by tropical modern architects over the last half century. Second, drawing predominantly on interview material, I describe the environmental aesthetics that such techniques afford users of (predominantly domestic) tropical modern built space. And, finally, I tease out a dominant cultural logic of these aesthetic domains that, I argue, continues to instantiate an ethnicized spatial politics of everyday life.

Building Tropical Modern Space:
Techniques, Materials, and Tropicality

Though each of Sri Lanka's tropical modern architects has their own design signature, there are certain common techniques for building space that can be identified across tropical modernism's variety. It is perhaps fair to say that these technical commonalities are what draw together a range of disparate structures *as* something like tropical modern architectural 'style'. One defining ideological characteristic of tropical modernism emerges from that self-consciously 'post-colonial' effort to mark an appropriate rupture from colonial building techniques and this has been manifested in a challenge to open out the colonial house. Central within this ongoing ideological effort, however, has been a set of more material techniques and challenges that in different ways has driven modern architects to develop something like a tropical modern style of building. These are a concern for vernacularizing materials, as well as temporalizing objects, and due attention to climatic and physical tropicality, as well as the necessity to confront the environmental relationships between structure and site.

Opening out the Colonial House

As I have stressed in Chapter 5, architects Geoffrey Bawa's and Minnette de Silva's ruptures with colonial design and architecture were guided by an adaptive desire stylistically to enter architectural modernity on their own regional terms. This meant that their work was characterized by appropriative negotiation more than wholesale rejection of built colonial modernities. Early on, perhaps the central design problematic through which this was materially negotiated was the new urban house. Early Sri Lankan tropical modernists like de Silva and Bawa sought an opening out of the form that had come to characterize colonial bungalows, or what the architect Valentine Gunasekera once referred to as the 'PWD [Public Works Department] box' (quoted in Pieris 2007a: 48).

The problem of the colonial house for Sri Lanka's modernists was a combination of form and changing (sub)urban context. The bungalows that were built through the nineteenth and early twentieth centuries to house a growing number of British civil servants represented a model of country life in the colonies where house and garden were islands of civility and nostalgia. What Valentine Gunesekera stressed was a 'feared condition of the outdoors' (ibid.) resulted in structures with small windows and wood shutters that enabled the excision of the noxious outside from inside. Roofs and walls combined to enclose human life, keeping the nuclear (colonial or elite) family safe from the unruliness of what lay beyond the garden. As pressure on space increased through the early twentieth century, plot sizes decreased feeding an ever more unfavourable balance between house and garden size. Through the middle of the twentieth century, the suburbs of Colombo and Kandy grew even greater as an emergent university-educated Ceylonese middle class encroached on the cities' peripheries placing even more pressure on plot sizes.

There were various architectural responses to these dual problems of form and context from the late 1940s and 1950s onwards. For example, for Valentine Gunesekera the solution was the so-called American or Californian style sweeping Colombo's suburbs, whilst for Minnette de Silva it was a more obvious conversation between the international style and Kandyan architectural heritage. Common across these experimentations, however, was the desire physically to open out the colonial house, a desire fuelled by an apparent utopian freedom to imagine and fashion built space deemed more appropriate to this post-war and post-independent context by drawing upon a pastiche of elements of good design and materials. This kind of critical aesthetic reorientation towards the local and regional was an effort at fashioning a built environment more relevant to a 'post-colonial' value system (ibid.: 45). Though, as I have stressed in Chapter 5, despite its eclectic international influences and secularizing intent, this critical aesthetic reorientation was founded upon nostalgia for a pre-coloniality that was commonly understood as Sinhala.

The adaptation of the colonial house involved a number of quite simple steps to make domestic buildings more climatically and culturally suitable: clearing away bare-bulb lighting in favour of the cheaper circulation of natural light, for example; opening walls to maximize transparency and ventilation, thereby also solving the problem of mould growing on walls without drip ledges. The use of asbestos and cement as well facilitated a reduction in roof work and expenditure. For those who followed the American style this led to new gently sloped rooflines comprising continuous asbestos sheeting. For others who chose to preserve the large overhanging eaves of colonial bungalows, a common tactic was to uncouple the roof from what had been the colonial house's main structural features: walls. This was an innovation that led to a new and lasting kind of architectural orientation; as one architect put it, 'All you need is the roof, the rest is irrelevant' (conversation with Kaushik Bannerjea, 4 September 2006).

All of these techniques were aimed at opening out the house in the realization that the colonial bungalow, traditionally built within generous grounds with clear distinctions between protected inside space and outside gardens, was no longer suitable for a different style of middle-class metropolitan life in fast-growing post-independent Colombo or Kandy where space and privacy were at a premium. Geoffrey Bawa and Minnette de Silva in particular began to draw upon traditional design elements from Ceylon's past in order to open out the modern house, turning the colonial house inside out as it were to achieve new styles of urban living with high levels of openness, ventilation, durability, and transparency, yet also privacy.

The house Geoffrey Bawa completed for Osmund and Ena de Silva in 1962 in the heart of Colombo offers an excellent example of this effort, and for many commentators it marks the point at which Bawa's work began to exhibit a confident and successful negotiation of the traditional in order to push the Sri Lankan architectural modern. The house was designed around an internal courtyard that afforded a great deal of openness and transparency through the main living areas (for images, see ArchNet 'Osmund and Ena de Silva house [by Geoffrey Bawa]'). Though courtyards were commonly also found in Dutch and Moor housing in Ceylon from as far back as the seventeenth century, and though the courtyard house has in different contexts been identified with Hindu domestic spatiality (see Bryden 2004), in Sri Lanka's tropical modern architecture, the courtyard feature became narrativized as a reinterpretation of the *medu midula* – a main feature of Kandyan Sinhala domestic architecture. The main living room, which flowed into the *medu midula*, became less of a room and more a pavilion, recalling Kandyan dynastic architecture. The pitched, triple-tiled roof with large overhanging eaves that extend way beyond the wall lines created verandah spaces and loggias that extend geometrically through the length and breadth of the property, accentuating a sense of transparency and the through flow of air. All of these techniques were driven by an effort to break through the box of the urban house, connecting house with garden in seamless fashion to create a fluid, liveable space of comfortable proportion. The effect at the Osmund and Ena de Silva house, as David Robson writes, is that 'Space flows from inside to outside and long vistas range across a series of indoor and outdoor "rooms" to create the illusion of infinite space on a relatively small plot' (Robson 2002: 75).

Architecturally, tropical modern architecture works hard at this illusion of infinity, from the smallest of details. As, for example, in the porch extension at Lunuganga (Figure 5.3), which opens out to spectacular views on two sides and on another side backs onto a planted well (here, Bawa took care not to use glass to enclose the bottom frames of one dividing window so as to allow air to circulate around the upper back and neck area when seated, thus allowing the body to breathe) right through to more explicit attempts at manufacturing infinity. In tropical modern hospitality architecture, for example, the swimming pool of choice tends to be the 'infinity pool', which offers users views from within the pool that extend seamlessly to lake, reservoir, or sea beyond. Though infinity pools are not unique to this architecture, their frequent deployment by tropical modernists to manufacture infinity is noteworthy in this context.

But the illusion of infinite spatiality is, of course, just that: an illusion. At the Osmund and Ena de Silva's house, Geoffrey Bawa enclosed the plot with a perimeter wall that instantiated a desire for privacy in the growing metropolis. Contemporary tropical modern architecture is indeed still driven by this fundamental contradiction that speaks of the style's classed particularity despite its utopian aspirations. If one of the hallmarks of the architecture is a seamless connection of inside with outside, integral to the production of that aesthetic terrain – particularly within domestic architecture – is the plot's spatial delimitation from a real outside of working-class urban poverty. Though the increasing impermeability of the perimeter wall through the latter half of the twentieth century was to some extent inevitable in the context of increasing civil unrest and the Janatha Vimukthi Peramuna (JVP) threat in particular, both figuratively and physically the perimeter wall marks tropical modernism's classed exclusionisms despite its attempts at fashioning infinite space. Indeed, contemporary users of such domestic architecture are often explicit about their need for an aesthetic separation from an urban outside marked socio-economically, if not ethnically, as different. One resident in the Colombo outskirts who had commissioned a house from the architect Varuna de Silva stressed how 'the other side of the road is, I don't know what you call it, semi-urban slums, and we wanted that after we close the door, that we are inside and there is no connection with the outside'. Just a few minutes later in our conversation, he stressed that the house had a 'very open' relationship with nature: its greenery, small roof garden, and internal verandah (which accommodates a living tree) all provide a necessary aid to living in the urban jungle (Interview with Sanath, 14 September 2006). More important here than a rather obvious class identification architecturally instantiated, is due recognition that within contemporary tropical modernism the fluidity of living inside/out marks an implicit inseparability of nature/culture rather than any pretence of socio-economic inclusivity.

Despite these exclusions and illusions, the important point to emphasize is that this opening out has been anchored within that self-consciously 'post-colonial' ideological effort at recuperating a notion of tradition and the sacred that mapped onto the dominant Sinhala-Buddhist ethnos in post-independent Sri Lanka. For example, of her house for Mrs A. Amerasinghe in Colpetty in 1954, Minnette de Silva herself wrote the following explanatory notes that leave us in doubt about the idiomatic Sinhala-ness of the structural traditions she draws upon:

> House walls are pierced with openings influenced by traditional econom-ically designed air vents. There are few solid walls; the main structure is carried by reinforced concrete pillars with R.C. flat slab floors. The enclosing walls of louvered or sliding doors and windows or wood or wrought iron trellises direct every available air draught into the house. The roof space is utilized as an attic study. Note niches for pahana.

> Notes: the garden, courts and house flow into each other ...

> ('Pahanas' are oil lamps which are traditionally used for celebrations and temple lights in Sri Lanka.)

> During the 'Pirith Ceremony' (the blessing of the house by monks) the priest made us all laugh as his sermon consisted of consolation for the Amerasinghes as their house didn't appear to be finished, of course it was – he just didn't think there was enough decoration or walls to hold the thing up! (de Silva 1998: 233)

De Silva's anecdotal last paragraph is telling. First, participating in that same idiomatic ordinariness that Bawa used to describe his view at Lunuganga (Chapter 5), there is no doubt left between author and readers that both 'temple' and 'monks' were in fact Buddhist. The textual field surrounding the house is thus positioned in a particular kind of way. But, second, there is a telling temporal contrapuntality in her anecdote. Her amusement at the monk's inability to grasp that this opened-out house was in fact structurally complete, speaks an uneasy counterposition between what she believed to be formal religion on the one hand, and on the other, architectural sacred modernity. At the same time, the house itself requires blessing by a monk and the design integrates niches for ornamentalized emblems of Buddhist worship (as well as a shrine room not mentioned above). In these ways, the sacred moves seamlessly into the space of the modern, instantiating a sacredness that is no counterpoint to modernity but instead woven into its contours.

Vernacular Materialities and Historical Materials

This new appropriate mode of architectural praxis was also born from the proto-national social and economic context. From 1956 to 1976, Sri Lanka had a succession of socialist-nationalist governments, and in 1955, Ceylon was a founding member of the global non-aligned movement. Indeed, it was in a speech in Colombo in 1954, that Nehru first coined the phrase 'non-alignment'. The economics of non-alignment had a lasting impact on tropical modernism. In short, the likes of Bawa, de Silva, Gunasekera, and other architectural modernists since them built through times of severe material shortage and import restriction. Glass and steel, for example, were expensive and very difficult to get hold of, as were the modern conveniences sweeping European architectural modernism and interior design.

For the Osmund and Ena de Silva house, Geoffrey Bawa was heavily reliant upon locally produced materials and locally trained craftspeople, something that has remained stylistically integral to the look and feel of Sri Lankan tropical modern built space today. The de Silva house assumed a vernacular palette through the use of features like the prominent roof triple-clad with local tiles, the unpolished stone floor, and the presence of local millstones and water urns in the *medu midula*. It was this considered improvisation and adaptation within a particular South Asian socio-economic proto-national context that became integral to the development and evolution of a style synonymous with that self-consciously 'post-colonial' Sri Lankan national. As one of Bawa's former architectural partners put it:

> it became Sri Lankan because of the materials used, because back then in the 1960s of course we couldn't import materials. We had to be self-reliant and that political context that we had to go through made sure we had to deal with things our own way. (Interview with Channa Daswatte, 16 February 2005)

Importantly, though, this context also hastened the practical necessity of opening out the new urban house. The de Silvas were adamant that they could not afford imported air-conditioning systems, so economic necessity played a major role in Bawa's efforts to design a structure that was well ventilated and naturally cool.

The presence of vernacular materials within tropical modern built space does more, though. Certain kinds of vernacularizing objects also inscribe particular temporalities and memories within space (see DeSilvey 2007; Ramsay 2009). If tropical modernism is an iteration of *Sri Lankan* modernity, then vernacularizing ornamental or structural materials that so often go into the making or composition of the built space perform an important kind of historical and geographical rooting. The sheer range and referentiality of vernacularizing objects to be found across tropical modern structures is vast and thus not necessarily confined to a history of Sinhala arts and crafts; objects come from an array of different sources. Osmund and Ena de Silva's locally sourced mill-stones are one example of vernacularizing materials, though the trend of material reuse as a kind of aesthetic and diachronic rooting is far more widespread. For example, I met one couple who had reused the heavy teakwood doors from Colombo's Empire theatre built in the 1920s, and one of Bawa's former architectural partners had chosen to frame his own house around the original wood shutters used by Bawa in one of his earliest hotel projects, the Bentota Beach Hotel. If these objects have a varied tapestry of historical, social, and ethnic biographies, they all have in common one thing: an origin *in* the island.[1]

Choices regarding material reuse are significant. In an important sense it is the biographies of these 'second hand things' (Appadurai 1988; Gregson and Crewe 2003) placed in houses that animate the built spatial structures of which they are fashioned to be a part. The presence of vernacular materials and ornamental objects vertically roots tropical modern built space itself within the discrete space of nation state, in whatever sense that 'national' comes to be articulated. It enables Sri Lankan architectural modernity to be spoken as a modernity that is sensitively and spatially rooted historically. Aesthetically, it is precisely these kind of vernacular objects and their historicizing materialities that enable modern architectural effort to so often be spoken of as in some sense 'timeless'. Vernacular materials comprise yet another dimension of the extension of inside space outward, the bringing of the outside in, only temporally rather than spatially so.

Tropicality, Structure, and Site: An Environmental Architecture

Despite recent work that has effectively shown tropicality to be a way of seeing (see Lefaivre and Tzonis 2001; Driver and Martins 2005; Driver and Yeoh 2000), the biophysical materiality of continuous growth and extreme climatic events within the monsoonal zones of tropical South Asia present considerable architectural challenges. If the international style was mostly forged in climatically temperate regions, translations and adaptations in Sri Lanka had to cope with the lively super-fertile materiality of a tropical nature that positively crashes into and engulfs buildings.

Bawa's first architectural partner, Ulrik Plesner, had grown up with Scandinavian modernism in the early 1950s, so his own style upon arrival

---

1 Notwithstanding the geographical relationality of colonial and other materialities.

Figure 6.1 Weathered interior walls in the office of MICD (Murad Ismail and Channa Daswatte) architect's office, Colombo, by Murad Ismail and Channa Daswatte (author's photograph).

in Sri Lanka valued the clean lines of abstract functionalism. However, after a few early experiments (for example, the Wijewardene house, Colombo, 1959–64, and Bishop's College, Colombo), Bawa and Plesner soon became aware that the clean white and sharp-edged prismatic forms of international modernism were not at all suited to Sri Lanka's environmental extremes of humidity, monsoon, and aridity. Their early work was therefore driven by a process of adaptation to Sri Lanka's regional environmental and climatic particularities. They realized that instead of trying to achieve untrammelled, sharp, and sanitary colours and lines, the architect working in a hot and humid climate should accept the inevitability of decay and exploit the patinas that building with tropical nature resulted in. The organic textures of decay have since become part of tropical architectural modernity, such that a building's own aging process within its environmental context is worn on the outside, so to speak. Architects consciously choose materials and colours that can bear the environmental stress and evidence of weathering, and so enable outside to meld with inside; another way of turning the house or structure inside out. Figure 6.1, for example, shows the effects of this kind of aesthetics of tropical decay as it appears on a wall in the office of one contemporary tropical modern architectural practice, MICD (Murad Ismail and Channa Daswatte).

But experimentations in building with tropicality also fed the kind of structural innovations that have seen a stripping away of form characteristic of tropical modern architectural innovation. For example, when Plesner and

Figure 6.2 The Kandalama Hotel, by Geoffrey Bawa, 1991
(Source: Riza Jazeel).

Bawa were commissioned to build a new bungalow on an arid and rocky coconut estate at Polontalawa in 1963, an appropriately innovative solution for them was to pare the main structure back to a simple, gently pitched tile roof spanning two vast boulders. A development of that theme of trying to break through the box, this open pavilion was perhaps Bawa's boldest expression of the structural, roof-centric, simplicity *appropriate* to this geographically difficult tropical environmental context.

When Bawa was commissioned to build the Institute of Integral Education at Piliyandala near Colombo in 1978, he tackled the inevitable problem of keeping the large lecture theatre cool all year round by simply opening it on three sides, setting the rows of seats in from the perimeter of the theatre and using detachable rattan screens to protect against the seasonal monsoons. And this type of practical architectural consideration of tropical materiality and geographical context is perhaps nowhere more apparent than at Bawa's vast Kandalama Hotel, whose flat roofs and stark concrete frame appear to be carved into the rock face (Figure 6.2). In fact, not dissimilar to the use of the boulders at Polontalawa, it is the contours of the rock face itself that guide the unobtrusive structure's flow. The training of surrounding superabundant vegetation has also allowed the hotel visually to merge with the jungle such that envelope and site seem to become one, the structure itself evolving with site.

In tropical modern architectural praxis then, it is common for buildings to be designed to quickly and inconspicuously to settle into their surroundings.

Tropical modernists attempt to build with the natural environment, not to keep it out or tame it somehow. They build such that in five or ten years' time the inevitable onslaught of engulfing palms and wild grass, and the extremes of heat, rain, and aridity do not pose a problem to a building designed to become properly woven into its environmental context. However, despite the organic and fluid appearances of their end results, their labour in this capacity can also be regarded as a concerted attempt at carefully controlling, regulating, and planning a built space's relationship to place. In her exploration of Brazilian artistic tropical modernism, Nancy Leys Stepan suggests how similar artistic managements of tropical nature in mid-twentieth-century Brazil were aimed precisely at fashioning an appropriately Brazilian disposition to the natural world against a history of European tropical vision (Stepan 2001: 230). Similarly, if Sri Lanka's architectural tropical modernists work at creating the illusion that there is little between nature and social space, they do so to express something of an appropriately Sri Lanka human disposition to the natural world.

The net effect of building with tropicality like this is the production of structures that apparently exist in effortless harmony with site; timeless built space that for all intents and purposes emerges from the over-abundant surrounding tropical context. As one architect put it:

> They're commonplace buildings built from commonplace materials ... they become buildings that when you look at those buildings in the landscape they look like they've always been part of that landscape – commonplace. (Interview with Channa Daswatte, 16 February 2005)

The commonplace-ness of the buildings aims here at a similar idiomatic ordinariness that pervades Bawa's description of Lunuganga (Chapter 5). But the architect's use of the word 'landscape' is also revealing because he uses it to describe a landscape into which his work is woven, naturalized, thus ascribing to the architecture itself a painterly landscape quality, as if it too is painted into the canvas of space. The built space becomes the ordinary component of landscapes that cannot easily be divided into human and non-human parts. This architect was also eager to stress that one of the fundamental precepts of the tropical modern architecture Geoffrey Bawa helped forge is its ability to collapse any distance between subject and surrounding environment: 'Because he [Bawa] firmly believed that buildings were not meant to be seen, but they were meant to be background to people's lives ... So if you're in the building you hardly notice they're around' (Interview with Channa Daswatte, 16 February 2005).

Accordingly, one of the guiding principles of Sri Lanka's tropical modern architectural praxis is the attention to building spatial experience rather than visually prominent and symbolic structures. As I show in the next section, tropical modern architecture is foremost about building experiences through space and environment; the fluid connections between inside and outside become integral to this process. The various techniques and material concerns that I have explored in this section – combinations of overhanging eaves, *medu midulas*, open-walled structures, extended through-vistas, vernacular materialities, and temporalizing objects – have all evolved to become more than an ongoing 'post-colonial' ideological effort. They have become central to the attempt to build certain types of spatial experience. As the architect quoted above put it:

> the envelope [structure] is not as important as the space you build in. So when you say Geoffrey's contribution, that is … that your concern with the envelope should not be as much as your concern with the places you live in, what you walk through, what you inhabit.

A legacy that this architect stressed clearly pervades his own work:

> a lot of this philosophy comes out in [our] smaller work. Most of our houses look like nothing on earth, it's just a roof and columns, but what it is, it is about moving through the walls, moving past the columns, about the columns, and then engaging the outside, engaging the left space next to the columns and so on. So this is part of the way we work. (Interview with Channa Daswatte, 16 February 2005)

Living Inside/Out, or Producing the Sri Lankan Environment

> From the moment you arrive at the Kandalama hotel after a lurching drive through the jungle of central Sri Lanka, you know you are in an extraordinary place. The entrance is the mouth to a huge cavern set into the mountainside.
>
> The huge building is spread along the side of the rockface and covered by rich vegetation that continues to serve as the home for an astonishing variety of wildlife. The hotel was built in the early 1990s by the late Geoffrey Bawa, one of Asia's foremost architects. His effort to blend the massive hotel into its environment, to use the contours, materials and vegetation of the stunning surroundings, succeeds triumphantly.
>
> The passages linking the 160 plus rooms to the cavernous communal areas are open to the jungle, and at night guests share the space with bats, lizards, mongooses, huge moths, and fireflies. (*Observer* 2006)

This description of the Kandalama hotel (Figure 6.2), published in an English broadsheet newspaper, perhaps says more about European tropical vision than it does about the politics of experience in Sri Lankan tropical modern space. However, I begin this section with it because, first, simply it offers a helpful glimpse of the qualitative encounters with the non-human world that tropical modernism affords. Second, the journalist's assertion that Kandalama is an 'extraordinary place' sits in obvious tension with claims regarding the style's ordinariness. That shock of the 'extraordinary' here may just be one of scale: how can simplicity on such a vast scale not be extraordinary? But, heuristically, I want to suggest that for the tourist it also denotes difference; the 'extraordinariness' of the different ways-of-being that this built space affords. And third, published in the UK to a British readership, there is a sense here that the hotel is somehow allegorical: it stands in emblematic relation to the Sri Lankan national.

If tropical modern architects aim at building experience, then how can we understand the experiences they create? And what does such an understanding reveal about an ongoing spatial politics of tropical modernity? It is to the experiential domains of tropical modern built space that I turn in the rest of this chapter. Particularly, what I draw out in this section are the different characteristics of a kind of habitation that I refer to here as living inside/out.

Fluid Habitations

Fluid forms of habitation are the common and unsurprising effect of an architectural labour that foregrounds spatial experience over form, site over structure. Fluidity as an analogy for experience in and through tropical modern built space denotes a common aesthetic terrain wherein people feel their bodies are able to flow through built space, into and out of spaces loosely choreographed as one by the just as loose arrangement of formal structural components like walls, windows, and doors. If, as David Robson remarked of Bawa's Osmund and Ena de Silva house, 'Space flows from inside to outside and long vistas range across a series of indoor and outdoor "rooms" to create the illusion of infinite space' (Robson 2002), then fluidity is the aesthetic register through which that illusion convinces.

One resident who together with her family had commissioned the practice PWA (Phillip Weeraratne Architects) to design their modest suburban house in Colombo, stressed how fluidity was an aesthetic requirement in their negotiations with the architects. Having parted company with one architect at the design stage who had offered them a structure 'with far too many walls and far too many everything', she stressed how a central requirement that they put to PWA, the new architects, was that the house 'has to be open, and we don't need it to be ... there have to be fewer walls, there has to be a space that's more fluid' (Interview with Sharmini, 6 September 2006). Sharmini further emphasized how 'light was a pre-requisite in this house certainly, lots of natural light. And lots of air blowing through, you know; no air con. I mean we only have air conditioners in the bedrooms and we only use them some of the time'. When pushed on the connection between ventilation and her own expression, 'a space that's more fluid', she was more reflective:

> I hadn't thought about it but I guess it has to be, right? The air is fluid, the design is fluid, when you walk: physically you're fluid within it, right? Stepping in and out ... [points to a large opening in an upstairs wall that leads directly to a roof terrace] you know, because that could be a door or

a window, because the design ... I mean, what is it, you know? (Interview with Sharmini, 6 September 2006)

The difficulty Sharmini faces in attributing function to formal parts of her house hints at a re-categorization of normative structural properties that tropical modern built space achieves. (After all, spatially what formal purpose does a rendered wall with a five-foot hole in it serve?) There is also a tension between her effortless description of the conceptual blueprint for a house comprised of 'space that's more fluid' and her admission of not having thought much about the architectural production of fluidity. Rather than any negation of fluidity as such, this tension itself hints at a kind of a priori aesthetics, a spatial locution, that though rarely articulated is understood by and through a body intimately familiar with the coordinates of *fluid space*; what Rancière (2007: 13) calls a 'silent speech' whose marks are directly imprinted on a body by its history, 'more truthful than any discourse proffered by a mouth'. Sharmini knows what she means when she speaks of 'a space that's more fluid', even if she has not previously thought about it. Here, a particular distribution of the sensible breaks down not just perceptions of a normative house with clearly demarcated rooms and divisions between inside and outside, but also the structures of language available to describe *this* house, and *this* aesthetics, *this* difference. There are traces of the same structures of (silent) speech in David Robson's description of the illusion of infinite spatiality at the de Silva's house: the 'series of indoor and outdoor *rooms*' (Robson 2002; my emphasis) he describes must be qualified by scare quotes because the formal category 'room' is eroded, translated, taken elsewhere, by the architectural grammar of tropical modernity.

Experientially then, fluid habitations point to the architectural success of techniques of opening up the house. As the architect Channa Daswatte put it, 'it's all about that somehow there is no difference between what's out there from yourself, you are part of that and that as is much part of you' (Interview with Channa Daswatte, 16 February 2005). As I show below, the dominant cultural logic of this fluidity often hints at an ethnicization of space that brings tropical modern architecture into the domain of politics, but for now I merely want to emphasize the ordinariness of fluid spatial experience in and through tropical modern built space. Indeed, for his own home, Channa Daswatte had built the main house as a bridge, the main span of which provides overhead shelter to a dining 'room' open on two sides. The main living room that sits above the dining area and comprises the main span of the bridge can also be fully opened with the wooden shutters he salvaged from the Bentota Beach Hotel refit. Both rooms, he stressed, are designed such that the gentle southwest monsoonal breeze flows seamlessly through the plot and property, filling the space with a fluid form of ventilation, bringing the outside in, and offering precisely that environmental impression that 'you are part of that and that is much part of you'.

Bringing the outside in invariably shapes a particular kind of relationship between users of tropical modern built space and the environment beyond their 'walls'. This could be seen as the inevitability of having 'nature' inside; however, the problem with the formulation '"nature" inside' is that linguistically and ontologically it much too readily presupposes, first, a nature distinguishable from culture in a classically Cartesian tradition (see Berleant 1992), and second, an inside formally, spatially, demarcated from an outside by solid walls, doors, windows, or other such structures. The fluid spatiality of tropical modern architecture produces instead that kind of irreducible proximity with, and through, environment. Aesthetically, inside and outside fold into one.

Ravi and Ashley had designed a four-storey house (Ashley is an architect) in Colombo's wealthy Cinnamon Gardens that they stressed they wanted to be able to open out so that they could have a relationship with the environment. In describing his house to me, Ravi stressed how, within their small plot in an overcrowded suburb, they had chosen to build next to a large tree. At each level the vertical ascension of the house can be opened directly to the tree giving them, he stressed, an engagement with the tree and its bird and animal life, from trunk through to canopy (Interview with Ravi, 16 September 2006). In her house in Rajagiriya, another suburb of Colombo, Dharshenie told me how there is a time between 6.30 and 8.30 each weekday morning after her husband goes to work and the maids are pottering about when the house is open to sunlight, breeze, and the birds that begin to inhabit and sing on the roof terrace. This, for her, was a very special time when the house allows her to be her 'most free' (Interview with Dharshenie, 3 September 2006).

Many residents and users of tropical modern architecture spoke at length about the environmental relations their houses afforded them. Shiranika and Pradeep, who had commissioned PWA to build their two-storey suburban house, stressed that their main requirement was that they had to have a house 'with nature' (Interview with Shiranika and Pradeep, 8 September 2006). Emphasizing a desire for their home to fold outside and inside, they stressed that they asked the architects to build around existent trees on the plot so as not unnecessarily to remove flora that could otherwise be incorporated into the structure. Pradeep explained that this was because they were 'absolute nature lovers', and from the outset they were adamant that the house had to have 'that jungle feel' (ibid.). As our conversation progressed they also stressed that living in the house makes them feel pleasantly distant from the city, Pradeep again adding that here they feel 'nearer to the jungle' (ibid.). As if physically to emphasize the presence of the jungle in their home, Shiranika and Pradeep had chosen to hang wildlife photographs that they had taken on excursions to Ruhuna National Park. Narratively and materially, therefore, their house contained quite palpable aesthetic connections to Ruhuna National Park's own aesthetic domains. These connections with wildlife and environment, however, also played out in their everyday relationships with the animals that frequent the property: notably birds and wild squirrels which Shiranika feeds and which she now 'knows by name', as well as a porcupine who is a welcome and regular guest. Mindful of security and nuisance though, they remarked that their pet dogs both guarded and chased unwanted pests away.

Living with Animals: Guests and Pests

Living with animals like this is of course an inevitable part of the habitation of tropical modern architecture. Accordingly, most of the people I spoke with talked about the relationships with animals that their houses afforded them; some at length. Commonly, there were two sides to this relationship. The first – like Shiranika's relationship with the wild squirrels in her garden – being the delights of such proximity to the natural world, and the second being the inevitable problems that undomesticated animal and insect life causes in domestic space. Shiranika and Pradeep's enjoyment of the more charismatic animals that visit their house was balanced by the problems caused by considerably more unwelcome non-human guests that inside/out living invites. For example, they emphasized that the pond in their *medu midula*, which adjoins their dining room, is only ever full of water when they have guests, otherwise the water gets stagnant and attracts mosquitos. They have had monkeys that they chase from the property for fear that they might be rabid, and sometimes birds get into the living areas and need to be chased away by their dogs. All in all, they stressed, maintenance can be a problem in their house.

Indira still lives in the suburban house in Colombo that she had commissioned from Minnette de Silva in 1958; a commission that Minnette de Silva considered unusual at the time, first, because the family were practising Roman Catholics, and secondly, because the family were indifferent to security, enabling the architect, to open out completely the lower level (de Silva 1998: 302). Indira and her daughter continue to enjoy the animal life that Minnette de Silva's structural opening out has enabled, stressing an array of wildlife that over the years has incorporated the lower level of their house into their meanderings: toads, chameleons, geckos, tortoise, mongoose, snakes which use holes in the abrasive stone walls to shed their skins, and an abundance of birdlife, including a peacock whom they named Polly (that they regretted was eventually killed by the mongoose). Aware that this abundance of animal life is because of the opened-out design where, particularly on the lower level, 'house' and 'garden' are difficult to separate, they quipped that their dog had become the worst guard dog in the world, unable to distinguish outside from inside! But they also emphasized that they have to deal with flies, rats, and poll cats, and are hampered by constantly having to clear food and dirt away from surfaces for fear of ant infestations (Interview with Indira and daughter, 15 September 2006). As with all those I spoke with, though, the de Silvas

135

seemed to have no regrets about these kinds of trade-offs. They were more or less the inevitability of a tropical modern lifestyle.

Krishanti and Gitu live in a suburban courtyard house designed and built less than a decade ago by Channa Daswatte of MICD. Their house backs onto a marsh, and on this very small plot two of the house's four enclosing walls extend to the plot's perimeter leaving a very small garden area at the back. There is also an internal courtyard area which opens the centre of the house to the sky, so from the inside the house appears sizeable, open, and inside/out. Emphasizing both fluidity and a thirst for the Sri Lankan 'jungle', Krishanti stressed how they had instructed MICD to build something 'open, with an element of space … we wanted our house to be open and have that element of freedom', adding that 'whenever we have holidays we go to the jungle, so he [the architect] would have had that in mind as well' (Interview with Krishanti and Gitu, 12 September 2006). When asked how they felt about that relationship with the environment that the house has, their responses were laced with precisely the kind of tense acceptance where the delight of sharing space with wild animals can so easily become a problem:

> **TJ**: So now, what sort of relationship do you think the house has with nature?
>
> **Krishanti**: Too close for comfort [laughs]. There are too many bloody geckos! No it's really nice actually, the way it kind of blends into the garden, except it's spoilt a bit by having the security bars … [because the house backs onto a marsh, the windows have security bars that can be opened out].
>
> …
>
> **TJ**: Are there other animals coming in here?
>
> **Krishanti**: The garden is, like, full of birds in the morning and evening, it's really lovely; mainly because of the marsh. And then you get, actually, an owl. He hasn't come for a while. He perches on the fence and tries to hunt. And then you get a mongoose.
>
> **Gitu**: We have a lot of those little raptors.
>
> (Interview with Krishanti and Gitu, 12 September 2006)

What I want to stress through these extracts and examples is merely the tacit acceptance – the ordinariness – of a close relationship with the non-human world in and through tropical modern domestic built space. Dealing with non-human life in and through the home seems to pose equal measures of delight and inconvenience that together have become a part of the ordinary routines of tropical modern living, woven into the materialities and meanings of such space. And, indeed, tropical modern architects themselves will attempt to build with and around animal life, even going so far as to place the non-human other as architectural critic of sorts. Channa

Daswatte stressed how he consciously tries to create spaces through which animals can move without stopping (Interview with Channa Daswatte, 4 September 2006). For him, the building must become a series of passages through which life, both human and non-human, can move, though in the same breath he stressed that rats can be a problem! In this respect, I also recall a conversation (pre-dating this particular research) with a Sri Lankan architect about a house she had designed, on the first floor of which she had built a corner room enclosed by wooden shutters on two sides. When both sets of shutters were open, this corner of the house was completely open to the garden. She told me that the biggest architectural compliment she had ever received was from the parrots in the garden who feel free to fly through this space in order to get to the other side of the garden.

Charismatic Space

Because of inside/out living, users of tropical modern space often animate their built space with a particular kind of agency. Indeed, it is common for tropical modern space to be narrated as charismatic and emotionally moving in ways that suggest the space's material potential to enchant (see Bennett 2001). Though there is often a secular logic at work in these kinds of animations, and though of course it is not at all uncommon for any kind of architecture to be invested with degrees of agency, what I stress here are the aesthetic resonances between this kind of everyday enchantment and the idiomatic ordinariness of tropical modern space that I evoked in the last chapter. In other words, there is nothing exceptional about narrating tropical modern built space as charismatic in ways that place it in close proximity to the idiomatic 'blessedness' with which, for example, Geoffrey Bawa narrativized and thus enchanted Lunuganga. For example, Krishanti and Gitu were both keen to emphasize the degrees of relaxation that their house afforded them on a regular basis, stressing that when they come home after work they feel as though their tensions dissipate. But in stressing this they invest the house itself with a degree of charisma and agency:

Krishanti: You just come in and you feel it's all so … so calm …

Gitu: And also when we entertain … I mean it's quite a talking point, you know, when people sort of come in here and they sort of look at this, my God, this huge open space …

Krishanti: But I think the house likes entertaining, it likes having people, it comes alive, you know … I don't know, it's really difficult to explain.

(Interview with Krishanti and Gitu, 12 September 2006)

The house's personality also reveals itself through certain effects that the building facilitates, like, for example, their description of observing storms from the house:

Krishanti: And it's amazing when it rains, actually. When you have thunder-storms you feel as if the whole storm is, like, contained within. It's majestic, actually, when you watch from upstairs, and you can see the storm sweeping across the marsh, yes. And the way he has designed it is sort of cool, where the garden is at the back so that you get the whole effect a lot more … So all the sounds are magnified as well, the rain and water falling. All of those things are very much part of the whole. Sometimes scary, though, no?

Gitu: That's right, because the whole place is open and we have these huge [unglazed] windows. So if there's lightning or anything you see huge streaks of lightening … I mean it's really nice.

The degree of fear attached to the majesty of storms they experience from the house hints at a certain kind of relationship to and dialogue with their built space. As if Krishanti and Gitu live *with* their house, not simply in a material shell, but *with* an object that has its own charisma and animate potential. Sharmini also acknowledged a similar kind of relationship to her family's house:

Sharmini: … it's a noisy house … , there are noises at night. [I]t's a schizophrenic house … , and I think because, its schizophrenic because downstairs is like a whole different house to upstairs, they almost don't have a relationship other than being on top of each other … And I think it's also schizophrenic in the sense that you can be downstairs and alone and quite happy and it works really well during the night … Upstairs, I'd never sit here at night alone.

TJ: Why not?

Sharmini: It just doesn't have the right energy …

(Interview with Sharmini, 6 September 2006)

Though Sharmini articulates a not uncommon fear of certain domestic space-times, the logic of her expression implicates and animates the house itself, its energies and agency, its personality.

In closing this section, it is important to stress that for users of this built space the different experiential elements of living inside/out afforded by the architecture all bear a relation – albeit sometimes tense – to the sign of the Sri Lankan national. Sometimes this is equivocal and irreducible, like, for example, Indira's daughter's emphatic and proud assertion that for her 'Absolutely everything' about their house was Sri Lankan. At which point, however, her mother Indira remarked that Minnette de Silva was the only architect at that time in the late 1950s who would gladly design something so open plan for her (Interview with Indira and daughter, 15 September 2006). For others, however, the relationship between their houses and the national was less equivocal, which is unsurprising given that much contemporary tropical modern domestic architecture does not carry half as much allegorical weight and heritage value as does anything designed by the likes of an architect as iconic as Minnette de Silva. Nor, indeed, should we need to be reminded, does domestic architecture more generally carry the weight of national symbolism like grand public designs as do Bawa's Kandalama Hotel or Parliament building, for example. So, many users of domestic tropical modern built space seemed more aware of their own participation in a kind of art for art's sake, specifically a kind Universalist vanguardism typical of architectural modernism more generally. However, when pushed on this disposition to their houses most also revealed both pride and awareness that they were participating in a uniquely Sri Lankan articulation of modernism, not unlike Indira's recognition that her house is experimental, but *as* a modern Sri Lanka house.

The point to emphasize in closing this section is that tropical modern living in the Sri Lankan context has become ideologically, stylistically, and aesthetically 'national'. Just as the *Observer* describes ways of being that Bawa's Kandalama Hotel affords its visitors (the epithet to this section), living inside/out has come to be seen as 'very Sri Lankan'. As the architect Channa Daswatte put it: 'I think at the level of residential architecture, certainly a lot of what we have done has percolated and become part of the national psyche, of the approach to architecture' (Interview with Channa Daswatte, 16 September 2005). It is to the particular cultural logic of these aesthetics that have worked their way into the 'national psyche' that I turn in the last movement of this chapter.

The Politics of Oneness: The Cultural Logic of Inside/Out Living

In Chapter 5, I suggested how tropical modern architects themselves have located their buildings, techniques, and architectural experimentations within an avowedly 'post-colonial' vernacular cognate with the modernization of Sinhala-Buddhist arts and crafts. It follows then that the spatial experiences they build, those I have described in the previous section, can also be located within that narrative. However, experiences of tropical modern built space in the present must also be seen as in some senses greater than the formal qualities of architecture itself (see Larkin 2009). I say this to stress the simple fact that inside/out living, and fluid spatial experience, are common across many formally religious and aesthetic traditions: Hinduism, Sufism, and Christianity amongst them (for example, see Bryden 2004). It can also be consistent with entirely 'secular' aesthetic modalities of habitation: Californian mid-century modernism, for example. In other words, there is nothing inherently sacred, nor political, about living inside/out.

However, here I turn to non-secular narrativizations of inside/out living in a particular kind of way that more clearly reveal the built space's implication in the production of a dominant aesthetic field in everyday life, and therefore, I argue, in the production of a pervasive spatial politics of everyday life. If it is building techniques and ideologies that are primarily responsible for producing the kinds of experiences set out above, unpicking the dominant and residual cultural logic of those kinds of habitations is what reveals its often distinct, if subtle, spatial politics. What I suggest in this final section, then, is that inside/out habitation of tropical modern space often leads to powerful affective and narrative moments wherein an otherwise secular canvas of built space and environmental context is (re)inscribed as meaningful and agential social text. As I show here, these moments territorialize Sinhala-Buddhism within the dominant aesthetic practices set out above. If Henri Lefebvre sought to define 'the social text' as 'how *we* perceive the semantic field in everyday life, in a non-conceptual or pre-conceptual (affective or perceptive) manner' (Lefebvre 2002: 306; my emphasis; also see Edwards 2009: 232), then my point here is that built space participates in the aesthetic fabrication of that exclusive *we* in the Sri Lankan context.

When I accompanied two interns from the architectural practice MICD to Geoffrey Bawa's estate Lunuganga, we stayed in the pavilion house on Cinnamon Hill. Bawa's last substantial addition to the estate, the bungalow was built in 1992 and is a mature expression of the chapter of tropical modernism that Bawa helped forge in Sri Lanka. It is a simple structure comprising four roofed pavilions, three of which are bedrooms whose exterior walls contain rows of door and ceiling-height, weather-beaten window frames with wood shutters that, when open, leave just a thin insect mesh between sleeping guest and encroaching field and jungle. Bath and shower rooms are open to the sky, and trees grow from within the structure, reaching through wrought iron grates in walls and ceilings. The fourth pavilion is a living area, open on two sides and covered by a triple-tiled roof supported by pillars and a rendered back wall (Figure 5.2). Furthermore, the bungalow is located right in the middle of the atmosphere that Bawa alludes to in his descriptions of the view over Cinnamon Hill (see Chapter 5).

One evening, after dinner, the three of us sat in this living area and chatted about the estate. Curious, I asked one of my companions, Dinesh, how he felt being in a place like this. He paused before turning to ask his friend a question in Sinhala. 'Infinity', she replied. Dinesh thought a little longer before saying, 'I feel like my mind keeps making these connections, one after another, to infinity. It's difficult to explain, words can't really explain it. Actually, in Buddhism there's a good explanation for this.' He then proceeded to tell a story about the Lord Buddha, his disciple, attendant and monk, Ananda, and their conversations about the search for the sphere of the infinity of consciousness, before again stressing, 'I feel like my mind is growing and forging connections with something beyond myself.' Finally, he stressed that he thought only in this type of place could this happen.[2]

So, what of Dinesh's infinity? Though his is not a religious experience in any revelatory or doctrinal sense, he clearly tells us two things. First, that a Buddhist textuality and metaphysics plays a central role in the way he is

---

2 At the time (26 February 2005), I made notes on this encounter in my research diary, including an approximate transcript of the conversation.

constituted there and then, as a subject. And second, that this experience is ontologically linked to place, to *this* tropical modern built space. To grasp these Buddhist aesthetics from his testimony is to try more fully to grasp the aesthetic effects of the built space to which he accords agency in this moment of his becoming. Following Dinesh, it is to join the dots between *that* space and *this* experience, to take what, for the Eurocentric social sciences at least, is a challenging and uncertain descent into the ordinary dimensions of this space, a space that Bawa once described as 'blessed' (Chapter 5) and was built by him to produce the kind of inside/out living that Dinesh narrativizes *this* way.

The first part of Dinesh's formulation – 'I feel like my mind keeps making these connections, one after another, to infinity' – bares some striking similarities to an altogether different figure and trope in William Wordsworth, who in 'The Prelude' declares the scene before him as he stands at Mount Snowdon as the emblem of a mind that feeds upon infinity (see Wilner 2000). But to make such a straightforward connection is to lapse into a reductively comparative way of understanding Dinesh's infinity. Dinesh speaks his infinity very differently from a European romanticism that devours an infinity-as-object to keep the romantic self in tact. His, instead, is an undoing, an exteriorization of subjectivity. It is conjunctural. Produced at that time, and at that place. But definitely not by accident. He stresses that only in a place like Lunuganga could this happen, directly implicating tropical modernism in his becoming infinite. And his difficulty to find the English words to explain his experience, just like Bawa's use of the Sinhala script to describe this very space's 'blessedness' (Chapter 5), suggests an unnameable difference, an aesthetics, that Eurocentric knowledge cannot adequately bring into representation. In other words, Dinesh's self-narrative stalls as he senses my inability to understand the cultural logic of his behavioural text. As Talal Asad (2003: 83) remarks, to narrativize an experience we need not just the words with which to tell stories but also an audience able to hear and understand those words as we intend them.

Dinesh tells us that in Buddhism there's a good explanation for his experience, and being attentive to this (for it is absolutely my intention to listen to him) means thinking about the Buddhist biorhythms and aesthetics mobilized in this place, at that moment, that for Dinesh at the experiential level persistently deconstruct any logical opposition between the natural and the cultural. His becoming infinite signifies a participation in a metaphysics of oneness that is ordinary within Buddhism. Acknowledging the presence of these biorhythms is, once again, to 'de-transcendentalize the sacred', that is, to move the very ordinariness of this sacred modern Buddhist spatial formation towards imagination (Spivak 2008: 10). Here, at this moment, Dinesh experiences a universe composed of dharmas, something like energies or forces, which is an affective premise that conceives of modernist knowledge of the nature-object, or any object for that matter, as but a projection (see Klostermaier 1991; Epstein 2007; also see Chapter 1). Instead, Buddhist selves and biophysical worlds are understood as the purely relational emergence into objective existence of these dharmas. Participating in a Buddhist social text, then, requires a tacit acceptance that dharma is itself unknowable through subjective knowledge of object fields. Naturalistic reality – that is, a glimpse of dharma – is only graspable intuitively, as the self unravels. These are the metaphysical domains in which Dinesh locates his subjectivity, his becoming infinite. My aim here is not to assess either the validity or accuracy of his assertion. Such a judgement would immediately reinstantiate an implicitly comparative Eurocentric evaluation all over again. My aim instead is to listen and grasp Dinesh's own (non)self-fashioning (see Scott 1999: 208–15); the ways that he takes hold of his body's energies to impose upon them regularities, orders, sets of rules, values, and legibilities that themselves are spatially contingent. Because it bears repeating, for Dinesh only in this type of place could this happen.

In fact, it is apposite to ask whether the notion of subjectivity itself is a flexible enough concept-metaphor to grasp Dinesh's becoming infinite? In his work on colonial education, European knowledge and difference in mid-nineteenth-century British Bengal, Sanjay Seth (2007a; 2007b) usefully attends to the implicit comparativism that inheres in the very notion of subjectivity. He stresses how subjectivity has a teleology built into it, such that all its variants culminate in modern forms of liberal selfhood. Just as part of this book's argument is that the adjective 'religious' obscures a pervasive Buddhist aesthetics that is neither secular nor sacred, and similarly that 'nature' obscures non-dualistic Buddhist understandings of metaphysical oneness, Seth writes that the '"different" in "different subjectivity" is simultaneously enabled and obscured by the concept "subjectivity"' (2007a: 686). Like nature and religion, subjectivity itself is a categorization that works in the service of Eurocentrism to obscure other modes of personhood. Taking Dinesh's experience on the ordinary terms through which it is written moves towards the imagination other kinds of relationships between a self and Sri Lankan socius. In this case, a self that in and through moments and spaces like these lives with the prospect of its own undoing through the metaphysical principles on which it is written. Thereby, a self placed within the midst of an imagined social text that is intuitively, and very ordinarily, Buddhist, and thereby ethnically Sinhalese. This reading of the conjunctural relationship between tropical modern built space and experience continues the work of 'suspending oneself into the text of the other' (Spivak 2008: 23) that Chapter 3 began in Ruhuna National Park. And it aims at locating tropical modern architecture's production of experience – its inside/out habitations – within what Gayatri Spivak, borrowing from Deleuze and Guattari, has referred to as a 'miraculating agency', where 'as if by miracle one speaks as an agent of a culture or an agent of a sex or an agent of an ethnos et cetera …' (Spivak 1993: 6).

In all these senses, Dinesh's experience in and through the Cinnamon Hill bungalow at Lunuganga was both exemplary and rather ordinary. Rather than divine or revelatory religious experience, his mobilization of Buddhism as a metaphysical explanation enabled by his spatial present is a relatively common narrativization of tropical modern space. Indeed, it is precisely the ability of this kind of aesthetics to be at the same time both irreligious and Buddhist that enables it to dwell unproblematically in modern, ostensibly secular, architectural space. Sharmini, for example, was keen to stress that though she and her family are Buddhist, there is little that she could identify as sacred, or religious, about their house. However, she then went on to emphasize how each day her mother lights a lamp in the house's shrine area in the living room, she pays obeisance to a photograph of the Lord Buddha, and for a hour or so plays pirith tunes through a home stereo system: sounds that, as she put it, come to pervade the house 'energetically'. As she spoke it became clear that for Sharmini there is in fact a particular kind of sacred modern cultural logic to the aesthetics the house enables: a logic that she was at pains to distinguish from the more traditional forms of orthodox religious Buddhist veneration found in more devout households:

> I quite like it because Buddhism is about shedding a lot of attachments and I think that in this house actually you are able to shed a lot of attachments. You can become very detached, because you can just observe things and that's what Buddhism is kind of about: observing yourself, observing the things that happen. (Interview with Sharmini, 6 September 2006)

Though Sharmini is able to identify against a more regressive form of nominally religious worship, her own modernity still sits within a Buddhist idiom. Shiranika and Pradeep, on the other hand, who both were so keen to inscribe a kind of 'jungle' aesthetic to their own modes of living inside/out, went a little further as Pradeep explicitly identified as 'sacred' the modes of tranquillity and calmness that their house's proximity with the surrounding environment affords them. He also stressed that the house's imperative to live inside/out corroborated what for him was a Buddhist edict: never to harm a single living thing and nurture a love and respect for nature. Though Shiranika, his wife, identified as a Catholic, Pradeep described himself as a Buddhist who lights lamps in the house, despite not being really religious (Interview with Shiranika and Pradeep, 8 September 2006).

Drawing out these kinds of narrativizations that hint at a residual cultural logic to tropical modern experience reveals the kinds of habitation I have drawn out in this chapter to be neither religious nor secular metaphysical ways-of-being. Neither are they just facilitated by tropical modern space. Moreover, as ways-of-being they are located by some users within the space's very essence. Narratologically as well, for Sharmini, Dinesh, and Pradeep they *are* Buddhist ways-of-being, but in discernibly modern, rational, and irreligious ways. These are more moments and affective intensities where aesthetic states constitute instances of pure suspension, where form is experienced on its own terms, and a specific type of humanity is produced and educated (Rancière 2004: 24). The specific type of humanity I am gesturing towards here is a distribution of the sensible marked by, and marking, a cosmopolitan Buddhism, which, though ostensibly secular, in the Sri Lankan context is implicitly anchored to the hegemony of a Sinhala ethnos.

By drawing out this cultural logic to tropical modern experience, I mean in closing this chapter to show how a behavioural text might be decoded precisely by entering into the space of that text. The logic behind the experiences I have evoked – the contours, idiom, and meaningfulness of Dinesh's infinity, his oneness, for example – are from my perspective neither illusory, nor ontologically inaccurate. Nor is there anything to be gained in attempting to establish the validity (scientific or otherwise) of such experiential knowledge. Rather, in reading for the ordinary logic of tropical modern habitations and experiences, and in connecting them to the ideological and material work of architecture, I am interested in the contingent spatial production of bodily yearnings for the (non)self to be connected to the world in certain ways; what Talal Asad refers to as a desire to be controlled by the world in particular kinds of ways and not others: 'knowing the world practically and being known practically by it' (Asad 2003: 73). In an important sense then, the 'cultural' and 'physical' cease to dichotomise when spatial aesthetics are narrated in a particular kind of way. How a subject invests an affective intensity and its spatial production with meaning becomes a mode of living a relationship to the world (ibid.: 84). And, in this sense, each narrativization of living inside/out in and through tropical modern space is another moment in that space's inscription as Buddhist. Like the architect Channa Daswatte put it in a conversation we had regarding the relationships between Buddhism and tropical modernism, there *is* something sacred about tropical modern architecture, but that sacredness is merely 'inherent in good design'.

CHAPTER 7

Over-Determinations:
Architecture, Text, Politics

works of art are not received as single entities, but within the institutional frameworks and conditions that largely determine the function of the works.

Peter Bürger, *Theory of the Avant-garde* (1984), p. 12

Architecture is dependent on others at every stage of its journey from initial sketch to inhabitation.

Jeremy Till, *Architecture Depends* (2009), p. 45

Just moments after the architect Channa Daswatte spoke of a 'sacredness' inherent in good design (see Chapter 6), I asked him whether he thought there was anything at all political about tropical modernism in the context of Sri Lanka's national question. He was vehement that there was nothing either religious or political about the materiality of the architecture itself. However, at once he stressed that the problem is that tropical modern architecture can be, and has been, one of those things that Sinhala-Buddhist nationalists latch onto, co-opt, for their own political ends; like education was, like language was. His defence of the genre raises an important point. The admission that the architecture has been latched onto somehow, reveals what I want to show in this chapter is the very impossibility of artistic autonomy. In the context of its environmental resonances then, tropical modernity's aesthetic domains are always partly shaped by a myriad of extra-architectural factors and assemblages. With all the will in the world, contemporary architects like Channa Daswatte cannot control how their built spaces *come to mean* in a particular kind of way. Not only does the historical weight of the genre itself weigh down upon them, their work circulates through institutions, representational economies, and markets in ways that as I explore in this chapter over-determine the meaning of tropical modern materialities and environments, as well as the cultural logic of living inside/out that those materialities afford. As much as Bawa's and de Silva's early and self-conscious 'post-colonial' narrativizations of their style, it is these excessive constellations that forge tropical modernism's cultural and political effects. It is to some of these over-determining assemblages of Sri Lankan nature as it is experienced in and through tropical modern architecture that I turn in this chapter.

Critics of modernism have long noted the hollowness to any modernist movement's claims to artistic autonomy (also see Huyssen 1986). We know now that modernism is always connected with the vagaries of the institutional frameworks, force fields, and markets in and through which it emerges only to simultaneously disavow with claims it might make about its own artistic autonomy and thereby critical potential. If this is to make a critique of modernist movements, the more general point regarding how things come to mean in and through society is that, as Brian Larkin (2009: 167) puts it, 'A cultural text is not a container of a meaning that lies inside of it waiting for the critic to release it but is already mediated by the process of circulation itself and accrues meaning by virtue of that traffic across difference'. This point has been implicit, and at times explicit, in this book so far. For example, of Ruhuna National Park's dominant post-independent meanings and imaginations, Chapter 4 began by stressing it was precisely the ways it was made to circulate as a social text amongst a particular public that purified its landscape meanings as a culturally and historically Sinhala space of nature. In the conclusion to Chapter 5, I argued that popular imaginations regarding Geoffrey Bawa's work in particular have inevitably been swayed by his work for the Sri Lankan government in a number of grand designs that themselves were, directly or indirectly, connected with processes of post-independent (Sinhala) nation-building; the production of the *dharmistha* society. It is precisely these extra-architectural factors that inscribe and position Sri Lanka's tropical modern architecture within the particular kinds of spatial and environmental political domains that I have been evoking in this book.

In this very sense, we should be wary of the too easy impulse to locate architecture as a discrete professional practice, set apart from a world in which it is always already mired. Like Edward Said's (1983) insistence on the worldliness of texts, architecture too is in and of the world; pulled semantically and materially in this direction and that by a host of factors. Though it is true that national architectural institutions and their professional members might tell to themselves the lie of autonomy, in actual fact architecture is irredeemably immersed in the demands of a world at once social, political, and cultural. As Jeremy Till puts it, if '[t]he profession of architecture is internally defined and necessarily self-contained; the practice of architecture is a set of external networks, and necessarily dependent' (Till 2009: 161). As he also notes, because of this lie of autonomy that architecture can tell itself about itself, architects can reason that their creative artistry is seen to rise above the political world. However, the crux, as Till puts it in a way that resonates with Channa Daswatte's hauntingly melancholic mourning of tropical modernity's autonomy lost, is that 'just saying that something is not political does not mean that it actually isn't. Quite the opposite: the assumed innocence makes it vulnerable to appropriation' (ibid.: 162). Architecture's dependencies, therefore, have a considerable effect on how the environment is affectively, materially, and imaginatively produced. It is to these dependencies and over-determinations that I turn in this chapter.

Shifting and Indeterminate Dependencies

Tropical modern built space's aesthetic and political over-determinations are forged through a number of shifting and indeterminate dependencies. Though diffuse and disparate, this range of different and disparate extra-architectural factors upon which the meanings and politics of tropical modernism depends overlap and cross-pollinate one another on a regular basis. They are so entwined with the architecture itself that their designation as 'extra-architectural' is misleading in as much as it can erroneously imply that the architecture *can* exist in isolation from these excessive encounters with the world. In this chapter I highlight three kinds of assemblages that we can suggest the style depends upon: first, client demands; second, representational economies; and third, the conditions of a hospitality imperative that pervades tropical modern architecture, and, as I show, is deeply embedded within the contours of Sri Lankan nature more generally. Crucial to understanding them, however, is due recognition of their fluid and indeterminate implication in one another, the impossibility of their disaggregation. For example, what I will suggest below are a set of clientelistic relations that over-determine tropical modernism's environmental resonances, and further, that what the architecture does in and through contemporary Sri Lankan society cannot be thought of in isolation from the representational economies that come to bare upon tropical modernism's meaning. And, in turn, a certain kind of hospitality imperative is deeply implicated in both client demands and the representational poetics that shapes the market for tropical modernism. In reading what follows, then, due recognition of the shifting and indeterminate nature of these dependencies is paramount.

Client Demands

It is an obvious but no less important point to stress that buildings do not get conceived, let alone built, without a client base. Despite tropical modern architecture's status as artistic expression and vanguardist experimentation, architects have always been dependent on a market for their work. In Sri Lanka, this market has historically been confined to a relatively affluent, upper-middle-class section of Sri Lankan society, as well as the state and an abundance of hospitality corporations. As such, though Bawa and before him de Silva derived much of their creative élan from a notion of Sinhala 'folk culture' drawn from the creative gestations of the '43 Group, they have rarely built directly for that folk. Domestic commissions continue to come from a class that, if not consistently bourgeois, could certainly afford to commission architect-designed houses. These can be amongst the politically, economically, and culturally influential of Sri Lanka's population, and they are also part of a broader section of multi-ethnic upper-middle-class Sri Lankan society that requires an aesthetic separation from the visible traces of hardship and poverty that Sri Lanka's working classes, or folk, encounter daily (see Chapter 6).

Geographically, as well, because of twenty-six years of civil war and associated patterns of regional underdevelopment, commissions have also tended to be generated from either southern or central Sri Lanka and not from the north and east. In other words, the market is overwhelmingly located in parts of the country where the ethnic composition of local population structures comprise a statistical majority of Sinhala-Buddhist people. In these very simple terms, there is a certain statistical and biopolitical prejudice to the composition of the market upon which tropical modernists are dependent for their commissions.

This has manifested itself in terms of the client demands made of domestic architectural projects. If, for example, we return to the house that Geoffrey Bawa built for Osmund and Ena de Silva in Colombo in 1962, not only did Bawa here seek much of his design inspiration from a notion of tradition that for him seemed to be cognate with arts, crafts, and architectural heritage identified as Kandyan-Sinhala, his client also played a hands-on role in the ethnicized historical narrativization of her innovatively opened-out modern structure. According to David Robson:

> the de Silvas had one foot in the past and one in the future. Ena was conscious of the Aluvihara family traditions, though she hated the colonial-style bungalow that the architect Charles Gomez had built for her father at Aluvihara in 1956. She demanded a house that would incorporate traditional Kandyan features – an enclosing wall, open-sided rooms, verandahs, courtyards, a shrine room – but she also wanted a modern house with an office for her husband, a studio for her son, and guest wing for visitors. (Robson 2002: 74)

Such client-driven pressures merely illustrate how tropical modern architecture is an irredeemably relational and dependent venture that conceptually and materially is in and of a Sri Lankan world narratologically marked by Sinhala-Buddhist historiography. As such, the production of its environmental resonances must also be considered as embedded in this world. Referring to this majoritarian biopolitical prejudice of sorts is not to gloss over the many just as wealthy and influential Tamil, Muslim, or Burgher clients who also commission Sri Lanka's tropical modern architects. Indeed, a significant minority of my own small sample of interviewees identified as non-Buddhist. But this is not the point. Rather, the point is that there is a market-driven reason why alternative idiomatic placings and narrativizations of the style are extremely rare. Arguably, were it not for regional underdevelopment of the north and east owing to war since 1983 and civil unrest since the mid-1950s, tropical modernism may have found commissions in parts of the country where Tamil or Muslim populations outnumber Sinhalese, and we can speculate that had this been the case the architecture's narratological locatedness may have evolved differently. It did not. And, as it is, when clients demand an opened-out house, they demand an aesthetics framed by a dominant and situated understanding of the historical that is made to bare the allegorical weight of the national; what I refer to below as a 'hospitality imperative'.

This is perhaps even more marked if we jump scales from domestic to corporate clientele, particularly within the hospitality market. Channa Daswatte himself famously collaborated with Geoffrey Bawa on the Kandalama Hotel in 1991. The hotel (Figure 6.2) was built in the middle of the dry zone, in the tourist hotspot of Sri Lanka's so-called 'cultural triangle', which joins the ancient cities of Anuradhapura and Polonarruwa with the first-century BCE Buddhist, monastic cave complex at Dambulla. In the centre of the cultural triangle is the fifth-century rock palace Sigiriya built by King Kasyapa as a fortress protection and which can now be seen from the Kandalama Hotel. All of these heritage sights occupy significant places within a Sri Lanka historiographical formation sanctioned by those orientalist translations of the *Mahavamsa* outlined in Chapter 3. In other words, all mark cardinal points on a historical compass of the nation state written as foundationally Sinhala and Buddhist.

For Bawa and Daswatte, the aesthetic terrain they sought to build at Kandalama was in part framed by a conscious narrativization that capitalized on the hotel's location. Its drama was to be mobilized by the surrounding historical geographical context and a correspondent 'jungle' aesthetics (see Chapter 4) woven into places like this: 'What he [Bawa] wanted was a site that would offer mystery and suspense: visitors would be forced to make a long trek through the jungle to arrive at the edge of a tank, across which they would finally see Sigiriya in the distance' (Robson 2002: 200). At the same time, both Bawa and Daswatte wanted to engender in the building, and the jungle experiences it produces, a kind of historical disconnect so as precisely *not* historiographically to over-determine the hotel's meaning as a Sinhala-Buddhist revivalist structure:

> I mean, historical references are the last thing that [we wanted] … when we worked on it … In fact it sought to avoid such references. The idea was that we would create some kind of empty framework into which you could throw your references after a hard day seeing the sights …

That I think was one of the things we wanted to do with the Kandalama, and one of the few criticisms we had in the early days was that it was in the cultural triangle but it had no reference to Sri Lanka. (Interview with Channa Daswatte, 16 February 2005)

It is worth adding here that, by 'Sri Lanka', Daswatte means the dominant Sinhala historiography with which the cultural triangle is associated. He then went on to describe how the clients, Aitken Spence, placed him and Bawa under real pressure for around six months during the design process to make some narrative concession to the hegemonic and regional contexts. With some resistance, they eventually conceded to painting the area behind the reception with a large fresco reminiscent of the formal structures of medieval Sinhala temple wall painting. Its reference was the traditional shrine room arras and awnings replicated frequently on Buddhist cave temple walls and ceilings not filled with narrative panels. Though this non-secular historical reference is oblique, it still historicizes the Kandalama's materiality in an idiomatically Sinhala kind of way. Daswatte's story highlights the pressure that clients place on architects to bind their architecture to ever more explicitly Sinhala and Buddhist historiographical and aesthetic formations.

In a reversal or appropriation of a similar kind of client-driven pressure, another junior architect who worked at MICD, Robert Verrijt, spoke of a hotel project he was pitching to another corporation at Koggala Lake on Sri Lanka's southwest coast. His brief was to come up with something that utilized the lake and, as his client stressed to him, would be 'very Sri Lankan'. The ambitious design that Verrijt presented to his client involved tree houses, outdoor decking supported by stilts, pavilions that were to float on the lake, as well as a lakeside spa. Crucially, however, the whole complex was anchored by Verrijt's narrative reworking of the early twentieth-century author and scholar of Sinhalese and Buddhist folk culture and society, Martin Wickremasinghe, who himself became a figure in Sri Lanka's early twentieth-century Sinhala-Buddhist populist movement. Wickremasinghe wrote an autobiographical novel called *Ape Gama* (Our Village) (1940), which revolved around Koggala, the village of his birth. Verrijt stressed that not only was his lakeside hotel complex an interpretation of the utopian Sri Lankan village based on Wickremasinghe's novel, but this textual framing proved central to allaying his client's early fears that his ambitious design might not be Sri Lankan enough.

Both these stories illustrate the kinds of dependent relationships with paying and commissioning clients that effectively over-determine the meanings and aesthetic terrains that tropical modern architecture signifies. At the same time, both stories reveal the pressures that shape what contemporary architects associated with this style *are able* to continue to produce *as* modern architecture. Client-driven pressure presents a major challenge to the evolution of the genre in the simple sense that, for some architects, expectations and demands imposed in the market place prohibit experimental vanguardism in the here and now. It prevents ruptures and disarticulations

Figure 7.1 House in Colombo, by Varuna de Silva
(Source: Varuna de Silva).

with an engrained Sinhala and Buddhist cultural logic to tropical modern built space. It prevents autonomy. Channa Daswatte put it succinctly when he stressed how one particular client who had recently chastised one of his designs for being 'too modern',

> had an idyllic idea of Sri Lanka that has been processed through south-east Asia, which is now coming back to haunt us because that's what we do, which is a waste for me. It feels like I'm going back in time to something that we've done. Meanwhile we need to get on with it. But somehow there are clientele that are demanding that's what we should be doing. (Interview with Channa Daswatte, 16 February 2005)

On the other hand, as Robert Verrijt's manipulation of the Martin Wickremasinghe narrative at the Koggala lake hotel complex reveals, there are also contemporary tropical modern architects who use client demands and expectations strategically, sometimes to make their more abstract designs marketable by locating them within a particular semantic field. Another contemporary architect, Varuna de Silva, was referred to me as an example of someone whose vanguardist designs are pushing Sri Lankan architecture forward stylistically, in terms of both his choice of industrial materials not best suited to the tropics, like glass and steel, and his preference for the brutal aesthetic of straight lines and angles over curves and contours (see Figure 7.1). The architect who referred me to Varuna de Silva stressed that de Silva was known and sometimes teased amongst architects for producing buildings that were 'not very Sri Lankan'. When I spoke with de Silva, however, he was adamant that despite his brutalism his structures are very tropical, and hence very Sri Lankan, *because* of the attention he pays to opening the house, to having that fluid inside/out spatiality and environmental resonance that his clients demand in a tropical modern architectural market pervaded by the spectre and legacy of an opening out pioneered by the likes of Geoffrey Bawa and Minnette de Silva.

These different ways that architects deal with, and work towards, clientelistic demands and expectation all have one common effect: that is effectively to lock down meanings, helping to over-determine the cultural logic of the aesthetic fields and environmental resonances they produce. It is the pull of a market populated by clients who want their buildings to mean in a particular kind of way that is important here; clients whose aspirational desires seek out particular kinds of environmental resonances through the space they sponsor.

There is, however, another important market, another set of clients, that is, for tropical modern architecture that traffics in a lucrative but far more immaterial tropical modern style. I am referring here to the high-quality and glossy style books that showcase the design attributes and environmental historical aesthetics of Sri Lanka's best-known tropical modernists from Minnette de Silva onwards. Steadily, since around the mid-1980s, this market has been proliferated by an increasing number of prominent and now well-known publications that are rich in descriptive and evocative text narrating a history of the tropical style, and are usually punctuated by an abundance of high-quality photography. These publications are sold in a selection of boutique gift shops throughout Colombo, Kandy, and Galle, and are also available from some of the larger bookshops across the country. Though foreign tourism provides an inevitably good market for these publications, there is also a sizeable domestic market whose aspirations are catered to by this print culture.

These publications also play a role in over-determining the cultural logic of tropical modernism's meanings. Though this literature does comprise its own field and market of cultural production, it should also be seen not as external to tropical modern architecture but instead as woven into the ways its materialities mean. In this sense, it is worth stressing the closeness of text to the material architectural world and its environmental resonances; and it is not just that we can think of architecture *like* a text in the Saidian sense of a text's lively worldliness (Said 1983: 31–53). Rather – and as I come on to discuss in more detail below – Sri Lanka's tropical modern architecture is also inseparable in some senses from these texts (also see Cairns 2007; Scriver 2007).

In his book *Beyond Bawa: Modern Masterworks of Monsoon Asia* (2007), David Robson himself points to the early role of such texts in a conjunctural understanding of Geoffrey Bawa's career and legacy. He writes how 'moments of conjunction cannot be engineered and are often the result of happenstance; the world does not wake up to them until long after they occurred. Bawa's career was punctuated, indeed shaped, by a number of such conjunctions' (Robson 2007: 17). Robson means to emphasize the central role that events apparently disconnected from Bawa's material architectural work have played in its development. As he proceeds to stress, the publication of the first compendium of Bawa's architecture was one such 'happenstance' event, or one moment of conjunction:

> The third point of conjunction occurred in Singapore during the early 1980s. The Aga Khan's Trust for Culture established its own publishing house in Singapore in 1980 and rented space in the same building where architect William Lim had his office and his wife, Lena Lim, ran a book shop called Select Books. This event led to the publication of Bawa's 'White Book' in 1986 and later inspired a series of influential books. (Robson 2007: 17)

Robson refers here to the architectural journal *Mimar's* third monograph in its series on 'noteworthy developing world architects' (ibid.: 88), which was simply entitled *Geoffrey Bawa* (Brace Taylor 1986). If this publication was singularly important in Bawa's career, it was also the template for a plethora of lavishly produced and illustrated style books that now circulate around Sri Lanka's tropical modernism. Robson goes on to devote two of his ten chapters in *Beyond Bawa* to discussing the importance of these books (chapter 8, 'Two Books and an Exhibition' and chapter 9, 'More Books'), offering a sense of how the architecture itself is dependent upon this lively market and the aspirations it engenders. Ironically, though, perhaps the most influential and lavishly produced books that currently circulate around and pervade tropical modernism's semantic field are the three Thames and Hudson publications written by Robson himself: *Geoffrey Bawa: The Complete Works* (2002), *Beyond Bawa: Modern Masterworks of Monsoon Asia* (2007), and most recently *Bawa: The Sri Lanka Gardens* (2009). Though Robson writes himself out of the genre's textual field, these three quality publications remain very much part of the ongoing over-determination of tropical modern architecture's meanings; particularly Geoffrey Bawa's. No text – including this one – can stand outside its object of representation (see Jazeel and McFarlane 2010: 112–15).

Representational Economies

When I shadowed Dinesh and Ro, two architectural interns at MICD, we had a discussion about drawing. They showed me some architect's drawings of a project they were working on, renovations at an estate. The drawings looked fairly typical to my untrained eye: clean straight pen lines marking with precision and scalar accuracy an overhead view of the building and plot they were to work on, the whole plan liberally dotted with measurements denoting metered architectural modernity. 'It's dead,' Ro said, as she and Dinesh showed me this technical drawing.

In truth, of course, architectural and technical drawings are much more a part of the architectural process than style books. They partake in the formation and material realization of ideas. They are also, however, irreducibly textual, and in an important way they occupy a liminal space between architect and client. Drawings perform a relationality in and through which an abundance of meaning, memory, and cultural logic is negotiated. As Jeremy Till puts it, 'One might think that an architectural sketch has a certain innocence, but even those early marks are conditioned by previous experience and present expectations' (2009: 46).

Ro expanded on what she meant when she said the drawings were 'dead' by stressing that she does not like the clean, geometred, straight-line method of architectural drawing; it purges the plan of any sense of inside/out-ness and environmental fluidity in the spatialities that they work hard to produce. As a matter of course, what she and her colleagues do, she went on, is to over-score the clinical geometry of technical drawings with a free hand and impressionistic pen, lending to them a 'kind of shaky effect' that gives the drawings life, conveying that organic merging of structure and site that their clients expect from tropical modern architecture's environmental domains. But Ro's predilection for the 'shaky effect' in technical drawing is not an idiosyncratic quirk. Her and Dinesh told me how at the university their examiners look and give credit for this kind of 'eye' and disposition in their drawing abilities, and as a technique it is taught. It is called 'rendering' and it aims for an at once detailed but poetic depiction of spatial design. Its purpose, they went on, is twofold: first to avoid abstraction, and second, to convince clients by conveying to them the 'sense of place' they wish to convey.[1]

This 'way of drawing' has a genealogy within Sri Lankan tropical modernism that is particularly associated with the Bawa office (see Robson 2007: 49–60). Two of Bawa's former assistants, Laki Senanayake and Ismeth Raheem, were the first to render architectural drawings this way in the early 1960s. They, in turn, were influenced by an Australian artist, Donald Friend, who lived with Geoffrey Bawa's brother Bevis in the late 1950s. These techniques of drawing have been described as 'phenomenological' (Robson 2007: 49) in as much as they offer readers an invitation to imaginatively inhabit the design. They emerged out of a dissatisfaction with modern architecture's uneasy relationship with the natural world where trees, for example, were represented by architects simply as abstract shapes that graphically pinned down their location in a plot. This kind of abstraction many early tropical modernists deemed out of synch with the style's aims at opening out the house and creating a more fluid sense of space and environmental engagement. Senanayake 'used a dip pen whose line thickness could be varied with pressure. He drew each separate species of tree in meticulous detail and succeeded in capturing a sense of space and the interconnectedness of building and landscape' (ibid.).

---

1 All quotes from this conversation are reproduced from a transcript made in my research diary (27 February 2005).

Representationally, rendering continues to stand in a constitutive relationship to tropical modern architecture. The traffic in meaning promulgated through this established drawing technique, as Robson himself suggests, is not incidental to the architecture. It remains an essential expression of a philosophy and aesthetics of design, and has become somewhat of a *lingua franca* of tropical modernist expression (ibid.). Moreover, what I want to emphasize here is the necessity of understanding such representational components of tropical modern architecture not as before-the-event illustrations, or anticipations, of built space, but instead as 'constituent images of its meaning or meanings' (Daniels and Cosgrove 1988: 1). Drawing in this rendered style needs to be understood as a way of assembling form; it is productive of certain forms of inhabiting the material world (Rancière 2007: 91).

Rendering is particularly important in this respect because it is a way of drawing that has not been consigned to the traffic of architectural plans that scurry between client and architect. In lively and generative ways, rendering has also pervaded the style books and the role that these books have played in the emergence of tropical modernism's broader aesthetics and environmental resonances. In the late 1950s, Bawa's partner Ulrik Plesner struck a close friendship with his client Barbara Sansoni, founder of the now hugely successful Sri Lankan 'style' shop, Barefoot. Sansoni herself was an architectural enthusiast and the two began to take field excursions around the country with the aim of identifying good examples of medieval Sinhalese and colonial architecture. In the field they would photograph and draw buildings in order to record and 'measure' something of the country's architectural heritage (Robson 2007: 48). In doing so they were perhaps only partly aware of their active contribution to the authorship of that material cultural heritage. Importantly, they were accompanied by Laki Senanayake and Ismeth Raheem who were at that time developing their new rendered style of drawing. Together the four of them produced an abundance of photographs as well as rendered and impressionistic drawings of historical and vernacular buildings across Sri Lanka.

Through the 1960s, these drawings and notes were regularly published under the pseudonyms Simon and Claude in a series of newspaper articles in the *Daily Mirror*. The feature was entitled 'Collecting Old Buildings'. Eventually, a sample of the rendered drawings, notes, and impressions was published together in a 1978 book that, tellingly, was entitled *Viharas and Verandahs*. Reprinted in 2007 amidst a sea of other glossy architecture and style books, the title boldly frames the notion of Sri Lankan architectural heritage that its authors proffer between two emblematic markers of Sri Lanka history writing: the Sinhala-Buddhist and the colonial, respectively. If the Buddhist vihara was indigenous, vernacular, and somewhat passive, the colonial verandah was foreign, extra-local, and active in the sense of being an influence *upon* the former. The book's accessibility was limited by the price tag that its production quality demanded, however the drawings published over the years in the *Daily Mirror* ensured this architectural history writing became accessible to Sri Lanka's public at large. And it is important to stress that Plesner, Sansoni, Senanayake, and Raheem's turn towards the vernacular thought *as* Sinhala-Buddhist at that time was entirely in keeping with the explicitly 'post-colonial' recoveries of tradition being sought by Geoffrey Bawa through the late 1950s and 1960s, and before him Minnette de Silva.

This kind of extra-architectural discursive authorization of a vernacular towards which tropical modernists and their clients were turning, and from which they were learning, was further consolidated in 1998 with the publication of a far more comprehensive selection of these drawings and photographs. This time Sansoni and Plesner's original efforts were pulled together in a more ambitious book coauthored by the historian Ronald Lewcock, Barbara Sansoni, and Laki Senanayake. This just as beautifully produced book is perhaps best considered an evolution of *Viharas and Verandahs*, one that made its intentions at authoring a national architectural heritage of sorts explicit through its title: *The Architecture of an Island: the Living Heritage of Sri Lanka*. Though it was intended that the book would be less scholarly treatise than, as they wrote, 'an evocation of the excitement, pleasures and satisfaction of experiencing traditional buildings in Sri Lanka' (Lewcock, Sansoni, and Senanayake 1998: xxv), it is arguably much more traditionally anthropological in its format than its predecessor.

The Architecture of an Island is organized in thirteen separate sections covering different architectural styles that the authors map onto Sri Lanka's ethnic groupings. For example, sections included 'Sinhalese Vernacular Domestic Buildings', 'Hindu Secular Vernacular Buildings' and 'Moslem Vernacular Domestic Buildings'; 'Buddhist Temples', 'Hindu Temples', 'Mosques', and 'The Nineteenth Century Catholic Tradition'; and three separate sections on Portuguese, Dutch, and British colonial architectures. All of the ninety-five buildings covered in the book are depicted through a combination of photographs, sketches in the rendered style, and overhead plans that accompany a short descriptive text written with the distance and objectivity of the passive tense. And the sense of a *'living heritage'* that its title proclaims is enhanced by the frequent inclusion of people dwelling in the structures sketched; notably in this respect an abundance of impressionistically rendered Buddhist monks and villagers, testifying to the text's picturesque recuperation of the pre-colonial Sinhala-Buddhist.

The organization of the book does suggest a somewhat more plural, democratic, and multi-ethnic form of architectural history writing by virtue of its inclusion of sections on Moslem, Hindu, and Catholic structures. However, the balance does not. The overwhelming majority of pre-colonial structures covered (some 38 out of 44) are designated as somehow Sinhala or Buddhist. At the same time, and more importantly, the introductory essay explicitly frames the Sri Lankan vernacular around a familiar understanding of the primordial status of the Sinhala ethnos and Buddhist 'religion' in an island territory retroactively projected *as* the Sri Lankan nation state. It is worth reproducing here the first two paragraphs of the book, subheaded 'History and Geography':

> If we imagine that we are able to look down on Sri Lanka from the air as it was 2000 years ago, we would see spread out below us an island with a wide coastal belt of plains and low rising hills with, in the centre, the steep slopes of high hills and plateaux ... This was the cradle of the ancient Sinhalese people ... From our aerial view we could count a number of towns and ports, particularly the great port of Mantota, or Mantai, which served for the exchange of goods from the east ... This port, which lay on the straits on the west side of the island, also served as the main entrance from India; roads led from it fifty miles to Anuradhapura, the capital city built by the Sinhalese and the centre of Buddhist culture. To the east of the island another ancient port, Trincomalee ... In legend Shiva landed here.
>
> ... we would observe over a period of a few centuries the filtering of Hindu peoples in to a narrow region at the extreme northern tip of the island, the Jaffna peninsula ... Buddhism dominated the area at this time (as place names, monastic ruins and inscriptions testify), but it eventually became saturated with the culture and civilization of Tamil people from southern India. (Lewcock, Sansoni, and Senanayake 1998: xvii)

There is little by way of nationalist, or indeed political, intent in these stage-setting passages. This is certainly not the nationalist co-optation of architecture that the architect Channa Daswatte bemoans at the beginning of this chapter. Textually, however, these paragraphs participate in a worldly historiography that achieves certain imaginative effects. The primacy of the Sinhala ethnos is established within a nation state that never was, for Sri Lanka *as* nation state is of course a formation of colonial and political modernity that meant little 2,000 years ago (see Jazeel 2009b). Equally, if there is a reality to Buddhism's primacy within this 'cradle of the ancient Sinhalese people', then Shiva's landing at Trincomalee is relegated to the unreality of 'legend'. And, further, the arrival of Tamil civilization and culture does no more than 'saturate' a pre-existent Sinhala and Buddhist polity; itself a variation on the hydraulic metaphors so often used to couple immigration with geographical imaginaries of invasion.

My intention here is not to accuse. Indeed, none of this architectural history writing is surprising given the Sinhala-Buddhist historiographical formation that emerged from nineteenth-century orientalist translations of the *Mahavamsa* and subsequent colonial archaeological praxis (see Chapter 3). This was also the same form of history writing that was consolidated aesthetically through the '43 Group's modernism (see Chapter 5). However, when texts of 'Culture' like this enter the public domain, they can rarely dispossess themselves of the social and political context in which they were forged. As Said has famously put it, 'check[ing] your politics at the door before you enter' (Said 1993: xiv) is simply impossible. Both architecturally and environmentally, the point to stress is that through these texts this rooting of the Sinhala ethnos primordially *in* island space, whilst routing Tamil, Muslim, and European otherness through invasion and arrival, comes to pervade the very fabric of an ordinary Sri Lankan architectural vernacular. In other words, the *idea* of a Sri Lankan vernacular is firmly textualized, historicized, and anchored as Sinhala and Buddhist in ways that today have become strikingly consistent in a by now abundant extra-architectural style literature.

David Robson's books (2002; 2007; 2009), the 'White Book' (Brace Taylor 1986), Minnette de Silva's book (1998), Anura Ratnavibhushana's book (2009), as well as a number of other style books, all similarly participate in such historiographical narrations of Sri Lanka's tropical modern architecture. Cultural texts, like this host of dossiers on architectural heritage and modernity, do not stand outside the meaning of tropical modern built space and its environmental aesthetics. They inevitably shape the cultural logic of its materialities and aesthetic fields in the present, naturalizing the architectural vernacular that is recuperated through modernism as Sinhala and Buddhist in persuasive ways. Aesthetically, architecture depends on such representational economies, which like too many words over-determines meaning, inscribing political value by dint of the powerful combinations it authorizes (Rancière 2007: 33–67). These texts make architecture mean in particular – that is to say, Sinhala-Buddhist historiographical – ways.

The Conditions of Hospitality

Guests who are able to rent the expensive suites at Geoffrey Bawa's Lighthouse Hotel in Galle, his Bentota Beach house, or even a room at Lunuganga, will find that their rooms come equipped with one of these style books. Whether or not they choose to read or leaf through them, the placing of the books within material tropical modern built space suggests an active over-determination of the meaning of that space in all the ways sketched above. There is little doubt that tropical modern architecture is enticing. Its inside/out aesthetics are seductive, comfortable, and tranquil in the most hospitable of ways, and as a consequence the architecture enjoys a sizeable market in the hospitality industry. But in an important sense, and as I have been stressing throughout this chapter, such buildings are rarely untouched by the vagaries of their own representational fields. If placing style books within guest rooms is just one tangible example of how the style literature is consciously mobilized in ways that, knowingly or not, shape the meanings of tropical modern built space, it is one that hints at a tendency of the architecture itself to participate in a broader hospitality imperative which is as common in houses and government commissions as it is in hotels.

In a narrow sense, we can suggest that the books placed in the hotel rooms instruct guests on how to make sense of their experience. In a broader sense, the books stand for the over-determination of such built space: quite literally, they are indicative of the ways that such texts cannot stand outside the material built spaces they reference. Through such textual mobilizations, tropical modern built space therefore also has little chance of standing outside a hospitality narrative that asserts the primacy of a sovereign host, whose right to be the host is legitimated by its vertical *rooting* in a Sinhala-Buddhist historicization of tradition, the vernacular, and importantly the environmental resonances of the built space itself. These are the architecture's conditions of hospitality that work in a kind of double imperative (see Derrida and Dufourmantelle 2000). They historically condition a Sinhala-Buddhist meaning of the aesthetic domains guests are entreated to enjoy in and through hospitality architecture and its environmental resonances, and in doing so they simultaneously configure a guest's relationship of sameness or difference to this host space. Ultimately, this is a spatial relationship of conditional hospitality. Built space itself hosts through the logic of the architectural over-determinations thus far explored in this chapter.

This kind of tension has also been visible through the previous chapters in this section, not always in 'extra-architectural' ways. Minnette de Silva's recuperation of a quite ethnically and historically particular sense of a Sinhala vernacular to-be-recovered (Chapter 5), for example, Geoffrey Bawa's composition and narrativization of the view over Cinnamon Hill at Lunuganga (Chapter 5), as well as his state commissions during President Jayawardena's political fashioning of the *dharmishta* society (Chapter 5), and the pervasive cultural logic narrated by various residents of contemporary tropical modern space (Chapter 6). All rely on a certain kind of anchoring of geographical imagination and experience within a sacred modernity that finds its historical lineage in Buddhist aesthetics and Sinhala ethnicity. And in similar kinds of ways these conditions of hospitality have been common to the ongoing management and protection of Ruhuna National Park's nature and landscape, which as Part I showed has also been historiographically inscribed. Sri Lankan nature, in other words, regularly participates in such conditions of hospitality that seem to instantiate a cosmopolitan Sinhala-Buddhist nationalism.

Politically, what is at play with the over-determination of these aesthetic domains is a slippery relationship between the particular and the universal. By universal here I refer specifically to the idea of 'the national', that is to say the political articulation of a geographical unit of universal comparability: the nation state. By particular, on the other hand, I refer simply to the content of that national. In these terms, the particularities of an explicitly and self-consciously 'post-colonial' national by definition claim universality for themselves (see Jeganathan 2009: 55). This is to stress how the particular is made to slide over the universal, replacing modes of universal thought and categorization ushered in through colonial modernity. This is precisely how spatializations of alternative kinds of ordinariness and modernity are instantiated as new, post-enlightenment distributions of the sensible. Understandings and experiences of modern translations of a Buddhist aesthetics rooted in an indigenous Sinhala tradition – experiences, that is, that cannot be named by the enlightenment's sacred/secular binary, nor by the nature/culture binary – constitute the new taken-for-granteds of a national environmental tradition. This process can rightly be seen as the replacement of one particular with another, the colonial with the anti-colonial (or, at least, self-consciously 'post-colonial') in the place of the universal, so to speak. In terms of Sri Lanka's contemporary politics of difference, this is also what constitutes an 'episte-mological orientation to the world' (Jeganathan 2009: 55) that places tropical modern built space and its environmental aesthetics within the domain of politics.

At stake here is not just the way that tropical modern architecture's hospitality narrative makes room for difference; allowing the non-Sinhala, non-Buddhist, to experience and partake in its sacred modern aesthetic domains. Rather, at stake are the ways that the sovereign historiographical assumptions written into tropical modern built space (architecturally or extra-architecturally) help create the very conditions wherein non-Sinhala otherness emerges *as* difference in relation to a Sinhala subjectivity that at the same time can thereby emerge *as* host. In Derrida's own excavation of the hospitality narrative, it is precisely this dependent relationship between host and guest that sees the emergence of host *as* host, and guest *as* guest: 'Strange logic, but so enlightening for us, that of an impatient master awaiting his guest as liberator' (Derrida 2000: 123). The arrival of the guest, of otherness, liberates the host *to be* a sovereign host, in charge and in command of the space on which this relationship is calculated and performed (also see Barnett 2005; Dikeç 2002). Derrida's concerns were, of course, to explore the philosophical contradictions embedded within an apparently familiar and responsible Western concept like hospitality. However, in ways that are useful for this particular intervention into the environmental aesthetic consti-tution of the political, he also hints at the importance of aesthetic practice in hospitality's double and contradictory imperative, particularly when he implicates language's vital role:

> In the broad sense, the language in which the foreigner is addressed or in which he is heard, if he is, is the ensemble of culture, it is the values, the norms, the meanings that inhabit the language. Speaking the same language is not only a linguistic operation. It's a matter of *ethos* generally. (Derrida 2000: 133)

In this very sense, then, the aesthetically Buddhist distributions of the sensible that tropical modern built space curates – including those accepted historiographical narrativizations of a Sri Lankan architectural vernacular and heritage *as* principally Sinhala – partake in the production and emergence of an ethnicized identity politics in the Sri Lankan context. These are the effects of the particular sliding over the universal, of Sri Lankan modern architecture becoming idiomatically and aesthetically Sinhala.

In 1991, just a year after its publication, David Robson wrote a short review of the *Lunuganga* book (Bawa, Bon, and Sansoni 1990). The favourable review published in Sri Lanka's *Observer* newspaper was a fitting testament to a beautifully crafted text. For my purposes, however, one line towards the end of the review stands out. Describing Bawa's use of Lunuganga, the estate, Robson writes how:

> Here he has held court, drawing together a circle of painters, designers and architects and plotting with them to write a new chapter in the history of *Sinhalese* art and architecture. (Robson 1991, pag. not known; my emphasis)

If the sentence is familiar, it is because word for word it prefigures a sentence penned in the chapter on Lunuganga in his book *Geoffrey Bawa: The Complete Works* (Robson 2002: 238); a sentence that I have also included as part of a quote early in Chapter 5:

> Here he held court, drawing together a circle of painters, designers and architects and plotting with them to write new chapters in the history of *Sri Lankan* art and architecture. (Robson 2002: 238 quoted above, Chapter 5; my emphasis)

Nearly. Because, of course, readers will note that in Robson's 2002 version, 'Sinhalese' has been substituted for 'Sri Lankan'. Robson's reuse of his own writing is certainly not uncommon within academic labour (I include myself here). Moreover, I use this as an example of the subtle, often barely noticeable ways that the particular slides over the universal in tropical modern architecture's semantic fields. Here, 'Sinhala' ethnicity and the 'Sri Lankan' national are locked, interchangeable, problematically entwined in ways that first create, then crowd, otherness within the space of the postcolonial national. In such ways does tropical modern architecture participate in a banal spatial politics of everyday life in Sri Lanka.

But, in concluding this section, we can also look more optimistically on Robson's entanglement of the particular within the universal. After all, in the eleven years between these two publications he chooses to substitute 'Sinhalese' with 'Sri Lankan'. Though we can read this as entanglement, a sliding of the particular over the universal, it may also be interpreted as a sliding of the universal over the particular, the 'Sri Lankan' over the 'Sinhalese', not the other way around. In other words, the editing process has arguably seen a democratic opening of the aesthetic and artistic domains with which Robson inscribes Lunuganga as tropical modern built space. Not a closure. If, as I have argued in Chapter 5, tropical modern space is implicated in the constitution of subjectivities and identities, then this opening suggests the possibilities of progressive reconstellations and recalculations of tropical modern architecture's hospitality narratives to-come. Aesthetically, as I want to suggest in the conclusion to this part of the book, despite the over-determinations covered in this chapter there is much purchase in this kind of optimistic emphasis on iteration, becoming differently, and futurity, as they might be thought through the politics of Sri Lankan nature. Indeed, the engagements with existent aesthetic and spatial constitutions of the political in the context of Sri Lankan nature to which this book has committed, aims precisely at making space for such critical openings.

Conclusion: Aesthetics as Openings

> What remains to be explored further is the role of the relational within aesthetic experience. In contrast to focussing on how an autonomous object emanates the very elements that lead to the transcendent experience of a viewing subject, how we might, for example, expand on … work on artists who engage dialogically with a community, who foster an experience that leads to the radiation, touch, conversion of an aesthetic's distributive value – an attentive looking – into the caring for the other? (Min 2009: 33–34)

To stress that human engagement with the natural environment can be considered *as* aesthetic is not just to gesture towards realms of experience, or distributions of the sensible, that transcend the nature/culture binary. It is also to take the arrangement and choreography of those environmental experiences seriously, in the knowledge that aesthetics might be critically regarded as incomplete environmental encounters in the most hopeful of ways. As Sussette Min suggests in the epithet to this conclusion, aesthetic experience generally can be thought as encounters full with the potential to progressively remake the meanings of objects encountered. Such a disposition to the environment as aesthetics holds forth the potential to enlarge the space of politics that Sri Lankan nature provides; to remake nature as space of critical and political opening through encounter.

Paradise (Figure 7.2) was a temporary installation by the Sri Lankan Tamil artist Thamotharampillai Shanaathanan, produced during an artists' retreat at *Lunuganga* as part of a workshop in 2003. The striking environmental installation comprised a large oversized bed placed centrally on Cinnamon Hill, right in the middle ground of Geoffrey Bawa's favourite view that Chapter 5 focussed on in depth. Its title, *Paradise*, accentuates the sense of comfort, depth of feeling, and seduction that the architect has choreographed to inhere in this space. In fact, *Paradise* seems to echo in some sense the sentiments expressed by the delivery driver that Geoffrey Bawa was so keen to quote in the closing section of the book *Lunuganga*: 'but this is a very blessed place' (in Bawa, Bon, and Sansoni 1990: 219; also see Chapter 5, above).

Shanaathanan produced *Paradise* during a two-week international artist's workshop organized by the contemporary Sri Lankan art collective, *theertha*, with which Shanaathanan has been a close collaborator since its inception in 2000. The collective stresses as one of its core objectives the challenge of exploring 'the possibilities of exchanging ideas and knowledge across ethnic, regional and artistic borders, in the context of contemporary critical art practice in Sri Lanka' (theertha 2009). As a collective it emerged from, and continues to support, the Sri Lankan art movement popularly known as the 90s trend. The 90s trend can be seen as a response to the '43 Group, in so far as part of their work's élan has been to mount what one of its proponents, Jagath Weerasinghe, has stressed is 'a major theoretical assault on almost all the established ideas of art-making in Sri Lanka' (Weerasinghe 2005: 183).

Figure 7.2 *Paradise*, a temporary installation at Lunuganga by
Thamotharampillai Shanaathanan, 2003 (Source: Anoli Perera and Sasanka
Perera, reproduced with permission of the artist).

The work has been characterized by critical intervention. And, as such, it is
forthrightly an issue-driven art provocatively forged by, as Weerasinghe puts
it, 'a group of people living with memories of violence, dispossession and
despair, on the one hand, and, on the other, as the casualties of the alluringly
strange beauty and evasive nature of urban culture' (ibid.).

Paradise is, of course, not an urban piece as such. In the context of this
book, however, I use it because it raises an important critical question over
Lunuganga's own 'alluringly strange' environmental beauty, and specifically,
as I want to suggest, of the sacred modernity woven into Geoffrey Bawa's view
over Cinnamon Hill. The thing about Shanaathanan's *Paradise* is that beneath its
sumptuous and seductive red velvet facade are the bristlingly hard surfaces of
military sandbacks. In other words, it is made from the very same material as
those shot proof staples of Sri Lanka's once nationwide military checkpoints,
where citizens' identities are rendered transparent to the hegemonic gaze of
the state. Not only is it hard to the touch, and therefore hardly seductive, it is
also a material reminder of the military power the state has deployed in order
to secure its ethnicizing hegemony. *Paradise* is an aesthetic illusion of sorts,
and in this very sense speaks to what I have been suggesting through this part
of the book is tropical modernity's aesthetic seduction; a seduction that in
fact hides a much more uneasy discomfort. We can read this discomfort both

in terms of the classed exclusions that Lunuganga undeniably instantiates, but also and in the context of my arguments, given the artist Shanaathanan's own biography we can read this discomfort in terms of the ethnicized politics and conditions of hospitality embedded within the estate's aesthetic composition.

Thamothampillai Shanaathanan was born in Jaffna, where he now teaches Fine Art at the University of Jaffna. Though he trained at the College of Art, University of Delhi, he was denied entrance to Colombo's Institute of Aesthetic Studies at the University of Kelaniya because instruction there was in Sinhala only, not his native tongue, Tamil (Jeganathan 2004: 197–98). His access to Sri Lanka's art spaces has been a journey through such commonplace marginalizations and dispossessions (see, for example, Shanaathanan 2011), and *Paradise* stands as one more intervention into the deceptively seductive and ordinary mechanics that marginalize non-Sinhala otherness in Sri Lanka. In the context of this book's intervention around the spatial politics of Sri Lankan environment and nature, from Ruhuna National Park through modern, environmental architecture, *Paradise* highlights the political exclusions of Sri Lankan nature's 'alluringly strange beauty' (Weerasinghe 2005: 183). Like other work that emerged from Sri Lanka's 90s art movement, the installation can in fact be read as the articulation of desire for a liberation of sorts:

> first, from a tradition which was signified as 'genuinely Sri Lankan' within the anti-colonial and nation-building projects of the early and mid-20th century; and second, from the confusing belief of art as 'self' or the 'soul's' expression, where 'self' or 'soul' is defined as an apolitical existence. (Weerasinghe 2005: 184)

In this sense, *Paradise*'s intervention is its very intervention. By this, I mean that its critical purchase is precisely that it encourages us to think hard, perhaps to think differently, about the ways that Lunuganga means. It encourages modes of 'attentive looking' that as Susette Min urges in the epithet to this conclusion open a critical space *for* politics. In this very sense it opens tropical modernity to the potential of aesthetic reconstellations in the light of the knowledge that the work of architecture, just like the work of art, is not apolitical. *Paradise* urges us to consider the work involved in fashioning an environmental aesthetics more comfortable within tropical modern architecture all the way back, so to speak. That is to say, going forward in a post-war context, how can the naturalizations and relationships to nature that are promulgated by Sri Lanka's tropical modern architecture be aesthetically hospitable in more ethnically inclusive and less identitarian ways? Perhaps part of the answer here is to see Shanaathanan's intervention when we see and experience tropical modernism itself (Jeganathan 2004: 200); or, to put this differently, to allow such critical aesthetic openings to proliferate the architecture as a matter of course, as a matter for the fashioning of new more critical ordinaries in the future.

To be clear, this critical environmental and aesthetic work is not in any sense antithetical to, or a betrayal of, an architectural genre whose very foundations are built upon the suturing of this and that. Indeed, such interrogations are precisely what might enable architects themselves to move creatively forward without having to bear the burden of building the emblematically and allegorically 'Sri Lankan' in idiomatically restrictive ways. Such an approach, as Vicky Bell suggests, 'instead of attempting to determine what we should do on the basis of what we essentially are, attempts, by analyzing what we have been constituted to be, to ask what we might become' (Bell 1999: 123). It is to reject environment and nature as essential and unchangeable, but instead embrace the potential for their critical reconstellation.

Conclusion:
Sri Lankan Nature as Problem Space

Not long ago, I boarded a Sri Lankan Airlines flight at Katunayake International Airport in Colombo, bound for London Heathrow. I had been on a short visit from the UK, one of the aims of which was to discuss draft sections of this book with colleagues and friends in Colombo. The politics of Sri Lanka's nature was very much on my mind. It was the front cover of the Sri Lankan Airlines in-flight magazine, *Serendib*, that first caught my attention: a high-resolution photograph of a wild leopard in Ruhuna National Park drinking from a water pool. Beneath was a list of features inside the magazine, which, in what seemed a striking and fortuitous coincidence, read like a partial reflection of the contents of this manuscript. As well as a feature on leopard spotting in Ruhuna, there was an article on Geoffrey Bawa's garden retreat Lunuganga, another on tropical modern architecture, as well as a feature on Sri Lanka's network of national nature reserves. There were more nature pieces as well, including a feature on the wildlife photographer Chitral Jayatileke, and a guide to Blue Whale watching in Sri Lanka.

I should not have been surprised by *Serendib*'s contents. As I stressed in the introduction to this book, nature is something of on obsession in Sri Lanka. Like most in-flight magazines of national air carriers, the magazine seems to take as one its aims the promotion of Sri Lanka to tourists and travellers alike. Sri Lanka's wildlife, nature, and its tropical environmental aesthetics – as the Editorial to that issue put it, the 'harmony that exists in [its] nature' (Peaple 2009: 4) – are some of the country's most marketable and alluring assets. And accordingly Sri Lanka makes strong claims about the history of its natural assets and the harmonizing aesthetics they afford. For example, the title of the feature in *Serendib* on the country's network of nature reserves asks, with some rhetorical panache: 'Sri Lanka's Wildlife Parks: Were these the world's first wildlife reserves?' In answer to this question, the piece begins with a familiar legend in Sri Lankan wildlife and conservation discourse;

one that serves historiographically and ethnically to locate the origins of a national obsession with nature, and as a result invest the history of Sri Lanka's modern environment and wildlife conservation praxis with the ethnicized concepts and presuppositions of a political present (Guha 1997: 3). It stresses in unequivocal terms how:

> Buddhism was brought to Sri Lanka in 306 BC when the missionary monk Arahat Mahinda was sent by Indian Emperor Asoka to convey the Buddha's message to his Sri Lankan counterpart, King Devanampiya Tissa.
>
> On arriving in the capital city of Lanka, the monk came upon the king hunting deer in the royal hunting preserve. Stopping the king in his tracks, he preached the message of the Buddha – which among other concepts, advocates the sanctity of all living beings. The monk also informed the king that all mammals, birds, and other creatures should enjoy the same right as his people to live in the land. (Wijesinha 2009: 48)

This book has been an exploration of the political effects of these kinds of Buddhist realist and historical claims as they are made aesthetically manifest in Sri Lankan nature and the environment. I have shown how in the context of a pervasive Sinhala-Buddhist hegemony in contemporary Sri Lanka, such historiographical claims do have definite affective capacities as they are spun through the fabric and praxis of everyday life and space.

To be sure, Ruhuna National Park and tropical modern architecture do not exhaust the sites through which Sri Lankan nature and its resonances are made present for human consumption and experience. In this sense, this book is a signpost for further work on the spatial politics of other sites of Sri Lankan nature. The two parts that do comprise this book present an inevitably partial exploration of the ethnicizing spatial politics of Sri Lankan nature. However, taken together, park and architecture offer two sections of what I suggest is a continuous thread through an aesthetic and spatial domain whose political affects are located in the realities that landscape and biodiversity experiences, as well as environmental resonances and tropicalities, are commonly thought to name: those aesthetic and spatial domains I have called Sri Lanka's sacred modernity.

The book has shown how, in different ways, through both park and architecture, an environmental aesthetics is made present. I have argued that in and through these environmental aesthetics a commonly accepted sense of the reality of historical and non-secular narratives of national origin is instantiated, the likes of which also find voice in the *Serendib* article referred to above. To make this argument is to point towards a spatialized hegemony that masquerades as the innocently apolitical and pre-ontological fabric of everyday life in Sri Lanka: the natural world. In teasing out this hegemony, my argument has not simply been that metaphysically Buddhist and historically Sinhala signatures are inscribed in Sri Lanka's pre-existent landscape and environment. Rather, by mobilizing the register of aesthetics to describe the political work of the natural environment, and particularly Jacques Rancière's notion of the distribution of the sensible, my argument has been that the very fabric of space itself is produced in its completeness as Sinhala and Buddhist, all the way back. It is, I suggest, the production of space as a totality – a distribution of the sensible – *through* Sri Lanka's obsession with a particular kind of Sinhala and Buddhist environmental aesthetics that constitutes a political terrain that does the work of hegemony. In this sense, Rancière's phrase 'the distribution of the sensible' is appropriate. In its original French iteration, 'le partage du sensible', the verb 'partage' suggests at one and the same time something shared, common, and consistent that is nevertheless also partitioned, separated, and divided into different constituent parts. That is why in the context of Sri Lankan nature and environment sites as diverse as park and architecture are yoked together in this book. At one and the same time, they are very different sites that together articulate a common structure of feeling.

A large part of this work has concerned a historical excavation of sorts: not to unearth a 'history' itself, but an excavation of the history writing that has become manifest in that common domain of Sri Lanka's natural landscapes and environments. As the chapters have argued, a particular kind of historical refrain is deeply implicated in the production of the spaces through which Sri Lankan nature is so often made present for human consumption. Even in secular and scientific spaces of wildlife conservation and biodiversity, Buddhist myths of origin, primacy, and rationality have gained strong footholds; they have become naturalized. If this historically and culturally locates wildlife conservation more generally, as I have shown, Ruhuna National Park's popular histories are more firmly pulled into the ethnicizing orbit of a cyclical history of Sinhala sovereignty, Tamil invasion, and Sinhala reconquest. Aesthetically, tropical modern architecture's deployment and narrativization of a Sri Lankan vernacular that is congruent with the Sinhala arts and crafts movement is what enables the same hegemonic historical refrain within Sri Lankan modernism. My argument through this book has been that understanding how this history writing becomes manifest in sites of nature and their environ-mental resonances – that is, how this history makes itself palpably present *as* a distribution of the sensible, an a priori spatialization – is a step towards understanding how the coordinates of a common-sense political reality that conceives Sri Lanka as a naturally/historically Sinhala and Buddhist nation are achieved. As I have shown, it is to understand how colonial and anti-colonial historiography make sense of the material present, as well as how their historical refrains make the spatial present seem like so much common sense.

My focus on aesthetics is not just a means of bringing into representation the non-binary formations that the concepts 'nature' and 'religion' cannot quite name. The focus on the aesthetic dimensions of environment also opens ways of thinking about nature as an ethnicizing process. I choose the word 'ethnicizing' carefully here so as not to reinstantiate the actuality or authenticity of spurious and essential ethnic groupings in the Sri Lankan context. Whilst the book has by necessity worked through the reality of Sri

Lanka's heavily ethnicized political present, seeking particularly to work through the cultural logic of the Sinhala ethnic grouping that over-determines understandings of contemporary Sri Lankan society, it has also committed to elucidating ethnic grouping itself as a product of colonial historiography and anti-colonial, or self-consciously 'post-colonial', group fashioning. Sri Lankan nature is one more spatial and representational mechanism through which the common-sense logic of ethnic grouping is cemented, or put to work. That is precisely why connections, or for that matter disconnections, with nature's aesthetic domains become *ethnicizing processes*. The reality of Sri Lankan nature as it is experienced helps cement the divisive political realities of ethnic and religious grouping in the Sri Lankan context. To stress this is not to reify ethnic logic itself, but instead to understand ethnicity as a contingent event and relational process in which an aesthetics of Sri Lankan nature is heavily implicated. Nature and environment themselves become key to understanding what Rogers Bruebaker describes as the 'tacit, taken-for-granted background knowledge, embodied in persons and embedded in institutionalized routines and practices, through which people recognize and experience objects, places, persons, actions, or situations as ethnically, racially, or nationally marked or meaningful' (Bruebaker 2006: 17).

It is worth re-emphasizing in closing that Sri Lankan nature is, and has always been, accommodating. Sites of nature and environment do not exclude in explicit terms. Rather, and on the contrary, park and architecture particularly are actually very accommodating spaces. That is to say, they are sites in and through which diversity is encouraged. For example, even during Ruhuna National Park's years of closure due to LTTE presence, the state worked to secure the landscape for the use of all its citizenry (Chapter 4). Similarly, as we have seen, tropical modern architecture's main proponents make claims that the style learns from all of Sri Lanka history (Chapter 5). If Sri Lankan nature is accommodating, however, what this book has shown are the tolerant parameters through which it accommodates. The environmental structures of feeling I have evoked variously naturalize Sinhala history and Buddhist aesthetics. In doing so, the primacy of the Sinhala host is empowered to tolerate a Tamil or Muslim presence within Sri Lanka's environmental terrain. In other words, it is precisely the cosmopolitan claims surrounding Sri Lankan environment and nature that inscribe within its topographies a particular kind of ethnicized sovereignty. In effect, then, this book has delineated environmental mechanisms that operate a kind of governmentalization of power that simultaneously depoliticizes and organizes the social (Brown 2006: 13). It has sketched the contours of a tolerant nature that in the Sri Lankan context 'does not simply address identity but abets in its production; it also abets in the conflation of culture with ethnicity or race' (ibid.: 14). *Sacred Modernity* has sought to excavate a buried order of politics: one that masquerades as ontological naturalness.

More work is inevitably required on the formation of ethnicized non-Sinhala communities in the light of the arguments this book sets forth. If I have paid particular attention to the hegemony of Sri Lankan nature and its association with Sinhala ethnicity and group formation, questions remain concerning how Tamil and Muslim ethnic groupings are not only created in the face of that Sinhala and Buddhist environmental aesthetics, but also how such ethnicized groups and individuals subsequently navigate within and relationally negotiate those environmental aesthetics at the affective and symbolic levels. In other words, if Sri Lankan nature tolerates, how does it feel to so be tolerated?

It has not been my intention in this book to address that question directly, neither has it been within the scope of the critical interventions and research I have set out here. However, by tracing the political contours of space that previously have escaped the attention of critical (or indeed uncritical) political discourse, I hope to have delineated a new kind of 'problem space' (Scott 1999: 3–20; 2004: 2–6) in the hope of working towards a geographical understanding of the continued ethnicization of Sri Lankan politics and society. For even though civil war is now over, militarily crushed as the LTTE have been, now more than ever Sri Lankan society continues to be unequally stratified and severed along the lines of ethnicity and religion. Ethnicized thought and communitarianism are rife in post-conflict Sri Lanka, and new understandings of the political work of ordinary social gestations are urgently required. This book has attempted to open a space for critical thinking around how Sri Lanka's ethnicized common sense is dynamically produced through the fabric of everyday, ordinary, and apparently pre-political natural environments and landscapes. Part of that challenge, as I have shown, has been to bring those ethnicizing environmental aesthetics into representation on terms true to the singularity of their difference, such that an aesthetic hegemony, its politics, and its filling in of the social order, can be acknowledged and critically engaged rather than translated out of recognition by the unthinking Eurocentrism of words like 'nature' and 'religion'. Having traced the chalk outlines of this new problem space, let us hope that at the very least the depoliticization of Sri Lanka's obsession with nature desists.

Bibliography

Abeysekara, A., 2002, *Colors of the Robe: Religion, Identity and Difference* (Columbia, SC: University of South Carolina Press).

Abeywardene, R., and S. Bulathsinhala, 1995, 'Terrorists Infiltrate Yala', *The Island* (Sri Lankan newspaper), 14 November 1995, Associated Newspapers of Ceylon Ltd archive, Lake House, Colombo, Sri Lanka, from clippings file on 'Yala'.

Abeywardene, R., and P. Sahabandu, 1996, 'The Tiger Stalks Yala', *The Island* (Sri Lankan newspaper), 21 July 1996, Associated Newspapers of Ceylon Ltd archive, Lake House, Colombo, Sri Lanka, from clippings file on 'Yala'.

Abu El-Haj, N., 1998, 'Translating Truths: Nationalism, Archaeological Practice and the Remaking of Past and Present in Contemporary Jerusalem', *American Ethnologist* 25(2): 166–88.

—, 2001, *Facts on the Ground: Archaeological Practice and Territorial Self-fashioning in Israeli Society* (Chicago and London: University of Chicago Press).

Adithiya, L. A., 1981, 'Fauna of the Mahavamsa', *Ancient Ceylon*, 4: 1–49.

Adorno, T., 2004 [1997] (trans. by Robert Hullot-Kentor) *Aesthetic Theory* (London and New York: Continuum).

Adorno, T., and M. Horkheimer, 1997 [1972] (trans. by John Cumming) *Dialectic of Enlightenment* (London and New York: Verso).

Agnew, J., 2006, 'Religion and Geopolitics', *Geopolitics*, 11: 183–91.

Amarasekera, P., 1998, 'Reviving Yala's Virile Charm', *Daily News* (Sri Lankan newspaper), 12 December 1998, Associated Newspapers of Ceylon Ltd archive, Lake House, Colombo, Sri Lanka, from clippings file on 'Yala'.

Anderson, P., 1984, 'Modernity and Revolution', *New Left Review*, 144: 96–113.

Angell, M., 1998, 'Understanding the Aryan Theory', in M. Tiruchelvam and C. S. Datthathreya (eds.), *Culture and Politics of Identity in Sri Lanka* (Colombo: International Centre for Ethnic Studies), 41–72.

Anon., 1874, 'Administration Report for the Southern Province, 1874', The National Archives, London, United Kingdom CO57/63.

Anon., 1943, 'Minutes of the 50th Annual General Meeting of the Ceylon Game and Fauna Protection Society, held at the Galle Face Hotel', *Loris*, 3(4): 130.

Appadurai, A (ed.), 1988, *The Social Life of Things: Commodities in Cultural Perspective* (Cambridge University Press).

—, 1996, *Modernity at Large: Cultural Dimensions of Globalization* (Minneapolis, Minn. and London: University of Minnesota Press).

—, 2000, 'Grassroots Globalization and the Research Imagination', *Public Culture*, 12(1): 1–19.

ArchNet 'Geoffrey Bawa' <http://archnet.org/library/parties/one-party.jsp?party_id=73> (accessed 17 April 2012).

ArchNet 'Osmund and Ena de Silva house [by Geoffrey Bawa]' <http://archnet.org/library/sites/one-site.jsp?site_id=7283> (accessed 17 April 2012).

Asad, T., 2003, *Formations of the Secular: Christianity, Islam and Modernity* (Stanford, Calif.: Stanford University Press).

Baker, S., 1882, *The Rifle and Hound of Ceylon* (London: Longmans Green and Co.).

Barnes, T., and J. Duncan (eds.), 1992, *Writing Worlds: Discourse, Text and Metaphor in the Representation of Landscape* (London and New York: Routledge).

Barnett, C., 2005, 'Ways of Relating: Hospitality and the Acknowledgement of Otherness', *Progress in Human Geography*, 29: 1–17.

Barrell, J., 1983, *The Dark Side of the Landscape: The Rural Poor in English Painting, 1730–1840* (Cambridge University Press).

Barrow, I. J., 2008, *Surveying and Mapping in Colonial Sri Lanka* (Colombo: Vijitha Yapa Publications).

Batchelor, M., 1992, 'Even the Stones Smile: Selections from the Scriptures', in M. Batchelor and K. Brown (eds.), *Buddhism and Ecology* (Delhi: Motilal Banarsidass), 2–18.

Bawa, G., 1968, 'A Way of Building', *Times of Ceylon Annual*, Colombo.

Bawa, G., C. Bon, and D. Sansoni, 1990, *Lunuganga* (Singapore: Times Editions).

Bell, V., 1999, *Feminist Imagination* (London and New York: Sage).

Bender, B. (ed.), 1993, *Landscape: Politics and Perspectives* (Providence, RI and Oxford: Berg).

Bennett, Jane, 2001, *The Enchantment of Modern Life: Attachments, Crossings, and Ethics* (Princeton, NJ: Princeton University Press).

Berleant, A., 1992, *The Aesthetics of Environment* (Philadelphia: Temple University Press).

Berman, M., 1983, *All that is Solid Melts into Air: The Experience of Modernity* (London and New York: Verso).

Bhabha, H. (ed.), 1990, *Nation and Narration* (London and New York: Routledge).

Bibile, R., 1997, 'Kumana and the Pilgrim Path', *Loris*, 21 (3): 87–94.

Bingham, N., 2006, 'Bees, Butterflies, and Bacteria: Biotechnology and the Politics of Nonhuman Friendship', *Environment and Planning A*, 38: 483–98.

Birla, R., 2010, 'Postcolonial Studies: Now that's History', in R. C. Morris (ed.), *Can the Subaltern Speak? Reflections on the History of an Idea* (New York: Columbia University Press), 87–99.

Bozdogan, S., 2001, *Modernism and Nation-building: Turkish Architectural Culture in the Early Republic* (Seattle, Wash. and London: University of Washington Press).

Brace Taylor, B., 1986, *Geoffrey Bawa* (Singapore: Concept Media).

Brady, E., 2003, *Aesthetics of the Natural Environment* (Edinburgh University Press).

Braun, B., 2008, 'Environmental Issues: Inventive Life', *Progress in Human Geography*, 32 (5): 667–79.

Brayne, C. V., et al., 1934, 'Report of the Fauna and Flora Protection Committee, by C. V. Brayne (Chairman), W. E. Wait, H. L. Dowbiggin, A. B. Lushington, Lucius

Nicholls, A. J. Wickwar, August 20th, 1934', The National Archive, London, United Kingdom CO57/243.

Brennan, T., 1997, *At Home in the World: Cosmopolitanism Now* (Cambridge, Mass.: Harvard University Press).

—, 2003, 'Cosmopolitanism and Internationalism', in D. Archibugi (ed.), *Debating Cosmopolitics* (London and New York: Verso), 40–50.

Brown, W., 2006, *Regulating Aversion: Tolerance in the Age of Identity and Empire* (Princeton, NJ: Princeton University Press).

Bruebaker, R., 1996, *Nationalism Reframed: Nationhood and the National Question in the New Europe* (Cambridge University Press).

—, 2006, *Ethnicity without Groups* (Cambridge, Mass.: Harvard University Press).

Bryden, I., 2004, 'There is No Outer without Inner Space: Constructing the Haveli as Home', *Cultural Geographies*, 11: 26–41.

Buczaki, S., 2000, 'All Creatures Great and Small', unknown Sri Lankan newspaper, Associated Newspapers of Ceylon Ltd Archive, Lake House, Colombo, from clippings file on 'Yala'.

Bulathsinhala, S., 1995, 'Yala Terrorists to be Flushed Out', *The Island* (Sri Lankan newspaper), 15 November 1995, Associated Newspapers of Ceylon Ltd archive, Lake House, Colombo, Sri Lanka, from clippings file on 'Yala'.

Burger, P., 1984 (trans. by Michael Shaw) *Theory of the Avant-garde* (Minneapolis, Minn. and London: University of Minnesota Press).

Cairns, S., 2007, 'The Stone Books of Orientalism', in P. Scriver and V. Prakash (eds.), *Colonial Modernities: Building, Dwelling and Architecture in British India and Ceylon* (London and New York: Routledge), 51–65.

Canclini, N. G., 1995 (trans. by Christopher L. Chiappari and Silvia L. Lopez) *Hybrid Cultures: Strategies for Entering and Leaving Modernity* (Minneapolis, Minn. and London: University of Minnesota Press).

Carroll, N., 1996, 'On Being Moved by Nature: Between Religion and Natural History', in S. Kemal and I. Gaskell (eds.), *Landscape, Natural Beauty and the Arts* (Cambridge University Press), 244–66.

Carruthers, J., 2003, 'Past and Future Landscape Ideology: The Kalahari Game Park', in W. Beinart and J. McGregor (eds.), *Social History and African Environments* (Coumbus, Ohio: Ohio University Press), 255–66.

Carter, H. F., 1925, 'Report on "Kataragama" fever: its nature, causes and control, July 20 to August 4, 1925', The National Archives, London, United Kingdom, CO57/215.

Carter, P., 1987, *The Road to Botany Bay: An Essay in Spatial History* (London and Boston: Faber and Faber).

Chakrabarty, D., 2000, *Provincializing Europe: Postcolonial Thought and Historical Difference* (Princeton, NJ: Princeton University Press).

—, 2002, *Habitations of Modernity: Essays in the Wake of Subaltern Studies* (University of Chicago Press).

Chatterjee, P., 1995, 'Alternative Histories, Alternative Nations: Nationalism and Modern Historiography in Bengal', in P. R. Schmidt and T. C. Patterson (eds.), *Making Alternative Histories: The Practice of Archaeology and History in Non-Western Settings* (Santa Fe, NM: School of American Research Press), 229–54.

—, 2004, *The Politics of the Governed: Reflections on Popular Politics in Most of the World* (New York: Columbia University Press).

Clark, N., 2005a, 'Disaster and Generosity', *Geographical Journal*, 171(4): 384–86.

—, 2005b, 'Ex-orbitant Globality', *Theory, Culture and Society*, 22(5): 165–85.

—, 2010, *Inhuman Nature: Sociable Life on a Dynamic Planet* (London: Sage).

Cohn, B., 1996, *Colonialism and its Forms of Knowledge: The British in India* (Princeton, NJ: Princeton University Press).

Connell, R., 2008, *Southern Theory: the global dynamics of knowledge in Social Science* (Allen and Unwin: Sydney).

Coomaraswamy, A., 1908, *Medieval Sinhalese Art* (London: Essex House Press).

—, 1964 [1916], *Buddha and the Gospel of Buddhism* (New York and London: Harper Torchbooks).

Coombe, G., 1955, 'A Visit to Yala National Park', *Loris*, 7(2): 76–81.

Cosgrove, D., 1993, *The Palladian Landscape: Geographical Change and its Cultural Representations in Sixteenth-century Italy* (University Park, Pa.: Penn State Press).

—, 1995, 'Habitable Earth: Wilderness, Empire and Race in America', in D. Rothenburg (ed.), *Wild Ideas* (Minneapolis, Minn. and London: University of Minnesota Press), 27–41.

—, 1996, 'Ideas and Culture: A Response to Don Mitchell', *Transaction of the Institute of British Geographers*, 21: 572–82.

—, 1998, *Social Formation and Symbolic Landscape*, 2nd edn (Madison, Wis.: University of Wisconsin Press).

—, 2008, *Geography and Vision: Seeing, Imagining and Representing the World* (London and New York: I. B. Tauris).

Cosgrove, D., and S. Daniels (eds.), 1988, *The Iconography of Landscape: Essays on the Symbolic Representation, Design and Use of Past Environments* (Cambridge University Press).

Cosgrove, D., B. Roscoe, and S. Rycroft, 1996, 'Landscape and Identity at Ladybower Reservoir and Rutland Water', *Transactions of the Institute of British Geographers*, 21: 534–51.

Cronon, W., 1995, 'Introduction: In Search of Nature', in W. Cronon (ed.), *Uncommon Ground: Toward Reinventing Nature* (London and New York: W. W. Norton and Co.), 23–68.

Cronon, W., G. Miles, and J. Gitlin (eds.), 1992, *Under an Open Sky: Rethinking America's Western Past* (London and New York: W. W. Norton and Co.).

Curry, P., 2008, 'Nature Post-nature', *New Formations*, 64: 51–64.

D'A. Vincent, F., 1883, 'Forest Administration of Ceylon, Report on the Conservation and Administration of the Crown Forests in Ceylon, by F. D'A. Vincent (Indian Forest Service), 1883', The National Archive, London, United Kingdom CO57/88.

Daily News, 1990, 'My Own Native Land. Block II, Yala National Park', *Daily News* (Sri Lankan newspaper), 3 March 1990, Associated Newspapers of Ceylon Ltd archive, Lake House, Colombo, Sri Lanka, from clippings file on 'Yala'.

Daniels, S., 1994, *Fields of Vision: Landscape Imagery and National Identity in England and the United States* (Cambridge: Polity Press).

Daniels, S., and D. Cosgrove, 1988, 'Introduction: Iconography and Landscape', in D. Cosgrove and S. Daniels (eds.), *The Iconography of Landscape: Essays on the Symbolic Representation, Design and Use of Past Environments* (Cambridge University Press), 1–8.

de Alwis, W. L. E., 1967, *Administration Report of the Acting Warden, Department of Wildlife for 1966–7* (Colombo: Department of Wildlife Conservation Records Room).

de Certeau, M., 1984 (trans. by S. Rendall) *The Practice of Everyday Life* (Berkeley, Calif., and London: University of California Press).

de Lanerole, N., 1999, *A Reign of Ten Kings: Sri Lanka – the World, 500BC–1200AD* (Colombo: Ceylon Tourist Board).

de Mel, N., 2007, *Militarizing Sri Lanka: Popular Culture, Memory and Narrative in the Armed Conflict* (London: Sage).

de Mel, N., and K. N. Ruwanpura, 2006, *Gendering the Tsunami: Women's Experiences from Sri Lanka* (Colombo: International Centre for Ethnic Studies).

de Silva, J. A., 1951, 'Administration Report of the Conservator of Forests for 1950, by J. A. de Silva Esq., September 1951', The National Archives, London, United Kingdom DO109/11.

—, 1958, 'Administration Report of the Warden, Department of Wildlife Conservation, for 1957, by J. A. de Silva Esq., September 1958', The National Archives, London, United Kingdom DO109/50.

—, 1960, 'Administration Report of the Warden, Department of Wildlife Conservation, for 1959, by J. A. de Silva Esq., August 1960', The National Archives, London, United Kingdom DO109/62.

de Silva, K. M., 1981, *A History of Sri Lanka* (New Delhi and Oxford: Oxford University Press).

de Silva, M., 1998, *The Life and Work of an Asian Woman Architect* (Colombo: Smart Media Productions).

de Silva, M., and P. K. de Silva, 2004, *The Yala Wildlife Reserves: Biodiversity and Ecology* (Colombo: WHT Publications).

de Silva, P., 1998, *Environmental Philosophy and Ethics in Buddhism* (Basingstoke: Macmillan).

Derrida, J., 2001 [1997] (trans. by Mark Dooley and Michael Hughes) *On Cosmopolitanism and Forgiveness* (London and New York: Routledge).

—, 2002 (trans. by D. Willis) 'The animal that therefore I am (more to follow)', *Critical Inquiry*, 28(2): 369–418.

—, 2003, 'And say the animal responded', in C. Wolfe (ed.), *Zoontologies: The Question of the Animal* (Minneapolis, Minn. and London: University of Minnesota Press), 121–46.

Derrida, J., and A. Dufourmantelle, 2000 (trans. by Rachel Bowlby) *Of Hospitality* (Stanford, Calif.: Stanford University Press).

DeSilvey, C., 2007, 'Salvage Memory: Constellating Material Histories on a Hardscrabble Homestead', *Cultural Geographies*, 14: 401–24

Dewsbury, J., and P. Cloke, 2009, 'Spiritual Landscapes: Existence, Permanence and Immanence', *Social and Cultural Geography*, 10(6): 695–711.

Dikeç, M., 2002, 'Pera, Peras, Poros: Longings for Spaces of Hospitality', *Theory Culture and Society*, 19(1–2): 227–47.

—, 2005, 'Spaces, Politics, and the Political', *Environment and Planning D: Society and Space*, 23: 171–88.

Dikeç, M., N. Clark, and C. Barnett, 2009, 'Extending Hospitality: Giving Space, Taking Time', *Paragraph*, 32(1): 1–14.

Disanayaka, K., 1992, 'Dusk at Yala', *The Island* (Sri Lankan newspaper), 8 August 1992, Associated Newspapers of Ceylon Ltd archive, Lake House, Colombo, Sri Lanka.

Dixon, D., 2009, 'Creating the Semi-living: On Politics, Aesthetics and the More-than-Human', *Transactions of the Institute of British Geographers*, 34: 411–25.

Domosh, M., 1988, 'The Symbolism of the Skyscraper: Case Studies of New York's First Tall Buildings', *Journal of Urba history*, 14(3): 321–45.

—, 1989, 'A Method for Interpreting Landscape: A Case Study of the New York World Building', *Area*, 21(4): 347–55.

Driver, F., and D. Gilbert (eds.), 1999, *Imperial Cities: Landscape, Display, Identity* (Manchester University Press).

Driver, F., and L. Martins (eds.), 2005, *Tropical Visions in an Age of Empire* (University of Chicago Press).

Driver, F., and B. Yeoh (eds.), 2000, 'Constructing the Tropics', *Singapore Journal of Tropical Geography*, 21(1): 1–98.

Duncan, J., 1990, *The City as Text: The Politics of Landscape Interpretation in the Kandyan Kingdom* (Cambridge University Press).

—, 2007, *In the Shadows of the Tropics: Climate, Race and Biopower in Nineteenth-century Ceylon* (Aldershot: Ashgate).

Edwards, B. H., 2009, 'Social Text', *Social Text*, 27 (3 100): 231–34.

EelamWeb, 'National Flag of Tamil Eelam' <web.archive.org/web/20040803073155/ http://www.eelamweb.com/flag/> (accessed 7 July 2004).

Epstein, Mark, 2007, *Psychotherapy Without the Self: A Buddhist Perspective* (New Haven, Conn.: Yale University Press).

Fernando, H., 1998, 'Pronounced Safe', *Sunday Times Plus* (Sri Lankan newspaper), 16 August 1998, Associated Newspapers of Ceylon Ltd archive, Lake House, Colombo, Sri Lanka, from clippings file on 'Yala'.

Fernando, S., 1996, 'Tigers Prowling around Yala', *The Island* (Sri Lankan newspaper), 17 July 1996, Associated Newspapers of Ceylon Ltd archive, Lake House, Colombo, Sri Lanka, from clippings file on 'Yala'.

Fisher, F. C., 1874, 'Papers Relating to the Working of the Game Ordinance, No. 6 of 1872, by F. C. Fisher (Assistant Government Agent of Tangalle)', The National Archives, London, United Kingdom CO57/84.

Foster, J., 2008, *'Washed with Sun': Landscape and the Making of White South Africa* (Pittsburgh, Pa.: University of Pittsburgh Press).

Foucault, M., 2007 [1978] (trans. by Graham Burchell) *Security, Territory, Population: Lectures at the College de France, 1977–78* (Basingstoke: Palgrave Macmillan).

Frampton, K., 1983, 'Towards a Critical Regionalism: Six Points for an Architecture of Resistance', in H. Foster (ed.), *The Anti-Aesthetic: Essays on Postmodern Culture* (Seattle, Wash.: Bay Press), 16–30.

Gamage, C., 1998, *Buddhism and Sensuality: As Recorded in the Therevada Canon* (Colombo: Karunaratne and Sons Ltd).

Gaonkar, D. P. (ed.), 2001, *Alternative Modernities* (Durham, NC and London: Duke University Press).

Gidwani, V., 2006, 'What's Left? Subaltern Cosmopolitanism as Politics', *Antipode*, 38: 8–21.

Godakumara, C. E., 1967, 'Administration Report of the Archaeological Commissioner for the Financial Year 1964–65, by C. E. Godakumara MA, PhD, DLit. (London)', The National Archives of Sri Lanka, Colombo.

Gokhale, B. G., 1979, 'Aesthetic Ideas in Early Buddhism', *Ancient Ceylon*, 3: 135–43.

Gold, J. R., 1997, *The Experience of Modernism: Modern Architects and the Future City, 1928–1953* (London and New York: E and FN Spon).

Green, M. J. B., 1990, *IUCN Directory of South Asian Protected Areas* (Cambridge: IUCN – The World Conservation Union).

Gregory, W. H., 1875, 'Address of His Excellency, the Right Honorable W. H. Gregory on Closing the Session of the Legislative Council, 6th January 1875', The National Archives, London, United Kingdom CO57/64.

Gregson, N., and L. Crewe, 2003, *Second-hand Cultures* (Oxford: Berg).

Guha, R., 1997, *Dominance without Hegemony: History and Power in Colonial India* (Cambridge, Mass.: Harvard University Press).

—, 1999 [1983], *Elementary Aspects of Peasant Insurgency in Colonial India* (Durham, NC and London: Duke University Press).

—, 2002, *History at the Limit of World History* (New York: Columbia University Press).

Harley, J. B., 1988, 'Maps, Knowledge and Power', in D. Cosgrove and S. Daniels (eds.), *The Iconography of Landscape: Essays on the Symbolic Representation, Design and Use of Past Environments* (Cambridge University Press), 277–312.

Herbert, W. H., 1874, '"Annual Administration Report for 1873" by T. Steele (Assistant Government Agent for Hambantota), in "Ceylon Administration Reports 1873", by William Henry Herbert, Government Printer, Ceylon, 1874', The National Archives, United Kingdom, CO57/62.

Hinchliffe, S., 2003, 'Inhabiting: Landscapes and Natures', in K. Anderson, et al. (eds.), *Handbook of Cultural Geography* (London: Sage), 207–26.

—, 2007, *Geographies of Nature: Societies, Environments, Ecologies* (London: Sage) .

Hirsch, E., and M. O'Hanlon (eds.), 1995, *The Anthropology of Landscape: Perspectives on Place and Space* (Oxford: Berg).

Holloway, J., and O. Valins, 2002, 'Editorial: Placing Religion and Spirituality in Geography', *Social and Cultural Geography*, 3(1): 5–9.

Howitt, R., and S. Suchet-Pearson, 2006, 'Rethinking the Building Blocks: Ontological Pluralism and the Idea of 'Management'', *Geografiska Annaler b*, 88(3): 323–35.

Hudson, P. J., 1936, 'Administration Report on the Hambantota District for 1935, by P. J. Hudson, Assistant Government Agent, January 31, 1936', The National Archives, London, United Kingdom CO57/246.

Huggan, G., 2008, *Interdisciplinary Measures: Literature and the Future of Postcolonial Studies* (Liverpool University Press).

Huyssen, A., 1986, *After the Great Divide: Modernism, Mass Culture, Postmodernism* (Bloomington, Ind.: Indiana University Press).

Hyndman, J., and M. de Alwis, 2004, 'Bodies, Shrines and Roads: Violence (Im)mobility and Displacement in Sri Lanka', *Gender Place and Culture*, 11(4): 535–57.

Imrie, R., 1996, *Disability and the City: International Perspectives* (London: Paul Chapman Publishing).

Island, The, 1986, 'Disturbing Signs', *The Island* (Sri Lankan newspaper), 19 August 1986, Associated Newspapers of Ceylon Ltd archive, Lake House, Colombo, Sri Lanka, from clippings file on 'Yala'.

—, 1996, 'Yala – Another Casualty?', *The Island* (Sri Lankan newspaper), precise date unknown, Associated Newspapers of Ceylon Ltd archive, Lake House, Colombo, Sri Lanka, from clippings file on 'Yala'.

Ismail, Q., 2005, *Abiding by Sri Lanka: On Peace, Place and Post-coloniality* (Minneapolis, Minn. and London: University of Minnesota Press).

Jacobs, J. M., 1996, *Edge of Empire: Postcolonialism and the City* (London and New York: Routledge).

—, 2006, 'A Geography of Big Things', *Cultural Geographies*, 13(1): 1–27.

Jameson, F., 1997, 'The Constraints of Postmodernism', in N. Leach (ed.), *Architecture: A Reader in Cultural Theory* (London and New York: Routledge), 247–55.

—, 2002, *A Singular Modernity: Essay on the Ontology of the Present* (London and New York: Verso).

Jayawardene, H. W. (ed.), 1993, *Yala National Park* (Colombo: Fauna International Trust).

Jazeel, T., 2005, ''Nature', Nationhood and the Poetics of Meaning in Ruhuna (Yala) National Park', *Cultural Geographies*, 12(2): 199–228.

—, 2006, 'Postcolonial Geographies of Privilege: Transnational Politics of Personhood and the 'Sri Lankan Women's Association in the UK'', *Transactions, Institute of British Geographers*, 31(1): 19–33.

—, 2007, 'Spectres of Tolerance: Living Together beyond Cosmopolitanism', *Cultural Geographies*, 14(4): 617–24.

—, 2009a, 'Governmentality', *Social Text*, 27 (3 100): 136–40.

—, 2009b, 'Reading the Geography of Sri Lankan Island-ness: Colonial Repetitions, Postcolonial Possibilities', *Contemporary South Asia*, 17(4): 399–414.

—, 2009c, 'Geography, Spatial Politics, and Productions of the National in Michael Ondaatje's *Anil's Ghost*, in C. Brun and T. Jazeel (eds.), *Spatialising Politics: Culture and Geography in Postcolonial Sri Lanka* (London: Sage), 122–45.

—, 2011, 'Spatializing Difference beyond Cosmopolitanism: Rethinking Planetary Futures', *Theory, Culture and Society*, 28(5): 75–97.

Jazeel, T., and C. McFarlane, 2010, 'The Limits of Responsibility: A Postcolonial Politics of Academic Knowledge Production', *Transactions, Institute of British Geographers*, 35(1): 109–24.

Jazeel, T., and K. Ruwanpura, 2009, 'Dissent: Sri Lanka's New Minority?', *Political Geography*, 28(7): 385–87.

Jeganathan, P., 1995, 'Authorizing History, Ordering Land: The Conquest of Anuradhpaura', in P. Jeganathan and Q. Ismail (eds.), *Unmaking the Nation: The Politics of Identity and History in Modern Sri Lanka* (Colombo: Social Scientist's Association), 106–36.

—, 2002, 'Walking Through Violence: 'Everyday Life' and Anthropology', in D. P. Mines and S. Lamb (eds.), *Everyday Life in South Asia* (Bloomington, Ind.: Indiana University Press), 357–65.

—, 2004, 'Disco-*very*: Anthropology, Nationalist Thought, Thamotharampillai Shanaathanan, and an Uncertain Descent into the Ordinary', in N. L. Whitehead (ed.), *Violence* (Santa Fe, NM: School of American Research Press), 185–202.

—, 2009, 'The Postnational, Inhabitation and the Work of Melancholia', *Economic and Political Weekly* (7 March), 44(10): 54–57.

Johnson, A., 2007, 'Everydayness and Subalternity', *South Atlantic Quarterly*, 106: 21–38.

Kaufman, E., 1998, ''Naturalizing the Nation': The Rise of Naturalistic Nationalism in the United States and Canada', *Comparative Studies in Society and History*, 40(4): 666–95.

Kemal, S., and I. Gaskell (eds.), 1996, *Landscape, Natural Beauty and the Arts* (Cambridge University Press).

Kemper, S., 1991, *The Presence of the Past: Chronicles, Politics and Culture in Sinhala Life* (Ithaca, NY: Cornell University Press).

King, A. J., 1984, *The Bungalow: The Production of a Global Culture* (London: Routledge and Keegan Paul).

—, 2004, *Spaces of Global Cultures: Architecture and Urban Identity* (London and New York: Routledge).

Klostermaier, Klaus, 1991, 'The Nature of Buddhism', *Asian Philosophy*, 1(1): 29–37.

Kong, L., 1990, 'Geography and Religion: Trends and Prospects', *Progress in Human Geography*, 14(3): 355–71.

Larkin, B., 2009, 'National Allegory', *Social Text*, 27 (3 100): 164–68.

Latour, B., 2005, *Reassembling the Social* (Oxford University Press).

Leatherbarrow, D., 2004, *Topographical Stories: Studies in Landscape and Architecture* (Philadelphia, Pa.: University of Pennsylvania Press).

Lees, L., 2006, 'Towards a Critical Geography of Architecture: The Case of an Ersatz Colosseum', *Ecumene*, 8(1): 51–86.

Lees, L., and R. Baxter, 2011, 'A 'Building Event' of Fear: Thinking Through the Geography of Architecture', *Social and Cultural Geographies*, 12(2): 107–22.

Lefaivre, L., and A. Tzonis, 2001, 'The Suppression and Rethinking of Regionalism and Tropicalism after 1945', in A. Tzonis, B. Stagno, and L. Lefaivre, *Tropical Architecture: Critical Regionalism in the Age of Globalization* (Chichester and New York: Wiley-Academic).

Lefebvre, H., 1991, *The Production of Space* (Oxford University Press).

—, 2002 (trans. by John Moore), *Critique of Everyday Life*, vol. 2, *Foundations for a Sociology of the Everyday* (London: Verso).

Legg, S., 2007, *Spaces of Colonialism: Delhi's Urban Governmentalities* (Oxford: Blackwell Publishing).

Lewcock, R., B. Sansoni, and L. Senanayake, 1998, *The Architecture of an Island: The Living Heritage of Sri Lanka* (Colombo: Barefoot (Pvt.) Ltd).

Lewis, 1898, 'Letter to Governor Ridgeway Sending Report by Mr. Lewis in each of Mr. Le Messurier's Allegations, 27/8/1898', The National Archives, London, United Kingdom CO54/648.

Longhurst, R., 1998, '(Re)presenting Shopping Centres and Bodies: Questions of Pregnancy', in R. Ainley (ed.), *New Frontiers of Space, Bodies and Gender* (London and New York: Routledge), 20–34.

Lorimer, J., and S. Whatmore, 2009, 'After 'the King of Beasts': Samuel Baker and the Embodied Historical Geographies of Elephant Hunting in mid-Nineteenth-century Ceylon', *Journal of Historical Geography*, 35: 668–89.

MacKenzie, J. M., 1988, *The Empire of Nature: Hunting, Conservation and British Imperialism* (Manchester University Press).

McFarlane, C., 2006, 'Crossing borders: development, learning and the north-south divide', *Third World Quarterly*, 27: 1413–1437.

McNeill, D., 2005, 'Skyscraper Geography', *Progress in Human Geography*, 29: 41–55.

Madden, F., and Darwin, J. (eds.), 1994, *The Dependent Empire, 1900–1948: Colonies, Protectorates and Mandates, Select Documents on the Constitutional History of the British Empire and Commonwealth*, vol. 7 (Westport, Conn. and London: Greenwood Press).

Marx, K., and F. Engels, 1972, 'Manifesto of the Communist Party', in R. C. Tucker (ed.), *The Marx–Engels Reader* (New York: W. W. Norton), 469–500.

Massey, D., 1994, *Space, Place and Gender* (Minneapolis, Minn. and London: University of Minnesota Press).

—, 2005, *For Space* (London: Sage).

—, 2008, 'When Theory Meets Politics', *Antipode*, 40: 492–97.

Matless, D., 1998, *Landscape and Englishness* (London: Reaktion).

Millington, E. T., 1914, 'Administration Report on the Hambantota District for 1912–13, by E. T. Millington, Assistant Government Agent Hambantota District', The National Archives, London, United Kingdom CO57/185.

Min, S., 2009, 'Aesthetics', *Social Text*, 27 (3 100): 27–34.

Mitchell, D., 2000, *Cultural Geography: A Critical Introduction* (Oxford: Blackwell Publishing).

Mitchell, W. J. T. (ed.), 2002, *Landscape and Power* (University of Chicago Press).

Morris, R. C., 2000, *In the Place of Origins: Modernity and its Mediums in Northern Thailand* (Durham, NC and London: Duke University Press).

Mufti, A., 2005. 'Global Comparativism', *Critical Inquiry*, 31: 472–89.

Nalbantoglu, G. B., and C. T. Wong (eds.), 1997, *Postcolonial Space(s)* (New York: Princeton Architectural Press).

Nandy, A., 2002, *Time Warps: Silent and Evasive Pasts in Indian Politics and Religion* (New Brunswick, NJ: Rutgers University Press).

Nash, C., 1999, 'Irish Placenames: Post-colonial Locations', *Transactions, Institute of British Geographers*, 24: 457–80.

National Atlas of Sri Lanka, 1988 (Colombo: The Survey Department).

Neumann, R., 2002, *Imposing Wilderness: Struggles over Livelihood and Nature Preservation in Africa* (Berkeley, Calif.: University of California Press).

Nicholas, C. W., 1954, 'Administration Report of the Warden, Department of Wildlife for 1953', The National Archives, London, United Kingdom DO109/27.

—, 1956, 'Administration Report of the Warden, Department of Wild Life Conservation, for 1955', The National Archives, London, United Kingdom DO109/29.

Obeyesekere, G., 1970, 'Religious Symbolism and Political Change in Sri Lanka', *Modern Ceylon Studies*, 1.

Ondaatje, M., 2000, *Anil's Ghost* (New York: Vintage).

Panwar, H. S. and W. M. R. S. Wickeramasinghe, 1997, 'Management Plan Yala Protected Area Complex [Ruhuna National Park Block I to V, Yala Strict Natural Reserve, and Kataragama, Katagamuwa and Nimalawa Sanctuaries], Plan period: 1998–2007, Vol. 1' (Colombo: Department of Wildlife Conservation Record Room).

Park, C., 1994, *Sacred Worlds: An Introduction to Geography and Religion* (London and New York: Routledge).

—, 2004, 'Religion and Geography', in J. Hinnells (ed.), *Routledge Companion to the Study of Religions* (London and New York: Routledge), 439–55.

Parnavitarna, S., 1934, Annual Report of the Archaeological Survey of Ceylon for 1934, by S. Parnavitarna Esq.', The National Archives, London, United Kingdom CO57/24.

Peaple, S., 2009, 'Editorial', *Serendib: The Magazine of Sri Lankan Airlines* (November and December): 4.

Perera, N., 1998, *Society and Space: Colonialism, Nationalism and Postcolonial Identity in Sri Lanka* (Boulder, Colo.: Westview Press).

—, 2002, 'Indigenising the Colonial City: Late Nineteenth-century Colombo and its Landscape', *Urban Studies*, 39(9): 1703–721.

—, 2005, 'The Making of a National Capital: Conflicts, Contradictions, and Contestations in Sri Jayawardhanapura', in M. E. Geisler (ed.), *National Symbols, Fractured Identities: Contesting the National Narrative* (Middlebury, Vt.: Middlebury College), 241–72.

Perera, S., 1999, *The World According to Me: An Interpretation of the Ordinary, the Common and the Mundane* (Colombo: International Centre for Ethnic Studies).

Pieris, A., 2007a, *Imagining Modernity: The Architecture of Valentine Gunasekera* (Colombo: Stamford Lake (Pvt.) Ltd and Social Scientist's Association).

—, 2007b, 'The Trouser Under the Cloth: Personal Space in Colonial Modern Ceylon', in P. Scriver and V. Prakash (eds.), *Colonial Modernities: Building, Dwelling and Architecture in British India and Ceylon* (London and New York: Routledge), 199–218.

—, 2011, 'Tropical Cosmopolitanism? The Untoward Legacy of the American Style in Postindependence Ceylon/Sri Lanka', *Singapore Journal of Tropical Geography*, 32: 332–49.

Pieris, M., 1996, 'Wildlife in the Jataka', *Loris*, 21(2): 45–47.

Plesner, U., 1993, 'Falling in Love with Sri Lanka', *Mirror Magazine, Sunday*, 3 January

1993, Associated Newpapers of Ceylon Ltd, archive: Lake House, Colombo, clippings file on 'Architecture'.

Prakash, G., 1999, *Another Reason: Science and the Imagination of Modern India* (Princeton, NJ: Princeton University Press).

Prins, S. R., 2008, 'The Bawa's Green Mansions', *Sunday Times Plus* (Sri Lankan newspaper), 14 December 2008 <http://sundaytimes.lk/081214/Plus/sunday-timesplus_01.html> (accessed 15 January 2009).

Ramsay, N., 2009, 'Taking Place: Refracted Enchantment and the Habitual Spaces of the Tourist Souvenir', *Social and Cultural Geography*, 10(2): 197–217.

Rancière, J., 2004 (trans. by Gabriel Rockhill), *The Politics of Aesthetics* (London: Continuum).

—, 2006 (trans. by John Roffe), 'Thinking between Disciplines: An Aesthetics of Knowledge', *Parrhesia*, 1: 1–12.

—, 2007 (trans. by Gregory Elliot), *The Future of the Image* (London and New York: Verso).

—, 2009, 'The Aesthetic Dimension: Aesthetics, Politics, Knowledge', *Critical Inquiry*, 36: 1–19.

Ratnavibhushana, A., 2009, *Creating Simplicity: Sri Lankan Tropical Design, Architecture, Landscaping* (Colombo: Vijitha Yapa Publications).

Robson, D., 1991, 'Lunuganga – The Story of a Garden', *Observer* (Sri Lankan newspaper), 1 September 1991, Associated Newspapers of Ceylon Ltd archive, Lake House, Colombo, Sri Lanka, from clippings file on 'Lunuganga'.

—, 2002, *Geoffrey Bawa: The Complete Works* (London: Thames and Hudson).

—, 2007, *Beyond Bawa: Modern Masterworks of Monsoon Asia* (London: Thames and Hudson).

—, 2009, *Bawa: The Sri Lanka Gardens* (London: Thames and Hudson).

Rodaway, P., 1994, *Sensuous Geographies: Body, Sense, and Place* (London: Routledge).

Rodrigo, S., 1996, 'The Yala Bungalow – A Loving Requiem', *The Island* (Sri Lankan newspaper), 21 July 1996, Associated Newspapers of Ceylon Ltd archive, Lake House, Colombo, Sri Lanka, from clippings file on 'Yala'.

Rose, G., 1993, *Feminism and Geography: The Limits of Geographical Knowledge* (Minneapolis, Minn. and London: University of Minnesota Press).

S.K.R., 1970, 'The Silent Living of Ruhuna National Park – Yala', *Loris*, 12(1): 18–20.

Said, E., 1983, *The World, the Text, and the Critic* (Cambridge, Mass.: Harvard University Press).

—, 1993, *Culture and Imperialism* (New York: Vintage Books).

Samaraweera, C. S., 1970, 'Yala in History', *Loris*, 12(1): 18–20.

Sansoni, B., 2007 [1978], *Viharas and Veradahs, Ceylon* (Colombo: Barefoot (Pvt.) Ltd).

Sauer, C. O., 1925, 'The Morphology of Landscape', *University of California Publications in Geography*, 2(2): 19–53.

Schama, S., 1995, *Landscape and Memory* (New York: Alfred Knopf).

Schmidt, P. R., and T. C. Patterson (eds.), 1995, *Making Alternative Histories: The Practice of Archaeology and History in Non-Western Settings* (Santa Fe, NM: School of American Research Press).

Scott, D., 1995, 'Colonial Governmentality', *Social Text*, 43: 191–220.

—, 1999, *Refashioning Futures: Criticism after Postcoloniality* (Princeton, NJ: Princeton University Press).

—, 2004, *Conscripts of Modernity: The Tragedy of Colonial Enlightenment* (Durham, NC and London: Duke University Press).

Scriver, P., 2007, 'Stones and Texts: The Architectural Iconography of Colonial Indian and its Modern Contexts', in P. Scriver and V. Prakash (eds.), *Colonial Modernities: Building, Dwelling and Architecture in British India and Ceylon* (London and New York: Routledge), 27–50.

Scriver P., and V. Prakash (eds.), *Colonial Modernities: Building, Dwelling and Architecture in British India and Ceylon* (London and New York: Routledge)

Senanayake, D. S., 1934, *Agriculture and Patriotism* (Colombo: Cave).

Seth, S., 2007a, 'Changing the Subject: Western Knowledge and the Question of Difference', *Comparative Studies in Society and History*, 49(2): 666–88.

—, 2007b, *Subject Lessons: The Western Education of Colonial India* (Durham, NC and London: Duke University Press).

Shanaathanan, T., 2011, *The Incomplete Thombu* (Amsterdam and Santa Monica, Calif.: Raking Leaves).

Shohat, E., and R. Stam, 1994, *Unthinking Eurocentrism* (London and New York: Routledge).

Sioh, M., 1998, 'Authorizing the Malaysian Rainforest: Configuring Space, Contesting Claims and Conquering Imaginaries', *Ecumene*, 5(2): 144–54.

Smith, N., 1984, *Uneven Development: Nature, Capital and the Production of Space* (Oxford: Blackwell Publishing).

Snaffle, 1894, *Gun, Rifle and Hound in East and West* (London: Chapman and Hall).

Soper, K., 1995, *What is Nature?* (Oxford: Blackwell Publishing).

Sopher, D., 1967, *Geography of Religions* (Englewood Cliffs, NJ: Prentice Hall).

Spivak, G. C., 1993, *Outside in the Teaching Machine* (London and New York: Routledge).

—, 1999, *A Critique of Postcolonial Reason: Toward a History of the Vanishing Present* (Cambridge, Mass.: Harvard University Press).

—, 2003, *Death of a Discipline* (New York: Columbia University Press).

—, 2008, *Other Asias* (Oxford: Blackwell Publishing).

—, 2011, 'Theory in the World: A General Introduction', in M. Chauí, *Between Conformity and Resistance: Essays on Politics, Culture, and the State*, trans. and ed. M. Conde (New York: Palgrave Macmillan), vii–xi.

—, 2012, *An Aesthetic Education in the Era of Globalization* (Cambridge, Mass.: Harvard University Press).

Stepan, Nancy Leys, 2001, *Picturing Tropical Nature* (Ithaca, NY: Cornell University Press).

Storey, H., 1907, *Hunting and Shooting in Ceylon* (London: Longmans, Green and Co.).

Sunday Leader, 1996, 'The Unofficial Reporter: No Terrorists in Yala Says Wildlife Man', *Sunday Leader* (Sri Lankan newspaper), 3 Novemeber 1996, Associated Newspapers of Ceylon Ltd archive, Lake House, Colombo, Sri Lanka, from clippings file on 'Yala'.

Sunday Observer, 1993, 'Ondaatje's Gift to Yala National Park', *Sunday Observer* (Sri Lankan newspaper), 14 February 1993, Associated Newspapers of Ceylon Ltd archive, Lake House, Colombo, Sri Lanka, from clippings file on 'Yala'.

Sunday Times, 1997, 'The Jungle Awakes', *Sunday Times Plus* (Sri Lankan newspaper), 9 November 1997, Associated Newspapers of Ceylon Ltd archive, Lake House, Colombo, Sri Lanka, from clippings file on 'Yala'.

Tambiah, S. J., 1992, *Buddhism Betrayed? Religion, Politics and Violence in Sri Lanka* (University of Chicago Press).

Taylor, C., 2001, 'Two Theories of Modernity', in D. P. Gaonkar (ed.), *Alternative Modernities* (Durham, NC and London: Duke University Press).

*t*heertha, 2009, 'International Artists Collective' <www.theertha.org/about-us-1> (accessed 18 January 2010).

Thrift, N., 2007, *Non-representational Theory: Space, Politics, Affect* (London and New York: Routledge).

Till, J., 2009, *Architecture Depends* (Cambridge, Mass. and London: MIT Press).

Tilley, C., 1989, 'Archaeology as Socio-political Action in the Present', in V. Pinsky and A. Wylie (eds.), *Critical Traditions in Contemporary Archaeology: Essays in the Philosophy, History and Socio-politics of Archaeology* (Cambridge University Press), 104–16.

—, 1994, *A Phenomenology of Landscape: Places, Paths and Monuments* (Oxford: Berg).

Tissamaharama Special Correspondent, 1996, 'Yala Sanctuary Should be Protected', *Daily News* (Sri Lankan newspaper), 23 November 1996, Associated Newspapers of Ceylon Ltd archive, Lake House, Colombo, Sri Lanka, from clippings file on 'Yala'.

Tuan, Y. F., 1991, 'Language and the Making of Place: A Narrative Descriptive Approach', *Annals of the Association of American Geographers*, 81(4): 684–96.

Uragoda, C., 1994, *Wildlife Conservation in Sri Lanka: A History of the Wildlife and Nature Protection Society of Sri Lanka* (Colombo: Centenary Publications).

Vale, Lawrence J., 1992, *Architecture, Power, and National Identity* (New Haven, Conn.: Yale University Press).

Varma, R., 2004, 'Provincializing the Global City: From Bombay to Mumbai', *Social Text*, 81: 65–89.

Wace, H., 1899, 'Revenue Administration Report of the Government Agent, Southern Province, May 1, 1899', The National Archives, London, United Kingdom, CO57/137.

Ward, H. G., Sir, 1855, 'Address of His Excellency, Sir Henry George Ward KGCMG, on the Opening of the Session of the Legislative Council – July 4th, 1855', The National Archives, London, United Kingdom CO57/21.

—, 1856, 'Minute on the Eastern Province, by Sir Henry George Ward', The National Archives, London, United Kingdom CO57/22.

Weerasinghe, J., 2005, 'Contemporary Art in Sri Lanka', in C. Turner (ed.), *Art and Social Change* (Canberra: Pandanus Books), 180–92.

Weiss, G., 2011, *The Cage: The Fight for Sri Lanka and the Last Days of the Tamil Tigers* (London: Bodley Head).

West, P., 2005, 'Translation, Value, and Space: Theorizing an Ethnographic and Engaged Environmental Anthropology', *American Anthropologist*, 107(4): 632–42.

Whatmore, S., 2002, *Hybrid Geography: Natures, Cultures, Spaces* (London: Sage).

—, 2006, 'Materialist Returns: Practicing Cultural Geographies in and for a More-than-Human World', *Cultural Geographies*, 13(4): 600–10.

Wickramasinghe, M., 2004 [1940], *Ape Game* (Sinhala language) (Rajagiriya: Sarasa).

Wijesinha, S., 2009, 'Sri Lanka's Wildlife Parks: Were these the World's First Wildlife Reserves?, *Serendib: The Magzine of Sri Lankan Airlines* (November and December): 48.

Williams, R., 1976, *Keywords: A Vocabulary of Culture and Society* (Oxford University Press).

—, 1977, *Marxism and Literature* (Oxford University Press).

Williams, S., 1996, 'Whither Yala? Tigers Make Inroads to South via Yala Park', *Midweek Mirror* (Sri Lankan newspaper), 30 November 1996, Associated Newspapers of Ceylon Ltd archive, Lake House, Colombo, Sri Lanka, from clippings file on 'Yala'.

Wilner, Joshua, 2000, Feeding on Infinity: Readings in the Romantic Rhetoric of Internalization (Baltimore, Md.: Johns Hopkins University Press).

Woolf, L., 1913 [2005], *The Village in the Jungle* (London: Eland books).

Woolf, P., 1988, 'Symbol of the Second Empire: Cultural Politics and the Paris Opera House', in D. Cosgrove and S. Daniels (eds.), *The Iconography of Landscape: Essays on the Symbolic Representation, Design and Use of Past Environments* (Cambridge University Press), 214–35.

Wylie, A., 1993, 'Facts and Fictions: Writing Archaeology in a Different Voice', *Canadian Journal of Archaeology*, 17: 5–12.

Wylie, J., 2005, 'A Single Day's Walking: Narrating Self and Landscape on the SouthWest Coast Path, *Transactions of the Institute of British Geographers*, 30(2): 234–47.

—, 2007, *Landscape* (London and New York: Routledge).

Wylie, J., and M. Rose, 2006, 'Animating Landscape', *Environment and Planning D: Society and Space*, 24(4): 475–79.

Yorgason, E., and V. Della Dora, 2009, 'Editorial: Geography, Religion and Emerging Paradigms: Problematizing the Dialogue', *Social and Cultural Geography*, 10(6): 629–37.

Zimmer, O., 1998, 'In Search of National Identity: Alpine Landscape and the Reconstruction of the Swiss Nation', *Comparative Studies in Society and History*, 40(4): 637–65.

Index

Printed and bound by CPI Group (UK) Ltd, Croydon, CR0 4YY

09/06/2025

14685792-0001